KU-525-973

Books are to be returned on or before
the last date below.

LIVERPOOL JOHN MOORES UNIVERSITY
Aldham Robarts L.R.C.
TEL 0151 231 3701/3634

LIVERPOOL JMU LIBRARY

3 1111 01137 6207

Media Audiences and Identity

Media Audiences and Identity

Self-Construction in the Fan Experience

Steve Bailey

© Steve Bailey 2005

All rights reserved. No reproduction, copy or transmission of this publication may be made without written permission.

No paragraph of this publication may be reproduced, copied or transmitted save with written permission or in accordance with the provisions of the Copyright, Designs and Patents Act 1988, or under the terms of any licence permitting limited copying issued by the Copyright Licensing Agency, 90 Tottenham Court Road, London W1T 4LP.

Any person who does any unauthorized act in relation to this publication may be liable to criminal prosecution and civil claims for damages.

The author has asserted his right to be identified as the author of this work in accordance with the Copyright, Designs and Patents Act 1988.

First published 2005 by
PALGRAVE MACMILLAN
Houndmills, Basingstoke, Hampshire RG21 6XS and
175 Fifth Avenue, New York, N. Y. 10010
Companies and representatives throughout the world

PALGRAVE MACMILLAN is the global academic imprint of the Palgrave Macmillan division of St. Martin's Press, LLC and of Palgrave Macmillan Ltd. Macmillan® is a registered trademark in the United States, United Kingdom and other countries. Palgrave is a registered trademark in the European Union and other countries.

ISBN-13: 978–1–4039–4542–6   hardback
ISBN-10: 1–4039–4542–X   hardback

This book is printed on paper suitable for recycling and made from fully managed and sustained forest sources.

A catalogue record for this book is available from the British Library.

Library of Congress Cataloging-in-Publication Data
Bailey, Steve, 1967–
    Media audiences and identity : self-construction in the fan experience / Steve Bailey.
        p. cm.
    Based on the author's doctoral dissertation, University of Illinois at Urbana-Champaign
    Includes bibliographical references and index.
    ISBN 1–4039–4542–X
    1. Identity (Psychology) and mass media. 2. Mass media–Audiences.
3. Mass media and culture. I. Title.

P96.I34B35 2005
302.23′019–dc22   2005042930

10   9   8   7   6   5   4   3   2   1
14   13   12   11   10   09   08   07   06   05

Printed and bound in Great Britain by
Antony Rowe Ltd, Chippenham and Eastbourne

Contents

Preface   vii

Introduction: Media, Culture and The Self   1

Chapter 1   Media and Self-Construction: Theoretical
             Issues   15

Chapter 2   Every Freak Needs a Show: Polyvalent Subjectivity
             and a Local Underground Film Scene   53

Chapter 3   'I Believe in Me': Self-Affirmation in the
             'Kiss Army'   101

Chapter 4   Screen Subjects and Cyber-Subjects: The Case
             of Futurama   157

Conclusion: Underground Hybridity, Popular Piety and Virtual
            Irony as Three Modes of Mediated Selfhood   202

Notes   215

Works Cited   218

Index   223

Preface

In the following book, I try to synthesize several strands of critical thought not often combined, including neo-pragmatist philosophy, contemporary media and cultural studies and psychoanalytic theory. There are two main reasons for this unorthodox alignment of scholarly approaches. First, it reflects the peculiarities of my own academic background, one that has followed a winding, sometimes looping path. Secondly and more importantly, it is intended as an argument for the value and even the necessity of breaking from standard analytical methods in addressing questions, such as those regarding the inter-section of media and social identity, that have frustrated more conventional strategies. The barriers imposed by disciplinary organization and institutional affiliation are not as significant, by any measure, as the value in overcoming them (or merely ignoring them) in the pursuit of a better understanding of the media saturated world we inhabit. The puzzlement that my collection of perspectives has occasionally generated was an occasional source of anxiety, but proved to be an inspiration as well and eventually led to the completion of this book.

As mentioned, this book is the result of a long and winding intellectual path and this path has made significant stops in four cities and two nations in the course of a dozen years. Its roots, particularly for the individual research sites, extend back to my adolescence and subsequent undergraduate training in the seventies and eighties. As a result, acknowledging all of the individuals who contributed to the project in some fashion would be impossible. However, a number of people deserve special mention for their particular help in realizing the project. First, my doctoral advisor, James Hay of the University of Illinois at Urbana-Champaign deserves first mention for his steadfast support and relentless scholarly engagement. The remaining members of my dissertation committee – Andrea Press (University of Illinois at Urbana-Champaign), Bert Kögler (University of North Florida) and Douglas Holt (Harvard University) – provided insight, encouragement and critique far beyond the call of duty. Peter Lunt (University College London), Sonia Livingstone (London School of Economics), Greg Dimitriadis (University at Buffalo) and Siamak Movahedi (University of Massachusetts at Boston) read earlier versions of sections of the manuscript and their commentaries were valuable indeed. An anonymous reviewer at Palgrave gave suggestions that played a key role in the revision process. Audience members at conferences organized by the National Communication Association (US), the Media Ecology Association and the British Psychoanalytic Society provided additional critical commentary on various aspects of the work. My current colleagues at York University were also helpful and I drew frequently upon their diverse perspectives on a number of issues crucial to the project. My brother John Bailey and mother Nancy Killen provided familial support. Herman of Toronto provided vocal support and companionship in the final stages of the project. Anita Michel provided love and support through the research and writing process and inspired me throughout. She deserves significant credit for its strengths and is blameless for its weaknesses. My father Ron Bailey did not live to see the completion of this book but his spirit inhabits it and for that reason he deserves gratitude even in his absence.

Steve Bailey

Introduction: Media, Culture and the Self

As we enter a new millennium, there is considerable evidence within popular culture of an increasing public preoccupation with the role of mass media in social life, especially when the impacts of such media appear particularly intense. Consider, for example, the international release of *Trekkies*, a semi-satirical ethnographic film examining the lives of particularly devout *Star Trek* audience members, themselves the subject of a considerable corpus of academic analysis.[1] Similarly, much of the large body of publicity surrounding the release of the fourth installment of the *Star Wars* series in 1999 (after a 16 year wait), *The Phantom Menace*, detailed the scale and intensity of *Star Wars* fandom, with numerous discussions of the keen anticipation of the new film, as well as affirmations of an unyielding dedication to the larger *Star Wars* saga among members of this subculture. The majority of the attention to media fandom appears to consist of either a smirking examination of the 'freak show' aspects of the culture, as with *Trekkies* and some of the *Star Wars* coverage, or an unquestioning celebration of the inventiveness and charm of American popular culture, as with much of the remainder of the reaction to *The Phantom Menace*. Even though a great deal of this discourse was quite shallow and hyperbolic, the intensity and prevalence of forms of media fandom, which has always been the subject – somewhat narcissistically – of popular media attention, is a particularly prominent element in recent coverage of a number of cultural phenomena.

This spate of popular attention was not limited merely to a condescending or celebratory coverage of the power of media in individual lives. A very different treatment of these issues emerged in regard to the question of youth violence, reaching an apex in the frenzy of media attention surrounding the shootings at Columbine High School in

1

Littleton, Colorado USA the same year. In this case, the popular coverage often focused on the search for an appropriate cultural villain – the Internet, rock music (Marilyn Manson, Rammstein, KMFDM), video games (Doom, Quake) – that might explain the massacre. Here, the image of harmless, laughable geeks who needed to 'get a life' was reversed in favor of a nearly apocalyptic vision of nihilistic monsters taking moral instruction from degenerate rock stars and receiving weapons training from video games. As with the former perspective, the latter is hardly new to the popular media; there is a long tradition of hysteria over the effects of popular culture on youth. However, the roughly concurrent and undeniably pervasive coverage of both *Star Wars* and the Columbine shootings provided a particularly stark illustration of the two attitudinal extremes of popular media self-reflection.

The academic world, of course, manifests its own ambivalent but often obsessive attitude towards the cultural significance of various popular media. This is most evident, perhaps, in the postmodern theoretical tradition, one with strong roots in the work of Marshall McLuhan and other prognosticators of paradigmatic shifts in society produced by the dissemination of popular media. In many cases (e.g., Baudrillard, Virilio, Kroker), a 'media culture' becomes one of the structuring assumptions of any attempt to theorize social relations. The fascination with media is additionally evident in a variety of other positions on the academic left – Marxist ideology theory, the approaches lumped together as 'cultural studies' and many variants of contemporary gender theory (e.g., queer theory and some recent feminism) – that have become enmeshed in a series of debates regarding the impact of the media, the relative activity or passivity of the audience, the subversive potential of media reception and production practices and other related issues.

Politically conservative academics, while perhaps less broadly interested in questions of media, have also offered a variety of perspectives on these issues. In both the neoconservative and communitarian schools, for example, there is a tendency to treat mass media as endangering traditional social forms and degrading public and personal morality. Others on the political right, such as Tyler Cowen, provide a free-market defense of the popular media, arguing in effect that it gives the people what they want. As Thomas Frank notes, the latter position is not without its similarities to the 'British Cultural Studies' paradigm in its populist inclinations and antipathy to the relative cultural pessimism of the Frankfurt School (Frank, no date, p. 10). While there is a general tendency on both the academic right and left towards a criticism of and concern for the prominence of popular media in social and private lives, neither political position appears to lead intrinsically into an optimistic or pessimistic stance on this question.

Recent technological developments, particularly those involving the Internet and cyberculture, have only exacerbated this situation; there is little sign of the fascination with media and their audiences waning in both the academic world and within a larger set of popular discourses. For all of this attention, however, there are a number of areas of inquiry that have yet to be adequately addressed in a thorough and systematic fashion. Research in the area of the social and individual engagement with mass media objects has a long history, of course, but this has not necessarily produced any definitive answers, theoretically or empirically, to a number of central questions; indeed, such definitive answers are probably impossible. However, there are avenues of analysis that may yield insights that can take us beyond these binaries and also move the study of popular media, and especially the process of audience engagement, further along. This is precisely the purpose of the following work, which takes the issue of media engagement as its central focus, with the explicit aim of providing an innovative set of theoretical and analytical strategies for dealing with these often daunting issues.

The goal of offering both theoretical and empirical insights demands a dual focus, with related but distinct strategies for building a theoretical apparatus and then mobilizing it in concrete media research, a process that inevitably loops back and informs the ongoing process of theory development. In this book, the theoretical work will be devoted primarily to creating a response to a preeminent challenge facing media theory: the development of an understanding of the social subject and social identity adequate for the task of contemporary media analysis. In dialogue with this effort, the empirical analyses will take aim at three very different modes of media fandom, conceived here as three modes of hermeneutic audience engagement. Each will be analyzed in light of a set of cultural contexts and the variety of socio-hermeneutic practices engendered therein, practices with real implications for both a theoretical and empirical understanding of the intersection of mass media and social identity.

The challenge of the subject in media research

The question of why 'the subject' is so critical to this analytical effort is an important one, particularly in establishing the foundational value of this area of theoretical work for the specific field of media studies. This can be answered, partially, by referring to David Morley's discussion of some dominant schools of media research – the 'media effects' tradition and the 'uses and gratifications' model – that encounter fundamental difficulties closely related to issues of subjectivity (Morley, 1992, pp. 47–71). In the former, the audience experience is considered in terms of a passive absorption of information, a 'hypodermic needle' (as it is commonly dubbed) model of reception, one that accords little or no significance to the ability of individuals and groups to do anything other than passively receive media messages (Morley, 1992, pp. 47–49). Here, the underlying concept of subjectivity mimics that of conventional behaviorist psychology, in which the individual exists only as a 'black box' upon which stimuli are enacted and to which she responds. The uses and gratifications approach that emerged, as Morley indicates, in response to the deficiencies of the former paradigm, moves toward the other pole, understanding audiences as highly empowered and intrinsically active bodies using media in a variety of very different ways (Morley, 1992, pp. 51–52). The problem with this approach – and here I agree completely with Morley – is that it relies upon a highly individualistic and 'insufficiently sociological' understanding of media reception, failing to consider the social nature of meaning production and assuming an excessive freedom in the meaning-making process (Morley, 1992, pp. 52–53). In this case, the 'subject problem' at the root of these shortcomings involves the use of an excessively individualized, self-knowing subject that is a variant, in many ways, of the classical subject that has been the object of so much criticism in recent philosophical and sociological work. The key, then, must be a negotiation between these two opposing models of social (or in the latter case, asocial) subjectivity. Morley turns to an emphasis on the material and cultural contingencies that produce everyday life in an attempt to overcome these vexing binaries; this is a largely successful attempt, but one that does not demand a substantive theorization of the social subject as such. I am interested in a more thorough theoretical response to this problem, one that requires confronting the issue of subjectivity directly and systematically, and one that could provide a grounding for new directions in the study of mass media.

Developing such a theoretical position, though, requires more than simply superseding the long standing tension between a behaviorist and a classical understanding of the subject. There is a second set of issues linked to the theoretical tradition associated with postmodernism – a heavily disputed term that can cover a vast array of positions, but from which certain coherent themes emerge – that are directly relevant to the issue of the subject and the mass media. Here, I would identify three central challenges to an effective theory of social subjectivity, particularly in regard to the study of media, posed by post-modernism: the imperiling of the very concept of the social subject; the demands raised by a symbolically complex cultural environment (a key tenet of much postmodern theory); and the question of contextualiz-ing the position of the mass media in a social world that can seem dom-inated by, or even reducible to, such media. While all of these issues will be explored in greater depth in the chapters that follow, I want to provide a brief account of each challenge as a means of introducing the overall project.

As Robert Dunn points out, the postmodern attack on any con-ventional understanding of subjectivity takes a variety of forms that can vary greatly in the degree with which they seek to displace the clas-sical subject (Dunn, 1998, pp. 65–68). I want to focus, though, on one important dimension of many of these strategies, which is a flattening of the social subject. In this case, the subject is denied a reflexive depth and instead posed as a highly contingent, characteristically fluid entity. While much of this description is quite sound and in fact empirically supportable through an examination of the symbolic networks in which modern subjects operate, the process of flattening also entails a severe restriction or even elimination of a properly hermeneutic dimen-sion to the subject; that is, the subject is not granted the possibility for the kind of self-reflection that depends upon the ability to tran-scend the immediacy and fluidity of social existence, even minimally. However, as I shall argue, restoring a hermeneutic dimension does not require a return to a classical subject nor does it demand giving up the notion that the subject is a dialogic, non-organic and highly contin-gent entity. Following the tradition of George Herbert Mead and the expansion of his work by Hans-Herbert Kögler, Ernst Tugendhat and others, I will propose a model of the hermeneutic social subject that can enact this restoration.

This theoretical move has particularly crucial implications for the study of media, as I will argue that forms of popular media serve a uniquely hermeneutic function in the contemporary social world. Indeed, the empirical research growing out of and informing this theo-retical work takes the self-reflective and self-constructing dimensions of the media experience as its focus; the ways that subjects engage symbolically with media texts and events will be analyzed in light of their specifically hermeneutic dimension. It is this aspect of the media audience experience that is missing in both the 'effects' and 'uses and gratifications' traditions, and also largely absent from the kind of 'cultural studies' approaches that seek to move beyond these more traditional schools of media research.

The second and closely related challenge posed by postmodernist theory involves the aforementioned assumption of a complex, fragmentary social environment, one that informs much of this theoretical tradition. The task here will be to produce an understanding of the social subject capable of taking this condition into account, especially in relation to the development and restriction of the kind of self-construction described above. To put it another way, one must account for the properly spatial contingencies in any symbolic-interpretive practice. Here, the Meadian tradition (as well as the more contemporary work of Appadurai) is particularly useful, as it is predicated upon an inextricable linkage between the material environment and the development of various forms of self-reflection, or as Erving Goffman would put it, between 'regions' and 'roles'. Secondly, such perspectives can also help construct a model of subjectivity that can match the fluxional character of the symbolic environment, as the Meadian model is built upon a subject that is intrinsically polyvalent, shifting between an array of symbolic orders. Indeed, Mead takes the very emergence of a subject qua subject as dependent upon the movement through a variety of socio-material contexts. Once again, it becomes evident that sharing many of the assumptions of social postmodernism does not automatically engender an elimination of some measure of subjective depth; in fact, such depth can be rendered theoretically consonant with this symbolic complexity.

The implications for the more specific domain of media analysis are significant here in that in many accounts of the postmodern condition, the mass media are posited as a major, perhaps even dominant contributor to the fragmentation of the socio-symbolic world – this is most evident in Jean Baudrillard's writing, but also appears in the work of Fredric Jameson, Arthur Kroker, and numerous others. Taking this formulation seriously, even in the service of a critical interrogation of its assumptions, thus demands a better understanding of the full dimensions of a 'media society', including the often elusive field of personal interpretive practices – one place that such an environment impacts the individual.

Of course, this focus carries a related danger, one that I will pose as the third challenge of postmodern theory, which is the proper contextualization of media experiences within a larger social field. Failing to do this risks a kind of 'media-ism', in which all elements of social (and individual) life appear as derived from, or even identical to, various media forms. Actually, the challenge here might best be characterized as twofold: first, there is the need to avoid the kind of hysterical – or, as Baudrillard would have it, 'fatal' – slide into a faith in the all-encompassing, quasi-metaphysical power of the mass media. This can be avoided with a reasonable level of attention to extra-media (e.g., political, economic, demographic, etc.) factors within the social environment, particularly as they function as contexts for experiences with media. The second aspect, though, involves the more theoretically and empirically challenging task of placing the media and related experiences in a larger context. Here, some of the less 'fatal' postmodern theory can be helpful, particularly the recent work of Arjun Appadurai, who attempts a spatial contextualization of the mass media with a larger social landscape. This process of contextualization is absolutely critical, particularly in light of the polysemic space/subject model noted above; the status of the media as an element in this heuristic certainly demands analysis, so an adequate understanding of a larger framework seems necessary, and would then meet this third challenge of postmodernity.

There are other obstacles to the kind of theoretical work on the subject proposed here, in this case involving disciplinary boundaries, particularly those associated with the study of various forms of communication. Much of theoretical work on communication stemming from the Meadian philosophical tradition has tended to focus on 'interpersonal' rather than 'mass' communication processes. This is not particularly surprising, as Mead places great weight on the interpersonal encounter and upon social situations involving physical co-presence. However, these approaches should not be limited to the analysis of such situations; indeed, Goffman – working within this tradition – moves into a discussion of mass media in later works such as *Gender Advertisements*, *Frame Analysis* and *Forms of Talk*. Others have extended this move, as with Meyrowitz's innovative, if flawed, use of symbolic interactionism to study media effects in his influential *No Sense of Place*; Robert Dunn has made a similar effort with Meadian perspectives in 1998's *Identity Crisis: A Social Critique of Postmodernity*. One of the principle tasks of the theoretical section that immediately follows this introduction, will be an extension of this line of thinking, particularly as it concerns questions of subjectivity.

Indeed, working from the Meadian tradition will enable a second act of intellectual boundary crossing, one involving the redeployment of

**LIVERPOOL JOHN MOORES UNIVERSITY
LEARNING SERVICES**

psychoanalytic theory. One interesting aspect of Mead's understanding of social selfhood is an odd similarity with that of Jacques Lacan, suggesting an intriguing fusion of neo-pragmatist and psychoanalytic models of the subject. Lacan's emphasis on the unstable, disruptive nature of desire adds another dimension to the analysis, one that might act as a corrective to Mead's somewhat orderly model of developing reflexivity and self-consciousness. Psychoanalytic theory, while hugely influential within cinema studies, has always enjoyed a rather marginal status within a larger field of media scholarship, partly due to increasing skepticism regarding its therapeutic and scientific value and partly because it has tended to be linked to purely textual modes of analysis. Understanding certain aspects of contemporary psychoanalytic theory within the larger framework of neo-pragmatism could serve to contextualize the emphasis of this tradition; like a similar treatment of postmodern theory, then, this would avoid an extension of important insights into all-encompassing, metaphysical claims. There is no reason why psychoanalytic cultural theory's focus – the psychosocial affective potency of aesthetic experiences – needs to be regarded as an 'either/or' proposition for media studies, and placing it in dialogue with the often consonant Meadian tradition can restore a place for it within a larger system of analysis.

The sites of analysis: the terrain of the hermeneutic subject

Following the chapter dedicated to a theoretical reconstruction of the social subject for the analysis of media, the book presents three specific cultural sites that are analyzed in terms of the subjective possibilities, particularly in light of the practices of self-construction and self-reflection, that are enabled and disabled within the same. These empirical investigations might be characterized as a 'collective case study', to refer to the distinction made by Robert E. Stake, who differentiates such studies, that are designed as a group to 'provide insight into an issue or refinement of theory', from 'intrinsic case studies' that are designed primarily for 'better understanding of this particular case' (Stake, 1994, p. 237). More specifically, the examples are offered in the spirit of Michael Burawoy's 'extended case method' in which empirical research serves a dialogical role, informing and reshaping theoretical work. They are not designed, then, as individual, free-standing analyses, even though each site may hold a certain contingent unity.

More precisely, each site takes aim a specific mode of engagement with a form of electronic media as it is manifested with a given audience/fan formation: a local avant-garde film scene, the discursive world of fans of the internationally popular rock band Kiss and the cyberspace audience community that emerged in response to the 1999 debut of the animated television series *Futurama*. This selection of analytical sites is designed, collectively, to examine a diverse set of practices that share a hermeneutic significance that can be best drawn out with the kinds of theoretical tools elucidated in Chapter 1. This diversity is manifested along three distinct axes, thus providing a kind of triangulating effect on – suitably enough – three levels: media, space and the more elusive field of cultural connotation.

In terms of media, the diversity is explicit: the objects of audience interest in the respective empirical analyses are film, popular music and television. While this distinction may seem obvious, it is also clear that the audience formations under analyses involve a variety of communicative practices tied to other media. The local film scene, for example, is closely linked to both alternative print culture (e.g., 'zines', alternative weekly newspapers) and to local independent radio stations as a means for promotion and discussion; likewise, the 'Kiss Army' appears discursively through an extremely broad array of materials: print magazines, websites and Internet forums, videos and publicity materials and even toys and comic books. The third site takes the very question of the intersection of media as a central focus, concentrating on the use of one screen media (the Internet) for the mobilization of audience discourses concerning another (television). While the starting point, then, may be different media, the three sites inevitably share an imbrication in a much broader variety of discourses and means of transmission.

In regard to the issue of the material and discursive spaces that structure each audience formation, there are similar surface distinctions, though these too will inevitably become somewhat muddied as the analysis proceeds. The first case, involving a local underground film scene, takes a relatively narrow media phenomenon as its object; of course, such a scene always exists within a variety of much larger contexts, including national and international cinema cultures. The second section pursues an explicitly broad, international audience culture; in fact, it might be thought of as defiantly international, with its geographic and demographic scale serving as a particular source of pride. The final audience formation, the *Futurama* cyber-community, lacks the conventional geographic orientation of either, taking place in the imaginary – but much discussed and certainly controversial – space of the Internet. In this aspect, it provides a complement to the more conventional spatial dynamics of the previous sites as well as offering some insight into the unique hermeneutic possibilities of the virtual world.

Finally, all three sites involve media objects with vastly different cultural implications. The underground film culture exists within a long tradition of elite avant-garde and counter-cultural cinema practices, and thus carries associations of aesthetic and sometimes political radicalism, a conscious stance in opposition to traditional mass media and, more generally, a culturally bohemian aura. This stands in utter contrast to the unabashed populist philistinism and mainstream ubiquity of Kiss fan culture, especially as it has evolved following the band's 1996 reunion and subsequent touring and recording career. The *Futurama* fan culture exists somewhere between the aforementioned, involving a national and fairly popular television program, but one with a highly cultic group of particularly devout fans – there was discussion of the program on the Internet before it had even debuted – and, through its associations with *The Simpsons* creator Matt Groening, status as 'quality television'. The focus on a virtual fan community also creates significant limits on the audience formation: a measure of technical and navigational savvy, access to technology and a working knowledge of the operating customs of the Internet are required for participation. However, in all three cases, the apparent cultural status of the objects of audience attention is inevitably subject to a very unstable symbolic economy, and these fan formations certainly do not display a uniform and predictable set of discursive practices. The processes of hermeneutic engagement intrinsic to each can never be deduced simply from a set of apparent cultural implications.

Indeed, it was the discovery, in previous research, of such a particular and uniquely hermeneutic set of practices that motivated me to develop a theoretical approach capable of providing a better foundation for the analysis of such cultural formations. In 1996, I began a project on Kiss fans that was intended to examine various aspects of this fan community, at the time quite small in comparison to the postreunion resurgence. After a significant period of research, including interviews and an analysis of fan discourse, I became increasingly dissatisfied with the analytical tools provided by the theoretical work informing my research – a mixture of 'British Cultural Studies', Marxist ideology theory and postmodernism. None of these approaches was appropriate for a thorough analysis of what I found to be the most striking aspect of this culture, the ways that being a Kiss fan served as a means for self-reflection and identity construction, and the interpretive frameworks that enabled such processes. Approaches placing great emphasis on 'practices' (e.g., British Cultural Studies and the related work of figures such as John Fiske) failed in the sense that they tended not to accord an adequate level of analytical depth to individual subjects, a move that makes the analysis of issues of 'the self' extremely difficult, and similar barriers existed with the similarly flat subject (or anti-subject) of postmodern theory. Traditional ideology theory, while suitable in its emphasis on subjectification, could not account for both the discursive contingencies and the interpretive freedom evident in such cultures; it was simply too rigid and univocal in its emphasis on top down discursive dissemination.

The aforementioned traditional media studies paradigms discussed by Morley were similarly flawed, largely for the reasons noted above: a behaviorist elimination of active subjectivity in the 'effects' tradition and a failure to account for the social character of meaning-making practices in the uses and gratifications model. What was needed, I believed, was a social-hermeneutic model of cultural interpretation and the audience experience. Not long after the initial research, I was by chance involved in a separate theoretical encounter with the work of Goffman and subsequently Mead, one that suggested a fruitful synthesis with some aspects of media and cultural studies. Mead's social-hermeneutic model of the self, composed of an 'I' and a 'me' continually in dialogue, was particularly helpful here, and an initial sketch of the theoretical work that is the focus of the first chapter of this book emerged.

My ethnographic work with the local film community began some time after these initial theoretical efforts, but again I found the hermeneutic dynamics of this cultural formation to be a prominent, fascinating and often overlooked aspect of such 'alternative' cultures. In this case, the film texts themselves were particularly interesting, as there was a tendency to take questions of the self and identity as an explicit theme. This then produced some interesting parallels with the larger dynamics of the culture itself, one in which an explicitly oppositional – aesthetic and in some cases political – stance is often a major component in participation within the culture. The multi-layered hermeneutic dynamic, with practices of the self apparent in the film texts, the discourse surrounding them and in the events and other activities associated with this media formation further stimulated my interest in this theoretical domain. As with the earlier research, it appeared that conventional approaches could never really elucidate the scope and depth of these practices; however, the model developed below seemed to be very much appropriate to address these concerns. In turn, the research and theory became involved in an increasingly dialogic relationship, though the immediate motivation, as mentioned, was an initial empirical crisis.

Self-disclosure: a secondary motivation for the research

It seems only fair that a work that purports to analyze the hermeneutic dimension of media experiences – experiences deeply connected to questions of 'the self' and social identity – involves at least a minimal degree of self-disclosure on the part of the author. More broadly, as Hammersley and Atkinson argue, any variant of social research involves participation in a social world and is thus in some sense 'participant observation' research (Hammersley and Atkinson, 1995, p. 16); certainly media research, particularly of the qualitative variety, is no exception, so some consideration of one's own position and experiences is appropriate. In this case, the issue is particularly relevant, as a second degree of motivation, beyond the initial fieldwork noted above, stems from my own experiences as a media audience member. These experiences, and especially my very intense engagement with popular music for over 25 years, also suggested a somewhat elusive but deeply subjective dimension to audience practices that tended to escape conventional academic analysis. At the same time, I was certainly not immune to the natural ambivalence of the progressive academic who is simultaneously an eager participant in what is ultimately a mode of consumption, even if its implications may be quite distinct from many other consumer practices. When I discovered reflections of my own experience in the audience formations I was researching as a scholar, there was a personal resonance that I cannot deny provided an additional impetus for the project.

There are more direct personal connections with all three research sites, and it is thus appropriate to acknowledge these links. These ties are most extensive in the case of the research on Kiss fans. In my early adolescence in the late seventies, I was a fan of the group, which was enjoying its peak popularity. Though my interests moved rather quickly to other performers and styles of music, and even to a conscious rejection of Kiss fandom as embarrassingly juvenile, I shared a common experience with many American males of that generation. This sparked my initial interest in studying current Kiss fans, as many members of this culture – and particularly the most devout fans – had experienced a roughly concurrent initial attachment to the band. Thus, my experiences provided me with a level of knowledge and lent a degree of empathetic understanding to the research.

While not as autobiographically resonant as my relationship with Kiss fandom, I have been engaged with various facets of the underground film scene through my entire adult life. There is a crucial difference here, though, as my involvement with this cultural formation emerged in light of academic work, as a film student at both undergraduate and graduate levels, and professional activities (to use the term loosely), as a participant in independent film production. The ties with an academic career, of which the current research is an important element, thus give this site a more immediate analytic significance; the kind of meta-reflection and systematicity intrinsic to an intellectual, academic perspective has an organic tie to the object of research, which is undeniably different from the return to a pre-professional, even pre-adolescent passion inherent in the Kiss research. It is similar to the earlier work, though, in that a fairly extensive personal history has provided me with a level of knowledge that is quite useful in guiding the research and providing a degree of native expertise.

In the case of the final site, the recency of *Futurama*'s debut and the expediency of its demise would make any extensive personal history impossible. However, I have been an avid viewer of *The Simpsons* and a fan of Matt Groening's work throughout his career as a cartoonist, and was certainly anticipating the premiere of the show. Secondly, I have been involved with Internet fan communities for a number of years, both for academic research and personal interest; generally, this has taken the form of observation rather than active participation, but it has provided me with a degree of familiarity with the nature of such formations. The affective dimension, though, that is an important element in my relationship with the aforementioned sites, is not as prominent in this case.

The point here is not that such autobiographical information can adequately function as the limits of, or even the foundation for, the type of analysis raised by the project at hand; indeed, I am largely in agreement with the critique of excessive self-involvement in some recent cultural studies research. Nonetheless, I cannot deny that an initially intuitive belief that various forms of popular culture hold a significance not easily accessible through the standard set of perspectives associated with the media and cultural studies traditions, a sense that was derived from my own experiences, spurred further academic interest. The level of personal attachment to forms of popular music, particularly, and the sense that this engagement was a critical element in the development of forms of self- and world-understanding, was always lurking behind my research into the reception practices of others. The attempt to get at one's own practices through those of others is itself a supremely hermeneutic gesture, of course, and is thus particularly appropriate for this project, even as such an attempt is not accorded a theoretical priority. Like the 'self', though, it is always seeping through, and there is little use in denying it in the service of a putative objectivity.

1
Media and Self-Construction: Theoretical Issues

In the introduction, I pointed to the tendency for both popular and academic analyses of mass media to fall into one side of a binary of activity/passivity in describing the relationship of the audience to forms of mass media. Secondly, through the work of Morley, I identified the issue of subjectivity – and the inadequate theorization of the same – as the source of at least some of this tendency toward oversimplification, and pointed to the challenges of such theorization in a postmodern cultural context. In this chapter, I want to elucidate a theoretical model, the 'hermeneutic social subject', that may meet some of these challenges. This model, rooted in the neo-pragmatist philosophical tradition, can provide the foundation for a more coherent and nuanced understanding of the power of mass media for practices of self-construction and self-reflection, topics rendered nearly invisible in the move toward 'de-subjectified' analytical approaches.

The chapter begins with an examination of some of the intellectual roots of the issue and an examination of varying perspectives on subjectivity, media and culture, with a particular focus on those that have been most influential on a tradition of cultural studies of mass media. This is followed by a discussion of the unique contribution of the aforementioned neo-pragmatist model, as well as its consonance with certain variants of contemporary psychoanalytic theory, a similarly neglected source of theoretical insight. Finally, the suitability of this model for understanding the formidable complexity of a contemporary media culture is explored through a repositioning of 'the postmodern' as a field of symbolic possibility rather than as a metaphysical fait accompli.

The subject in/and media culture: four key positions

Writing about the crisis in the contemporary theorization of the subject, Axel Honneth identifies two intellectual trends that have made the strongest contributions to the fall of the classical subject (Honneth, 1995, pp. 261–262). One is the Freudo-Nietzschean 'psychological critique', that renders the classical sense of an autonomous subject hopelessly naïve. The second, derived from both Sausserean and Wittgensteinian traditions, puts the subject at the mercy of linguistic systems that she can never master. Honneth adds that Claude Levi-Strauss and Michel Foucault, despite some philosophical differences, effectively continue this second line of attack. While Honneth's analysis is aimed at the broad fields of social theory and philosophy, the more limited domains of media and cultural studies (fields with their own sets of significant disciplinary disputes) are permeated by a similar distrust of the old-fashioned subject. While there is relatively less of the first, psychologistic line of attack, particularly in more recent cultural analysis – though the proto-Nietzschean approach inaugurated by Gilles Deleuze and Felix Guattari might fit within this category – the reduction of the subject to linguistic, discursive and/or symbolic features is quite commonly accepted within much recent critical theory and practice. As many contemporary approaches to media and culture emerged quite a while after the debates over the classical subject seemed settled, many key assumptions associated with an 'anti-subject' theoretical position appear unquestioned; throwing off the Cartesian shackles was never an issue, let alone a controversy.

As Stuart Hall argued in a recent essay, the widespread popularity of such theories does not automatically require 'an abandonment or abolition of the "the subject" but a reconceptualization – thinking it in a new, displaced or decentered position within the paradigm' (Hall, 1996, p. 2). Hall later points to the work of Judith Butler and other identity theorists as profitably taking up the question of subjectivity, and hopes for a renewed inquiry to explicate the social production of subjects (Hall, 1996, p. 16). While Hall briefly suggests that a less deterministic sense of the suturing of the subject in terms of *articulation* would help advance the understanding of subjectivization, the scheme remains undeveloped in the essay. I will argue that there are other, more fruitful ways of reconceptualizing the subject to facilitate a better understanding of contemporary culture, but I am certainly in agreement with Hall's call for a renewed interest in this area. However, before moving to such a reconceptualization, it is important to sift through some of the most important work addressing issues of social subjectivity and mass culture. While the classical subject, as Honneth points out, may be dead, the means of coping with this loss – so to speak – vary widely and have a considerable theoretical relevance. To do this, I want to look at two pairs of opposing positions, one fairly recent and the other a few decades old, that have been particularly influential for media studies.[1]

The first is an explicit theoretical debate, in this case between two Marxist intellectuals, French philosopher Louis Althusser and British historian E.P. Thompson. Althusser is seldom given credit for the magnitude of his influence, partly for biographical reasons[2] and partly because he adhered to a rather draconian model of 'scientific' Marxist theoretical practice. Nonetheless, his model of ideology as 'the imaginary relationship of individuals to their conditions of existence' (Althusser, 1971, p. 162) and elucidation of a process of 'interpellation' in which individuals are 'hailed' by discourses provided by ideological apparati has had a profound influence on studies of media and popular culture. Althusser's understanding of subjectivity as created by discourse has informed a vast range of scholarship on mass media, from the film analysis of the '*Screen* Althusserians', critics associated with the preeminent British film journal in the seventies, to a good deal of current work within rhetorical studies and political communication. Indeed, it was the scope of Althusser's influence on Marxist cultural studies that inspired Thompson's explicit attack on this model of social subjectivity, although Thompson himself had been working within a radically different tradition of Marxist humanism for some time prior to this direct confrontation. It should be mentioned that Thompson, too, has had a major impact on studies of media and popular culture, as he, along with Raymond Williams and Richard Hoggart, is a founding figure in the 'British Cultural Studies' school.

Thompson's critique of Althusser is centered upon a defense of empirical historical work and a larger theoretical insistence on the importance of concepts such as 'experience' and 'value' in Marxist cultural analysis, concepts rejected within the Althusserian paradigm. Thompson additionally claims that, as a consequence of this rejection, Althusser has no room in his model for human agency, thus producing a theory totally incapable of explaining social change (Thompson, 1979, pp. 91–103). This elision is a particularly critical issue for Thompson, as he had dedicated much of his career as a historian to the question of how 'men make their own history', a major theme in his classic text of cultural history, *The Making of the English Working Class*. In essence, Thompson's critique centers on the nearly total passivity of

Althusser's interpellated subject and the resultant unwillingness to grant any flexibility in the response to and utilization of culture by the individual. This line of criticism is extended in an essay by Kevin McDonnell and Kevin Robins, entitled 'Marxist Cultural Theory: The Althusserian Smokescreen', that details the ways that this position assigns God-like powers to specific cultural objects and denies even the smallest role to individual human experience (Clarke, McDonnell, Robins and Seidler, 1980, pp. 73–174).

Perry Anderson, who offers the most extensive response to Thompson's critique, locates a number of fairly substantial problems in the latter's treatment of Althusser, issues additionally reflective of Thompson's own shortcomings. For one, there is a confusion by Thompson of agency with will and aspiration, a decision that forces Thompson to uphold a rather existential and voluntaristic sense of the human subject (Anderson, 1980, pp. 23–24). Secondly, according to Anderson, Thompson utilizes a wavering and sometimes contradictory sense of experience as a 'veritable limbeck of social life' (Anderson, 1980, p. 25), leaving him little room to address issues of ideology and knowledge that are of course central to Althusser's model. This point is repeated by Ted Benton, working explicitly within the Althusserian tradition, who finds Thompson's charges largely baseless, but acknowledges that Althusser fails to provide a fully theorized account of human historical agency (Benton, 1984, p. 215). This response can be understood as part of a broader critique of the approach characterized by Thompson and Williams as overemphasizing the active and unique character of human cultural participation and as reflective of an 'atomistic' individualism, to use the description of Slack and Whitt (Slack and Whitt, 1992, pp. 576–577). Indeed, Lawrence Grossberg has described the 'moment in which Williams is "saved" by rereading him through Althusserian structuralism' as a key development in the evolution of contemporary cultural studies, suggesting the importance of a possible synthesis of these two disparate positions. Grossberg's own response, a turn towards 'articulation' models of culture, will be discussed shortly, but there is one critical aspect of the Thompsonian critique of Althusser that demands further attention.

As noted, much of the critique of Althusser is directed at the hyper-determinism of the Althusserian model and, interestingly, this quality is sometimes linked to the profound influence of Lacanian psychoanalysis on his thought, with Althusser borrowing much of his understanding of interpellation from Lacan's model of the unconscious as a proto-linguistic structure. However, as a number of scholars have pointed out, Althusser's reading of Lacan is problematic, to put it mildly, and indeed his confusion regarding the Lacanian model may indicate some intriguing possibilities for understanding contemporary social subjectivity.

Terry Eagleton offers a particularly coherent elucidation of the problems with Althusser's use of Lacan in his book-length study of ideology. Eagleton notes Althusser's confusion of the 'ego' in Lacanian theory with the larger and more complex 'subject'. For Eagleton,

> The upshot of this misreading [the aforementioned confusion], then, is to render Althusser's subject a good deal more stable and coherent than Lacan's, since the buttoned-down ego is standing in here for the dishevelled unconscious ... the political implications of this misreading are clear: to expel desire from the subject is to mute its potentially rebellious clamour, ignoring the ways it may attain its allotted place in the social order only ambiguously and precariously. (Eagleton, 1991, p. 144)

It is evident from Eagleton's critique than many of the complaints of Thompson and other critics of Althusserian Marxism are in some sense derived from this initial misunderstanding. Slavoj Zizek, working from an explicitly Lacanian viewpoint, supports Eagleton's criticism, arguing that the 'Althusser-Lacan debate ... is theoretically more far-reaching' than the better-known Habermas-Foucault debate, and reiterates the distinctions between Lacan's unstable model of subjectivity and Althusser's 'process without a subject' model of history (Zizek, 1989, p. 3). The cultural determinism – or at least the retreat into an elitist and quasi-scientific 'theoretical practice' – and the philosophical stand against human agency are certainly bound up with Althusser's failure to acknowledge the unstable desires which permeate and fragment the Lacanian subject. Restoring this instability, this subjective polyvalence, will be a first step in the attempt to produce a fuller and more analytically useful model of the subject.

While the Althusser-Thompson 'debate'[3] may seem inextricably linked to an era of Marxist cultural analysis that has long passed, the fundamental terms of the debate are remarkably resilient. Certainly, they echo the debates within the American tradition of 'media effects' research – described in the introduction – between advocates of a 'powerful effects' model and scholars utilizing a 'uses and gratifications' approach. In these cases, there is little explicit discussion of subjectivity or human agency, as these terms and the debates surrounding them hold virtually no place in either tradition, but the fundamental assumptions regarding the passivity or activity of individuals in relation to systems of meaning-making and communication are remarkably similar. The confrontation between Althusser and Thompson is interesting precisely because it makes those concerns explicit, concerns that are at the heart of my own interest in rethinking questions of identity and mass media.

This debate continues in the work of two very influential figures loosely associated with the 'British Cultural Studies' tradition, John Fiske and Lawrence Grossberg, who provide a second pair of important opposing positions. In this case, there is a direct emphasis on questions of contemporary media culture. Concentrating on these contemporary examples allows a view of the theoretical development of two distinct positions within the 'British' tradition, one derived largely from the theories of Michel de Certeau and the other developed through Stuart Hall, Antonio Gramsi, Ernesto Laclau and Chantal Mouffe, and Deleuze and Guattari. I will argue that both attempt a theoretical route around traditional notions of subjectivity and thus the vexing binary described above, but neither ultimately resolves some fundamental questions.

Fiske's general position on popular culture is complex and controversial, but a key feature is his rejection of the problematic of 'subjectivity' in favor of a model of 'agency', a move explained in the following passage:

> ...theories of subjectivity put greater emphasis on the working of the forces of domination, which are usually explained by ideology theory, commodity theory, or psychoanalysis, whereas theories of agency focus more on how people cope with these forces. Because these forces of domination and discipline are relatively homogenous, subjectivity theories tend to emphasize what is common to all subjects of a particular social order, particularly their consciousness (and subconsciousness). But because the material conditions under which people actually live under these forces vary widely, theories of agency tend to stress diversity. (Fiske, 1994, p. 21)

Fiske's empirical research centers largely upon this question of agency; he examines a wide variety of media phenomena, from televised 'professional' wrestling (Fiske, 1989, pp. 83–89) to independent radical Black radio (Fiske, 1993, pp. 191–217), to uncover and analyze practices of everyday resistance. Fiske's understanding of everyday life, as well as his sense of both agency and 'the popular' is heavily influenced by the work of Michel de Certeau, and especially de Certeau's distinction between 'strategies' and 'tactics'. In de Certeau's work, the former reflects dominant modes of cultural action and interpretation and the latter describes practices that resist such domination and realize a measure of freedom (De Certeau, 1984, pp. 29–30). Fiske borrows this distinction to construct his own sense of 'popular pleasures, consist(ing) of both producerly pleasures of making one's own culture and the offensive pleasure of resisting the structures of domination' (Fiske, 1989, p. 58).

For Fiske, such popular pleasures are indicative of the importance of upholding this sense of agency against a model of subjective domination. As he argues, 'the necessity of negotiating one's way among these contradictory forces means that the members of elaborated societies are social agents rather than social subjects: the contradictions that characterize such societies and their practices require agency rather than subjectivity' (Fiske, 1993, p. 181). The tendency to emphasize agency has made Fiske's work the object of particularly intense – and in my view often quite excessive – criticism from a variety of scholars, including Meaghan Morris, Elspeth Probyn, John Frow and Grossberg himself, who bluntly states that Fiske 'construct(s) the everyday as if it were absolutely autonomous and its practices as if they were always forms of empowerment, resistance, and intervention' (Grossberg, 1997, p. 197). Probyn amplifies these comments, arguing that 'nowhere is resistance so all-consuming, and redemption so automatic as in the work of Fiske' (Probyn, 1993, p. 52). This critique, of course, echoes the aforementioned attacks on Thompson and Williams for their excessive stress on will against the imperatives of power structures, although in this case the blame is not placed on 'humanism' or 'existentialism' but on the use of a binaristic analytical system that fails to recognize the intertwining of popular and dominant interpretive modes.[4]

There is a deeper mode of binary thinking in Fiske's work, though, and one rarely noted by his numerous critics, but more critical to any reconsideration of subjectivity and social selfhood for media studies. As with the other sets of oppositions structuring Fiske's analysis, the subject/agent binary has the effect of flattening out the complexities of social existence into a simplified (subject=bad/agent=good) model. Part of this stems from Fiske's automatic identification of 'subject' with 'subjection'. However, as Michel Foucault notes in a 1984 interview, 'the subject' is not so much a substance as a form, and subjects can occupy a variety of positions, both 'subject to' discipline (as in the 'mad subject') and capable of 'self-constitution', albeit within the resources offered by 'his [sic] culture, his society, and his social group' (Foucault, 1989, p. 122). In a sense, Foucault is restoring a certain linguistic fullness to the term 'subject', as the term can refer both to the condition of being under authority ('subject to') and, in a stricter grammatical sense, to the object performing action in a sentence. One of the advantages of a more complex theory of subjectivity is the ability to account for this fullness, an attribute lost in the Fiskean model.

It is more than an issue of semantics, though, and Foucault's historical work – especially the later work – makes it clear that the various processes of subjectification imply more just than an enabling or constraining of social practice. These processes also produce modes of self-relation, ways of understanding one's position as a social subject and one's relation to the set of institutions, codes, norms and practices that constitute a social totality. The understanding of culture as producing modes of self-relation requires, at least minimally, a 'depth subject'. This is not the same, necessarily, as an 'existential subject'; it does not have to imply an authentic core beneath layers of socialized lamination. It does however require a minimal faith in the capacity for some mode of self-reflection and socially enabled self-understanding. This point is critical if one hopes to understand the social individual in regard to a plurality of codes, institutions and discourses. In his genealogical investigation of antiquity, Foucault dedicates a considerable space to understanding the ways that individuals had to manage multiple symbolic systems dealing with sexual, political and physical matters in a larger process of self-care (Foucault, 1985, pp. 39–68). This is clearly an issue that could not have been addressed through a more instrumental model of the individual and social action, as in an *agency* model; an individual instance of social practice is only a symptom here of a larger, multifaceted process of subjectification. While Foucault's point regarding the dual character of subjectivity will be important in my case for a neo-pragmatist social subject, the wider question of whether any form of subjectivity (or even agency) should be at the center of critical cultural analyses of media demands attention.

Grossberg is a leading advocate of a strong move away from such approaches, and his rejection of them is connected to a more general stance against 'Kantian' tendencies in social theory, including poststructuralism, that posit a primacy of 'meaning' and 'understanding' in all social practice (Grossberg, 1992, pp. 43–44). This tendency produces analysis aimed at understanding or 'decoding' the hidden truths of cultural texts, a process common to much ideology critique, as well as to traditional literary criticism. The consequences for social analysis, according to Grossberg, are a 'flatten[ing] [of] the possibilities of cultural relations and effects', and, more broadly, an elision of 'the real' from analysis through a displacement of it into the realm of representation (Grossberg, 1992, p. 44). As an alternative, Grossberg, working from a theoretical position initially developed by Hall, poses an *articulation* model of popular culture, describing it in the following terms,

> Thus the project of reconstructing historical contexts or organizations of practices [the task of articulation-based cultural studies], despite superficial similarities, is not a search for the underlying codes governing and determining human behavior. Nor is it the same as, for example, Williams' project of describing 'a structure of feeling'. It is not a description of experience, of what it felt like to live at a particular time and place. It is not a phenomenologically motivated attempt to capture a context of experience, or, as Foucault puts it, to grasp a '"whole society" in its "living reality."' The position I have presented here is not concerned with how people experience daily reality but with how they live and act in ways over which they may have no control and about which they may be unaware, experientially as well as consciously. In this project, experiences are not privileged, they are to be treated as facts among other facts. (Grossberg, 1992, pp. 62–63).

In addition to the explicit rejection of both Williams and Foucault, Grossberg's distance from Fiske's perspective is also quite clear. The renunciation of 'experience' as a special analytical category echoes the Althusserian polemic against Thompson, of course, but it also raises some significant questions about how such a model might regard issues of cultural identity, self-consciousness and subjectivity; simply positing them as 'facts among other facts' does not get one very far.

What, though, is the specific status of the subject/agent in Grossberg's model? It is perhaps easiest to begin by identifying three models of subjectivity explicitly rejected in the Grossbergian articulation model. As expected, Grossberg rejects the classical, Cartesian subject, who 'stands objectively poised outside of reality, (and is) the subject of rationality, language-use, creativity, and responsibility' (Grossberg, 1992, p. 117). As mentioned, the rejection of such a model of subjectivity is a standard assumption in cultural studies, as well as much current literary criticism, sociology, philosophy etc.; it is not surprising that it will not be 'the subject' of articulation theory.

Grossberg moves much further, though, rejecting a prominent alternative to the Cartesian subject: the 'interpellated subject', associated most closely with Althusser of course, but generally connected with a variety of positions including certain strains of functionalism and structuralism. This 'empty and weightless' individual is rejected for many of the reasons mentioned in the discussion of the Althusser-Thompson debate: no model of agency, no place for experience, and a resultant political pessimism (Grossberg, 1992, p. 120). Again, this is not particularly shocking, given Grossberg's intellectual roots in British Cultural Studies and especially Hall's work.

However, Grossberg takes this position still another step further, rejecting many of the alternatives to the interpellation model that attempt to preserve the sense of the socio-linguistically constructed subject without succumbing to an agency-inhibiting determinism. These include Kristeva's theory of a transcendent 'semiotic chora', as well as the later Foucault's self-caring subject, which are rejected, respectively, on the grounds of a metaphysical shakiness and a charge of ahistoricism (Grossberg, 1992, p. 121). Similarly, theories of 'incomplete interpellation' (the work of Zizek is not mentioned here but clearly fits within this paradigm) are discarded as too vague to be analytically useful (p. 120). Finally and most surprisingly, Deleuze and Guattari – important influences on other aspects of Grossberg's theoretical perspective – who locate a potential agency in the 'schizo' subject are deemed similarly naïve in regards to domination and politically unreliable in the intrinsic individualism of their understanding of the schizo (Grossberg, 1992, p. 121). Thus, Grossberg in due course rejects virtually any model of social subjectivity with even the slightest traces of a dreaded 'Kantianism', which in his view seems to include any model of the subject retaining a strong sense of the importance of mental, symbolic operations that are in some way individualized.

Grossberg does not avoid this area of inquiry entirely, though, and constructs the figure of the 'affective individual' to cover some of this ground. For Grossberg, the affective individual exists between subjection and empowerment, 'mov(ing) along different vectors... its course is determined by social, cultural, and historical knowledges, but its particular mobilities are never entirely directed or guaranteed' (Grossberg, 1992, p. 126). Similarly, the concept of the affective individual navigates between the stable, modern subject and the fragmented subject of post-structuralism: 'The affective individual is always a multiple, taking on the shape and color of the affective states through which it moves. Yet a certain coherence is always possible, and always effective, even if it is always fleeting' (Grossberg, 1992, p. 127). In the description of the affective individual, there is a great emphasis on the contingency of the process of affective investment, with 'no necessary correspondences between the various elements of this complex economy on individuality and agency' and 'nothing which guarantees which subjectivities or identities form nominal groups which are able to become historical agents' (Grossberg, 1992, p. 127). The process of transformation is left almost completely open – or to be less charitable vague – in Grossberg's theorization of the individual, subjectivity and agency. Clearly the process must depend on a material and/or discursive opening allowing for such a mobilization; however, any individual factors, for example consciousness or other social psychological factors, that might enable or constrain such a process – the heart of the 'ideology' model of social practice – are absent in any real form from this model.

This quality is evident in Grossberg's application of this theoretical standpoint to media culture. Take for example his description of forms of media fandom and the 'inauthentic authenticity' they reflect:

> Each creates a series of images of stars who embody not authentic instances of subjectivity and political resistance or even ideological statements, but temporary moods that can be appropriated by fans as temporary places rather than impossible identities, strategies by which individuals can continue to locate themselves within affective maps, and continue to make a difference, if not in the world, at least in their lives... Such strategies do not give us positions from which we can judge ourselves and the world, but as places in which we can temporarily install ourselves so that we can act, so that we can gain some control over our lives, so that we can negotiate the spaces between pain and comfort, between terror and boredom. (Grossberg, 1992, p. 232)

There is an interesting tension in the passage above (and the larger analysis) between the ways that modes of inauthenticity enable affective 'cartography' but fail to provide the ground for hermeneutic reflection – 'judging oneself and the world'. It may be that, as Grossberg argues, there has been a 'dissolution of what we might call the "anchoring effect" that articulates meaning and affect' (Grossberg, 1992, p. 223), but this does not necessarily engender a collapse of the process of generating a subjective self-reflexivity. It may mean that such a process is profoundly unstable and heavily fragmented but as even Grossberg admits, a 'fleeting coherence' is always possible. I would not quibble with his identification of such 'strategies' but I would argue that, at some point, a process of self- and world- understanding does take place; the distinction between a 'temporary installation' and a space of world and self-examination seems rather dubious. Any self-judgment, and especially one that takes account of the social generation of such a hermeneutic perspective is necessarily temporary. To deny that this is *ever* possible, it seems, would lead to a kind of post-structural behaviorism in which consciousness is folded into cognition and in which the possibility for a critical awareness appears to vanish.

To further explain the characterization of this model as 'behaviorist', I would argue that Grossberg's theoretical position tends to render the subject rather like the 'black box' of Watsonian psychological behaviorism. While we have the 'affective individual' drifting through various cultural attachments with differing degrees of investment, and a (collective or individual) agent taking advantage of the appropriate alignment of 'tendential forces' to enact meaningful cultural practice, the relationship between the former into the latter remains rather mysterious. Likewise, the formation of an admittedly transient subjective coherence is left undeveloped. Given the highly tentative and distinctly morphological character of the various affective investments individuals make, some sense of how a portfolio of investments – to extend the fiscal metaphor – with varying degrees of consonance and dissonance, is managed would seem to be critical to examining questions of ideology and social knowledge. Some of this gap can probably be explained by the commitment to a radical anti-Kantianism, but there are certainly ways of understanding subjectivity that are neither Kantian nor Cartesian, but that can account for a self-consciousness that is both unstable and evolving and also simultaneously capable of self-reflection and self-determination. Again, these will be explored in the following section, but appear here as absences which could help fill out the articulation model.

Ultimately, the work of Fiske and Grossberg reflects two very different positions regarding the relative activity/passivity of the media consumer – with a resultant political optimism and pessimism, respectively – and yet they share a similarly thin model of social subjectivity. For Fiske, this comes through an explicit rejection of the concept itself in favor of 'agency', while for Grossberg there is a conscious de-personalization of culture. I would argue, though, that both approaches reflect a side-stepping of questions regarding the subjective dimension of contemporary experiences with media rather than a strong case for ruling such questions out as irrelevant or hopelessly naïve. The consequences of subjectivity-based studies of popular culture identified by Fiske and Grossberg – a focus on domination or a Kantian idealism, respectively

– are simply not inevitable; likewise, an automatic assumption of passivity or activity or, more specifically, of dominance and resistance, is not an inevitable result of such an approach. The answer, I will argue, lies in the deployment of an adequate model of the social subject.

The I and the me(dia): the hermeneutic social subject and media studies

While the work of Grossberg and Fiske suggests, through its absences, the need for a more thorough reconsideration of issues of identity, particularly in relation to the study of media and culture, other recent scholars have made some intriguing steps in this direction. For instance, Elspeth Probyn's *Sexing the Self* and Toby Miller's *The Well-Tempered Self*, both published in 1993, take the issue of self-construction (as the titles would indicate) as a primary focus. Probyn works from feminist thought and the later Foucault to call for a renewed attention to the self and to clear a space for the category of social experience, which has largely vanished – despite its aforementioned fundamental role in early British Cultural Studies – from recent work on popular culture. Miller, on the other hand, provides a more 'top-down' analysis of the contemporary social subject in light of changing institutional contexts, particularly but not exclusively those related to state power. Both authors place a clear emphasis on the self-creating and self-disciplining aspects, respectively, of contemporary popular culture.

Although the emphases of their research are quite different, both Miller and Probyn turn to the later work of Foucault to understand the way that culture matters, so to speak, for the self. In Probyn's case, this involves enlisting Gilles Deleuze's notion of subjectivity in the late Foucault as kind of 'fold' in the social plane (Miller, 1993, pp. 127–132); popular media discourses, in Probyn's case the performance of comedian Sandra Bernhardt, thus provide instruments for a kind of folding process through which forms of self-understanding are possible (Probyn, 1993, p. 163). Miller, as noted, places greater stress on the social institutions – including the culture industries – that work to create 'well-tempered' selves; the dynamics of these selves mimic the musical structure of Bach's 'The Well-Tempered Clavier', famous for its use of a melodic tension between freedom and restriction (Miller, 1993, pp. ix–x). While Miller discusses the possibilities for the production of 'unruly' forms of selfhood, there is greater focus on the development of forms of cultural citizenship that support dominant institutions. In this respect, Probyn and Miller can be viewed as extending the continuum of passivity and activity evident in the Thompson/Althusser and Fiske/ Grossberg comparisons, with the former stressing individual experience and the personalization of popular cultural discourses and the latter emphasizing the shaping power of economic and political institutions. However, both add an analytical, symbolic depth to the operative model of the social subject lacking in the earlier work and thus open significant avenues for future research.

In a particularly intriguing passage in *The Well-Tempered Self,* Miller briefly engages the theoretical perspective on selfhood provided by the American pragmatist philosopher George Herbert Mead to understand how culture can work – even within formidable limitations – to create forms of self-reflexive understanding (Miller, 1993, pp. 207–208). While this brief observation is left otherwise undeveloped, particularly in specific reference to Mead's work, the recognition of Mead's potential contribution is noteworthy, as it will provide the foundation for my own exploration of the self-constructing possibilities of electronic media. Indeed, it may be telling that Miller's citation of Mead comes in a section of his book focusing on the complex, even contradictory dynamics of self-formation in contemporary culture, as Mead's understanding of the social-symbolic self is uniquely capable of recognizing this quality at a theoretical and an analytical level.

Before delving into the views of specific thinkers on the issue of 'the hermeneutic social subject', I want to lay out three central features of such a model that will then be elaborated through the subsequent discussion of Mead's work and its explication and expansion in Tugendhat, Kögler, Habermas and others. The first important characteristic is that the hermeneutic subject possesses at least the possibility for a degree of autonomy from the symbolic and material structures within which she operates. The second critical characteristic is that of contingency; if the hermeneutic subject cannot be reduced – as in Norbert Wiley's 'upward reduction' (Wiley, 1994, pp. 157–194) – to a set of social contexts, they are nonetheless the basis for the constitution of the subject (a seeming paradox which will be discussed later). The hermeneutic subject is most certainly not a return to a transparent, Cartesian subject; it is a socially constructed but irreducible sense of the subject. Thirdly and finally, the hermeneutic subject is predicated upon the possibility for at least some measure of critical-reflexive awareness of the structures and methods through which forms of social interpretation and action are both allowed and restricted. Like the subject herself, this awareness is highly contingent and not a natural social process nor is it in any way guaranteed.

Mead's work, perhaps most famous for its influence on Herbert Blumer and his symbolic interactionist followers, provides a number of challenges for the scholar attempting to integrate it within a more contemporary tradition of socio-cultural analysis. At a practical level, a full understanding of Mead's theoretical position is difficult, as what is arguably his most important work, *Mind, Self, and Society* was posthumously assembled from unpublished manuscripts and students' lecture notes (Mead, 1934, p. vi), leaving the work somewhat sketchy and certainly underdeveloped. There are other difficulties, though, that are more directly related to the substance of Mead's work. One is his rather limited sense of socialization and, especially, subjective development. As Anthony Giddens points out, 'the social in Mead's formulation is limited to familial figures and the "generalized other"; Mead did not elaborate a conception of a differentiated society nor any interpretation of social transformation' (Giddens, 1979, p. 50). Secondly, because Mead never developed some of the more dynamic implications of his theory of a social self, it was therefore easy for interpreters to neglect this aspect of his work, a move that encourages, as Giddens notes, a split between an interactional micro-sociology and a functionalist macro-sociology (Giddens, 1979, p. 254). Some of the narrowness of Mead's sense of 'the social' can be attributed to his having worked in the first few decades of the twentieth century, a context in which the breadth and complexity of the social-symbolic environment was far narrower. Certainly, there is little in Mead's theory per se that limits it to micro-sociological contexts.

Mead also tended to pose his theory in terms of *action*, describing himself as a 'social behaviorist'; indeed, one of Mead's most famous students was John B. Watson, a key figure in the school of thought known as psychological behaviorism. It is absolutely critical, though, not to equate Mead's work with that of behaviorism, at least as the latter is commonly understood. Mead explicitly distanced himself from Watsonian behaviorism (Cook, 1993, pp. 75–77), and once again there is little in his theory itself that would limit it to such a narrow understanding of social action. However as noted, Mead did not develop his theory to cover a more complex array of social practices, which again places a considerable burden of explication on any attempt to deploy Meadian theory in a contemporary context. In a sense, these limitations are most significant for the ways that they have tended to limit the use of Meadian theory to fields having a 'micro' focus, such as interpersonal communication and symbolic interactionist sociology, and have obscured his potential contribution to the study of media and popular culture.

The most notable feature of Mead's understanding of the development and functioning of identity is his division of the self into two distinct elements, the *I* and the *me*, that comprise, dialectically, the whole
self. Ian Burkitt offers a nice overview of this theoretical position:

> For Mead, there are two sides to the social self. There is the objective
> presence of the self within the group which acts as the stimulus to
> others; and then there is the subjective attitude of reflection which
> treats as an object the responses of the body to others in interaction.
> Mead had labeled these two faces of the self, which are continually
> in dialogue, the 'me' and the 'I'. Both faces are social and only
> emerge together in discourse, but the 'me' represents a unique iden-
> tity a self develops through seeing its form in the attitudes others
> take towards it, while the 'I' is the subjective attitude of reflection
> itself, which gazes on both the objective image of the self and its
> own responses. (Burkitt, 1991, p. 38)

Burkitt goes on to explain that this 'I' is radically different from the
Cartesian sense of a transcendental 'I' in that it emerges through social
interaction; it is not a 'primary reality' in the Kantian tradition, but
only appears through the thematization of 'me's' as 'objectified past
actions' (Burkitt, 1991, p. 40). While the 'I' is in some weak sense transcendental, as it exceeds individual 'me'-positions, it cannot exist independent of the social movement of the 'me'; in a logical sense, an 'I'
cannot reflect upon a 'me' until it emerges in social discourse. Though
Burkitt does not mention it above, Mead makes it clear that the I/me
dynamic is a distinctly social phenomenon and that it is not 'organismic' in the sense of a natural reaction of an animal to a given stimulus.
The play of the 'I' and the 'me' is a consequence of the individual's ability to 'tak(e) the attitude of the other... until this happens, he does not
appear as a self' (Mead, 1934, p. 195). This point is critical as it separates
Mead both from a behaviorism (in which 'self' would be wholly irrelevant) and from positing an essential, pre-given or wholly determined
self.

While Burkitt provides a nice gloss on the I/me dialectic, a number of
features demand further elucidation, and I will begin with the 'me'. For
Mead, 'the "me" is the conventional, habitual individual. It is always
there. It has to have those habits, those responses which everybody
[in an "organized community"] has; otherwise, the individual could
not be a member of the community' (Mead, 1934, p. 197). It is essential to recognize that this 'me' is not a stable, permanent feature, as it

is continually reworked, subject to membership in changing communities and the social acts of the individual. Without the complementary 'I', though, the 'me' – even given the limitations noted above – might appear to rule out autonomous social action. Its formation would appear rather like Althusserian processes of interpellation, and thus be subject to similar critiques for offering no apparent escape from conformity. However, the Meadian 'I' serves as a mechanism for understanding the novelty of social practice and the individual struggle for self-determination within a community or set of communities. Mead explains the 'I' in the following passage,

> ...it is the presence of those organized sets of attitudes that the constitute that 'me' to which he as an 'I' is responding. But what this response will be he does not know and nobody else knows. Perhaps he will make a brilliant move or an error. The response to that situation as it appears in his immediate experience is uncertain and it is that which constitutes the 'I'... the movement into the future is the step, so to speak, of the 'I'. It is something not given in the 'me'. (Mead, 1934, pp. 175, 177)

Again, it is important that the 'I', like the larger self, is not understood as a pre-existing entity that is reigned in by the oppressive 'me', but instead as a part of a mutually enabling pair. As George Cronk points out, 'the "me" is a necessary symbolic structure which renders the action of the "I" possible ...' (Cronk, 1987, p. 40); this interdependent character avoids both the possibility of a pure authenticity of the 'I' and of a total conformity of the 'me'.

Beyond the capacity for conceptualizing novel social action, the 'I' also serves as the mechanism for self-reflection, for the ability of the individual to become aware of the limitations associated with a particular 'me' position. This process, though, does not involve any direct access to the 'I' itself, as this would be impossible in that the 'I' can only appear to the individual as a post-construction, as a 'me'; a self-reflecting gaze upon the whole of the self would obviously be logically impossible as the agency of reflection cannot be located outside of the self, nor could it ever be able to turn in upon itself completely (Cronk, 1987, p. 38).

The issue of self-reflection and the potentially self-reflexive understanding of 'me' positions necessarily leads into Mead's concept of the mechanism for self-development and 'attitude-taking' that structures the play of the 'I' and the 'me'. It is here that Mead's sense of the 'role' becomes particularly important. 'Roles' are the connective tissue between the individual and society; they provide the means through which the self emerges and develops. The role is the mechanism that makes it possible for the symbolic structures of the community – those elements that comprise the 'me' – to become the enabling mechanism for the social action of the 'I'. 'Role' here is used to designate the process through which an individual can assume the perspective of an other, a process that would begin in childhood with physically proximate others. Eventually, the assumption of more complex roles involves the ability to assume the perspective of a 'generalized other', which is a synthetic set of community perspectives.

The organized community or social group which gives to the individual his unity of self may be called 'the generalized other'. The attitude of the generalized other is the attitude of the whole community... It is in the form of the generalized other that social process influences the behavior of the individuals involved in it and carrying it on, i.e., that the community enters as a determining factor into the individual's thinking; for it is in this form that the social process or community enters as a determining factor into the individual's thinking. (Mead, 1934, pp. 154–155).

The issue of the generalized other is pursued with particular vigor by the analytic philosopher Ernst Tugendhat, who links a kind of quest for additional 'generalized others' to the development of a critical self-consciousness. Tugendhat argues that Mead's sense of self-assertion depends upon a process in which the individual seeks to displace a generalized other or others in order to develop a set of norms more amenable to the demands of the 'I'. Tugendhat cites Mead's explanation of this process: 'The only way in which we can react against the disapproval of the entire community is by setting up a higher sort of community which in a certain sense out-votes the one we find' (Tugendhat, 1986, p. 253). This can be tied back into the question of the 'I' and the 'me' by recalling Mead's sense of the action of the 'I' as enabled by the mediation of multiple me (essentially role) positions. As Hans Joas explains, in the process of self-construction, multiple 'me's' must be synthesized into a single self (Joas, 1985, p. 158). The pluralization of generalized others through encounters with a diverse and often divergent set of socially generated expectations requires an increasingly complex I-me relation, a condition with significant cultural implications.

Mead addresses this question directly in *The Philosophy of the Present*, discussing the temporal dimension of such dialogical encounters with otherness:

> Now this [the 'conversation with oneself'] is possible only in the continual passage from attitude to attitude; but the fact that we do not remain simply within this passage is due to our coming back upon it in the role of the self and organizing the characters which we pick out into the patterns this social structure of the self puts at our disposal. The stretch of the present within which this self-consciousness finds itself is delimited by the particular social act in which we are engaged. (Mead, 1932, p. 87)

There is an unexpected but intriguing similarity here with Grossberg's aforementioned characterization of the 'affective individual'. The social actor moves through a set of attitudes, tied to a present experience, that structure social understanding, and, to use Grossberg's terminology, builds 'strategies by which individuals can continue to locate themselves within affective maps' (Grossberg, 1992, p. 232). However, Mead's understanding places a stronger emphasis on the continual encounter with past – at its zenith, he argues, in the aesthetic attitude – and the reconstructive task of activating the 'symbolic universals', as Mead puts it, to make sense of this past and to anticipate the movement of the future. The self – the I/me structure – provides the grounding for this task, with the 'I' moving into the future and the collected me-structures generating the symbolic possibilities for this action (the enabling function described above). Through the analytical mechanism of the role and his theory of time, Mead is able to create a level of depth to the practically generated experience of self without surrendering the primacy of social praxis. The impression of a 'black box' subject that appears in Grossberg's version of articulation theory is thus alleviated if one supplements such an understanding with a Meadian sense of the self-conscious social individual.

While, as noted, Mead's work has had almost no significant impact on critical studies of media culture, his work has inspired a noteworthy body of explication and expansion within recent German philosophy, and this work can add substantially to the analytic utility of Mead's hermeneutic model of the self. In addition to the discussion of the generalized other noted above, Tugendhat has provided a very useful elaboration of the dynamics of this self-construction in his *Self-Consciousness and Self-Determination*:

The following consequences can be drawn from these considerations [role theory]: First, a relation to oneself (i.e., to one's to-be) is contained in the assumption of roles, because roles as cooperative activities are constitutive of meaning. Second, the role is only an offer of meaning, and whether I make it my own depends on me. Thus, we also encounter the phenomenon of a yes/no position here, and we will see that this aspect of role behavior is crucial for Mead himself. The tension between identification and distance has relevance for the aspect of the self that he designates as 'I'. But taking a position toward roles is a relation to oneself, not because it involves taking a position toward something, but because it is taking a position toward possibilities of understanding *myself*; and here *myself* means my life. Even if one experiences a role that one occupies as not meaningful for oneself – for one's life – one relates precisely in this way to oneself, to one's life and its potential meaning. (Tugendhat, 1986, p. 243)

Here, Tugendhat identifies two important aspects of the process that are never discussed directly by Mead: the volitional character of role-playing and the way that such role-play constitutes a larger framework of autobiographical understanding. The refusal of a generalized other position, that is to say an identity, is itself an act of self-econstruction; the 'offer of meaning' does not guarantee acceptance of that offer. A course of attachments and distanciations, then, creates a meta-process of autobiographical understanding, one that requires he structural element of the 'I' as a means for reflecting upon this collection of other-encounters.

This point is more thoroughly pursued by Hans-Herbert Kögler, who mobilizes Mead for the understanding of a social reflexivity that can overcome the 'social dope' model of the individual[5] without the need for an idealist social subject or a post-structural asubjectivism. However, to build such a theoretical position – which has implications largely absent in Mead's work – Kögler needs to make an important modification of Meadian theory. This concerns Mead's naïve and idealist view of language and the process of understanding. As Kögler points out, Mead tends toward a 'transparency-theory of symbolic meaning' in which symbolic structures are merely mechanisms for the transmission of prior meanings; there is no sense, in Mead, of the ways that the 'relative autonomy' of a 'symbolic sphere' shapes social self-understanding (Kögler, 1996, pp. 193–200). This in turn leads Mead, who is otherwise very attentive to the social situatedness of understanding and action, to assume a kind of authenticity, particularly in regard to the movement of an 'I', in the reaction against the confining character of a given social norm (Kögler, 1996, p. 217). As Kögler points out, 'this conception would lead back into a pre-semiotic, metaphysical conception of bodily needs and desires, instead of assuming that even in this case [the refusal of social norms], our self-understanding has to be conceptualized as representing the internalization of symbolic structures' (Kögler, 1996, p. 217). However, by foregrounding the semiotic nature of Meadian role-play, Kögler argues that such potentially idealist and organismic connotations can be avoided. This move would also serve to re-emphasize the symbolic character of self-construction in Mead and potentially expand the range of 'others' that provide significant offers of meaning – to use Tugendhat's term – for a given individual.

   This expanded range of others is an important feature for Jurgen Habermas, perhaps the most famous contemporary interpreter of Mead. Habermas is particularly interested in the relevance of Mead's thinking for a modern social environment, the 'de-traditionalized lifeworld' in Habermasian terms, marked by an increasingly fluid process of identity formation. In his essay 'Individuation through Socialization: On Mead's Theory of Subjectivity', Habermas argues that Mead's theoretical position has a particular suitability for a social-symbolic context in which 'only a postconventional ego-identity could satisfy these demands [for social integration]. And such an ego-identity could only develop in the course of a progressive individuation' (Habermas, 1992, p. 197). Habermas further argues that Mead's model of the social self can counter the grim conclusion that the individual is merely 'the reproduction unit of the social' (Habermas, 1992, p. 199).[6] While Habermas' thus echoes Tugenhadt's and Kögler's stressing of the more dynamic quality of Mead's thought against any potentially deterministic implications, his work is important for its emphasis on the consonance between this dynamic model of selfhood and a similarly dynamic symbolic environment. This is a key point in any attempt to connect Meadian self-theory with the study of contemporary media as the proliferation of forms of electronic and virtual media has played a central role – one recognized by Habermas – in the creation of this 'lifeworld'.[7]

   As mentioned, Probyn and Miller, two scholars of contemporary media culture, turn to the later Foucault for an understanding of subjectivity and it is thus intriguing that Mead's theories intersect with this later work in some critical ways. I had mentioned Probyn's use of the Deleuzian reading of Foucault's subject as a 'fold', and this figure offers an interesting area of convergence. Deleuze understands Foucault's subject as built upon a sense of 'the inside as an operation of the outside: in all his work Foucault seems haunted by the theme of an inside which is merely the fold of an outside...' (Deleuze, 1988, p. 97). More specifically, Deleuze describes the Foucauldian process of subjectivation in the following passage,

> This derivative of differentiation must be understood in the sense in which the *relation to oneself* assumes an independent status. It is as if the relations of the outside folded back to create a doubling, allow a relation to oneself to emerge, and constitute an inside which is hollowed out and develops its own unique dimension ... This is the Greek version of the snag and the doubling: a differentiation that leads to a folding, a reflection. [italics in original] (Deleuze, 1988, p. 100)

Deleuze then concludes that 'Foucault's fundamental idea is that of a dimension of subjectivity derived from power and knowledge without being dependant on them' (Deleuze, 1988, p. 101), arguing that, in the later work, Foucault provides a model of the subject as derivative but possessive of an 'irreducible dimension' (Deleuze, 1988, p. 106).

Deleuze's reading of Foucault is important here because this 'folded' subject is quite close to Mead's I/me dialogue. In his lecture on 'The Problem of Society – How We Become Selves', Mead offers a view of the origins of the self strikingly compatible with Deleuze's Foucauldian model:

> A self can only arise where there is a social process within which this self has had its initiation. It arises within that process. For that process the communication and participation to which I have referred is essential. That is the way in which selves as such have arisen. That is where the individual is in a social process in which he is a part, where he does influence himself as he does others. There the self arises. And there he turns back upon himself, directs himself. He takes over those experiences which belong to his own organism. He identifies them with himself. (Mead, 1936, pp. 384–385).

The I/me dialogue and the emphasis on a form of role-play in the derivation of self is similarly echoed in the Foucauldian 'foldings' identified by Deleuze. Deleuze describes the Greek self as emerging from '[italics in original] *a relation which force has with itself, a power to affect itself, an affect of self on self* ... The relation with others must be doubled by a relation with oneself' (Deleuze, 1988, p. 101). The notion of self-generating and self-monitoring operations derived from the relation with others is similarly the basis of Mead's I/me schema. The 'affect of self on self' and the 'doubling' of social relations is at the heart of Mead's notion of an 'internal conversation' in which one assumes the attitudes of others in regard to the development of one's own thought and action. While Mead would never explain this process in terms of force – he clearly takes a more optimistic and less power-conscious view of 'subjectization' – the emphasis on an internal doubling of an outward relation is very similar to Foucault.

There is a more general similarity as well in the mutual orientation to discourse as a primary engine in the generation of this internal relation. In Mead, certainly, language serves as the locus for the generation of the self; in fact, it is Mead's rather unproblematic sense of language as a neutral medium that provokes Kögler's semiotic revision. In Foucault, the connection is less direct, but there is a similar emphasis on the role of a variety of discursive practices in generating and shaping self-relation. For example, in his discussion of Greek techniques of the self in *The Care of the Self*, Foucault describes the importance of 'notes which one takes on books or on conversations one has heard', 'the talks that one has with a confidant, with friends, with a guide or director', and the role of correspondence in shaping the self. 'Around the care of the self', Foucault concludes, 'there developed an entire activity of speaking and writing in which the work of oneself on oneself and communication with others were linked together' (Foucault, 1986, p. 51). In this case, the 'folding' of the outside is manifested through a doubling of communicative practices.

While Foucault focuses on classical antiquity in his analysis of this 'folded' subject and Mead, as noted, was working in the late nineteenth and early twentieth centuries, there is no reason that the range of communicative practices implicated in this 'turning back' needs to be limited to any particular medium or set of media. In this light, the affective potency of mediated discourses, a key quality of contemporary culture for the polemically anti-Foucauldian Grossberg, can be reconciled with a deeper and more hermeneutically rich model of the subject. Such affective forces create a field – or in Meadian terms, a set of generalized others – for the derivation of forms of selfhood through an internal utilization of these symbolic objects. While Foucault *describes* this process, Mead's position – particularly as expanded and modified by recent German thought – is uniquely equipped to offer a conceptual apparatus capable of *explaining* it.

Psychoanalytic interlude: Mead, Lacan and the psycho-social character of media

If Mead and Foucault can work in a complementary relationship in regard to issues of cultural self-construction, Mead's work has a similar and provocative resemblance to that of Jacques Lacan, arguably the most influential psychoanalytic theorist of the past 50 years and, as noted, a key (if misunderstood) influence on Althusser and his followers. Interestingly, the connection between Mead and Lacan is seldom made; Anthony Giddens notes a passing resemblance in the conceptual orientation of the two thinkers, but quickly dismisses any significant theoretical consonance (Giddens, 1979, p. 50). However, I would argue that there is a remarkable similarity in the way each conceives of the social development of the self, with Mead's I/me formulation – the 'I' as impulsive actor and the 'me' as conventionally adherent to symbolic norms – mirroring Lacan's sense of self-formation as rooted in otherness and reliant upon the deployment of social-symbolic structures, but always subject to a kind of psychic overflow. Lacan's anti-Cartesian view of the self as a sort of fiction and his argument that self-stability is achieved through symbolic anchoring similarly shares with Mead the notion of an essentially communicative process at the center of self-formation. Both also thought of reality as a kind of wild and unstable phenomenon, with Mead inheriting John Dewey's sense of reality as a 'blooming, buzzing confusion', and Lacan posing 'the real' as always beyond the reach of signification.[8] The crucial difference, of course, is that Mead did not operate with a Freudian psychoanalytic orientation towards the unconscious, and especially the paramount importance of desire, although his understanding of the process of self-formation certainly does not preclude the impact of these elements. In this sense, Lacan can help to correct, so to speak, Mead's rather orderly sense of self-development, and identify more precisely an openness, even a void, at the heart of the subject.

Of course, psychoanalytic theory is perhaps even less central to media studies than Meadian neo-pragmatism. While it hangs on, albeit tenuously, in literary and cinema studies, there is almost no significant place for psychoanalytically-inflected research in the study of other traditional objects of mass communication (television, popular music, virtual communication). Some of this is likely due to the tendency for recent psychoanalytic approaches to culture to have a text-oriented or even text-dominated focus. While textual analysis has fallen from favor in media studies to a vast array of competing strategies, from ethnographic analysis to political economy and institutional studies, psychoanalytic research has seldom followed suit. In this respect, an integration of Meadian and Lacanian perspectives could serve an additional function of helping to rejuvenate psychoanalytic theory by fusing it with an approach – neo-pragmatism – that places actual social experiences at the center of any analysis.

Lacan himself perceived forms of mediated communication as critical to the psychological character of contemporary life in a brief but highly suggestive passage in his groundbreaking 1953 essay, 'Function and Field of Speech and Language'. Here, Lacan refers quite explicitly to the potentially terrifying consequences of the proliferation of communication media. Referring to the 'loss' of the subject within communication, Lacan writes:

> There might be some point in measuring its [the 'language barrier'] thickness by the statistically determined total of pounds of printed paper, miles of record grooves, and hours of broadcasting that said culture produces per head of population in sectors A, B, and C of its domain... the resemblance between this situation [the 'thickness'] and the alienation of madness, in so far as the formula given above is authentic – that is, that here the subject is spoken rather than speaking – obviously derives from the demand, presupposed by psychoanalysis, for 'true' speech. (Lacan, 1977, p. 71)

Later, Lacan admits that this situation does not rule out the possibility for a creative subjectivity (Lacan, 1977, p. 72), but his comparison with the condition of insanity certainly suggests a rather dour view of this condition. While Lacan never developed this somewhat offhand analysis in any systematic fashion, it certainly raises the stakes on the Meadian notion of self-reflection as a perpetual dialogue deploying available symbolic tools. Here, the pluralization of these tools is more than just an issue of a 'de-traditionalized lifeworld' but also of a powerful recircuiting of desire.

Understanding symbolic self-construction as an issue of desire as well as socialization and the willful selection of a proper symbolic community will also move a neo-pragmatist approach a step further from more deterministic models (from Althusserianism to psychological behaviorism). One danger with Mead's work is that it can appear to naturalize processes of self-construction, and thus posit 'successful' socialization as conformity to social norms (Denzin, 1992, pp. 7–8). Similarly, both Richard Lichtman and Erving Goffman raise the concern that Mead's approach and especially his emphasis on the importance of role-play for self-development leaves little room for innovative human action (Cronk, 1973, pp. 319–320; Goffman, 1961, pp. 84–85). Certainly, Tugendhat's emphasis on volition and Kögler's on semiotics help to mitigate the residual determinism in Mead's model, but adding a Lacanian emphasis on the powerful desires that transect the symbolic fields that provide the groundwork for the self destabilizes the process further.

In this respect, Zizek's characterization of the late Foucauldian model of subjectivity and his Lacanian opposition to it may be useful given the aforementioned similarity of this figure with Mead's model. Zizek describes Foucault's model of a self-caring subject as part of a 'humanist-elitist tradition [in which] its closest realization would be the Renaissance ideal of the "all around" personality mastering the passions within himself and making his own life a work of art' (Zizek, 1989, p. 2); against this, Zizek poses Lacan's model of self-consciousness in which the highest form of self-awareness is a kind of 'subjective destitution' in which the individual realizes a distance from the mechanisms of self-formation and recognizes the ultimately incomplete nature of this process (Zizek, 1989, pp. 230–231). Zizek's attention to the fragility and instability of the process of subject formation – an instability caused by both the wild, asymbolic 'real' and the unpredictable character of desire – does not necessarily undermine the Meadian (or Foucauldian) understanding of self-formation. However, it does directly pose these characteristics against the tendency towards a too ordered understanding of the generation of forms of social selfhood and again mitigates any such tendencies in a neo-Meadian approach.

While Zizek's critique relates directly to the internal mechanisms of self-formation, other scholars with a psychoanalytic bent have pointed outwards to the cultural-symbolic conditions that produce selfhood in both the Meadian and Lacanian models. Both Kenneth Gergen and Robert Lifton, noted social psychologists in the post-Freudian tradition, have argued that the destabilized social sphere has produced a new mode of social selfhood, and both stress the role of mass media in creating this destabilization. Gergen characterizes this new mode of being as 'the saturated self', one characterized by 'multiphrenia', which he describes as 'the splitting of the individual into a multiplicity of self investments' (Gergen, 1991, p. 73). For Gergen, 'technologies of saturation' – especially communication technologies – have fundamentally reconfigured the social terrain in which a sense of self operates by providing a constant, often dizzying flow of information and opportunities for personal investment (see, for example, Gergen, 1991, pp. 48–49, though examples are scattered throughout *The Saturated Self*). Gergen notes that the dissemination of a variety of media are 'vitally expanding the range and variety of relationships available to the population', and later argues that such relationships have a impact equal to, or exceeding those of more conventional face-to-face encounters (Gergen, 1991, pp. 51, 54–56). Conceiving forms of media as 'relationships' suggests a compatibility with Mead's interactional self, of course, and it also implies the need to surrender hard boundaries between 'interpersonal' and 'mass' models of communication.

Lifton makes a less dramatic and less systematic but nonetheless similar claim about the effects of the mass media in the development of the 'protean self', his version of the social self that emerges in the late twentieth century. He uses the Homeric figure of Proteus as a metaphor for the contemporary self, which he argues reflects 'radical fluidity, functional wisdom, and a quest for at least minimal form' (Lifton, 1993, p. 5). The latter quality is particularly important, as Lifton explicitly states that this 'proteanism' does not involve the complete annihilation or dissolution of the self into symbolic or material contexts: 'Proteanism, then is a balancing act between responsive shapeshifting, on the one hand, and efforts to consolidate and cohere, on the other' (Lifton, 1993, p. 9). Like Gergen, Lifton places a considerable stress on the importance of mass media in producing these changes in the self. Working largely, if somewhat critically, from the writing of Marshall McLuhan, Lifton concludes that 'while that ["the twentieth-century"] self invokes defenses of withdrawal and numbing, it remains continuously bombarded by ideas and images and is in some measure recast by them, made more fluid in response to the surrounding fluidity' (Lifton, 1993, p. 21).

While Gergen and Lifton do not operate from a Lacanian perspective per se,[9] both add depth to a psycho-social picture of the self, particularly in relation to forms of mass media. The conception of the field of symbolic possibility created by forms of communication technology as holding both a conscious *and* an unconscious power for identity creation is a critical supplement to the more conventional sociological emphases of Mead and his followers. The rather unstable nature of desire, in the Lacanian (or virtually any post-Freudian) perspective, adds a dimension to the social processes through which forms of selfhood are generated and can work to create a kind of magnetic power, a hermeneutic grip, that is inaccessible through a purely conscious model of these processes. The specific dynamics of this field will be explored in the next section, but I raise the work of Gergen and Lifton at this point because they provide a kind of connective tissue between models of selfhood (the legacy of Mead) and models of a media-saturated symbolic environment (discussed below).

Media culture as generalized other and research site: postmodernism, fandom, and ethnographic research

The notion of mass media information systems constituting a generalized other – in the Meadian tradition – was first raised by Joshua Meyrowitz in the very influential 1985 book *No Sense of Place: The Impact of Electronic Media on Social Behavior*. Meyrowitz explores this notion briefly in an analysis of changing group identities in a media era, writing,

> The homogenized information networks fostered by electronic media offer individuals a comparatively holistic and a wider field within which to measure their relative lot. To use George Herbert Mead's term, electronic media alter one's 'generalized other' – the general sense of how people think and evaluate one's actions. The 'mediated generalized other' includes standards, values, and beliefs from outside traditional group spheres, and it thereby presents people with a new perspective from which to view their actions and identities. The new mediated generalized other bypasses face-to-face encounters in family and community and is shared by millions of others. (Meyrowitz, 1985, pp. 131–132)

Unfortunately, Meyrowitz does not pursue this line of thinking in an analytic sense, instead using the theoretical work of McLuhan and Goffman to supply a foundation for his argument that the mass media have profoundly affected a variety of social behaviors. Indeed, Meyrowitz's focus is not on the most fundamental function of a generalized other in the Meadian model – the generation of social identities. While he makes a very intriguing gesture in the direction of such research, and certainly deserves credit for first positing this rethinking of generalized otherness, his turn to other theoretical views leaves the point almost totally undeveloped in his work.

What I hope to do is follow through on this connection, motivated by the sense that the Meadian model (as described and modified above) can help to add both an analytical depth and an explanatory power to research on media and identity. The structural model of selfhood –

centered upon an I/me dialogue – is described above, but the other half of the social encounter, a symbolic field of 'meaning offers', demands elucidation. To do this, I want to turn to work within the tradition of cultural postmodernism to better understand the dynamics of this 'other'. As noted in the introduction, postmodern scholarship raises three substantive challenges to the study of contemporary media: the fragmentation of subjectivity, the complexity of the mediated environment and the placement of media within a larger social context. The first challenge has been addressed in the description of this neo-pragmatist model of the social subject. The second and third, though, merit further discussion; as the second will be the focus of extensive analysis, I want to address the third briefly.

One of the dangers of some postmodern scholarship, as noted, is the tendency to assign a kind of metaphysical power to mass media such that all social experiences and all material structures become reduced to epiphenomenon of a global media system; Jean Baudrillard's 'simulation' model is one early and very influential version of this line of thought. The world, in this model, becomes another mediated text (or set of texts) and reading this text becomes the primary critical enterprise. Recognizing the significance of media systems in the contemporary world, though, does not automatically demand the leap into such all-encompassing and hyperbolic claims. Perhaps the most interesting attempt to place mass media within a broader context is developed in recent work by anthropologist Arjun Appadurai, who uses a spatial/perspectival approach to situate encounters with mediated discourses.

Appadurai creates a model of global culture comprised of a set of analytic landscapes that collectively cover a wide range of socially significant practices and structures. This takes the form of five '-scapes', that collectively cover the dynamics of global cultural flows: ethnoscapes (roughly, physical location and migration), mediascapes (images, texts, etc.), technoscapes (dispersion of technology), financescapes (flow of global capital) and ideoscapes (political ideology, state politics) (Appadurai, 1996, pp. 33–43). As Appadurai explains, 'these landscapes thus are the building blocks of what (extending Benedict Anderson) I would like to call *imagined worlds*, that is, the multiple worlds that are constituted by the historically situated imaginations of persons and groups spread around the globe' (Appadurai, 1996, p. 33). The landscapes reflect a mediation of actual individuals and larger symbolic and imaginative structures, as they are 'inflected by the historical, linguistic, and political situatedness of different sorts of actors'. At the same time, they are heavily conditioned by a material global economy; the 'financescape', for example, could hardly be considered a mental construct per se, any more than a multinational corporation could be considered simply an imaginary object. The advantage of Appadurai's model is that it balances an emphasis on the importance of a social imagination in shaping experience with the recognition that such imaginative practices inevitably take place within a context that necessarily includes extra-semiotic material conditions. As Appadurai argues, 'the imagination ... has broken out of the expressive space of art, myth, and ritual and has now become a part of the quotidian mental work of ordinary people in many societies' (Appadurai, 1996, p. 5). At the same time, this dimension of everyday life does not inevitably lead to a kind of hostile takeover of the material world by technologies of communication and acts of signification – it is always embedded within this larger set of conditions.

That said, research on media culture necessarily involves the privileging of Appadurai's 'mediascape'; for him, the mediascapes,

> tend to be image-centered, narrative-based accounts of strips of reality, and what they offer to those who experience and transform them is a series of elements (such as characters, plots, and textual forms) out of which scripts can be formed of imagined lives, their own as well as those of others living in other places. These scripts can and do get disaggregated into complex sets of metaphors by which people live as they help to constitute narratives of the Other and protonarratives of possible lives, fantasies that could become prologomena to the desire for acquisition and movement. (Appadurai, 1996, p. 36)

Note the explicitly hermeneutic implications of the concept as it is described here, with 'possible lives' and 'narratives of the Other' emerging from the discursive flow. While never engaging a concept of 'audience' as such in his theoretical work, the mediascape is in fact the space of the audience experience, one in which individuals encounter symbolic worlds that open up imaginative possibilities for the self. The stress on the individuation of imaginative practices in Appadurai is also important here; as he argues, 'indeed, the individual actor is the last locus of this perspectival set of landscapes, for these landscapes are eventually navigated by agents who both experience and constitute larger formations, in part from their own sense of what these landscapes offer' (Appadurai, 1996, p. 33). Rather than eliding the individual – again, as an epiphenomenon of a metastatic 'media world' –

Appadurai emphasizes the contingencies of interpretive practices and their potential uniqueness.

While Appadurai's work is valuable for its contextual schema and emphasis on imaginative practices, it is not specifically concerned with issues of media and audience and thus never fully engages a critical question – *What does the mediascape look like?* In other words, while understanding this dimension of social experience as the space of interpretive practices of world-making and experiences of otherness, mapping the landscape – to extend his metaphor – requires a more precise focus on its particular symbolic character. It is thus appropriate, perhaps, that the most compelling work in this area tends to treat 'media culture' in a fundamentally environmental sense.

One of the most notable, and certainly the most notorious, of such perspectives is supplied by Baudrillard, who offers a particularly apocalyptic version of postmodern media culture in his most recent work. In this period of his career, Baudrillard presents a metaphysical case for the 'murder of reality' perpetrated by a technologically-driven, media-saturated culture. In this vision, the subject-object dynamic evaporates completely, a process he links with a kind of demented and intensified version of the Meadian role-play. For example, a recent discussion of the demise of otherness and the concurrent 'murder of reality', offers the following description of a strange new development in the area of intersubjectivity:

> We know people who, for want of being able to communicate, are victims of profuse otherness (as we speak of profuse sweating). They play all the roles at once, their own and the other person's; they both give and return, ask the questions and supply the answers. They embrace the other's presence so fully that no longer know the limits of their own. The other is merely a transitional object. The secondary gain from the loss of the other is an ability to transform oneself into anyone at all – through role-playing, virtual and computer games, through the new spectrality Marc Guillaume speaks of, with the age of Virtual Reality still to come, when we shall done otherness like a data suit. (Baudrillard, 1995, p. 127)

At this limit-point, the kind of subjective saturation described, for example, by Gergen mutates into a complete disappearance of the subject into the symbolic; even the 'other', which serves, in some sense, as the guarantor of a measure of individuality, becomes a mere place to inhabit, another 'suit' to be put on and taken off. The practical intersubjectivity at the heart of Meadian self-formation is now the instrument of the subject's demise and taking the role of the other becomes akin to the annihilation of the self. Early in the passage cited above, Baudrillard connects this annihilation to the will to communicate; this is prefigured in his earlier discussions of the interactive dynamics of the French mini-tel (a kind of ur-internet) system in 1985's *Cool Memories* (Baudrillard, 1990, p. 62), and in the warning that 'artificial intelligence and the hardware that supports will become a mental prosthesis for a species without the capacity of thought' in 1990's *The Transparency of Evil* (Baudrillard, 1993, p. 52). Beyond a somewhat superficial Luddite anti-technological impulse, Baudrillard suggests a deeper and more vexing issue – the expansion of 'communication' to the point at which the subject vanishes. It is worth noting here that Baudrillard, like both Lifton and Meyrowitz, derives his analysis at least partly from Marshall McLuhan's earlier work on television, although Baudrillard is unique in pushing these premises to such dramatic conclusions.

Baudrillard's argument is useful not as an empirical diagnosis of contemporary culture but rather as posing a kind of worst case scenario for selfhood within the context of pervasive and powerful communication systems. In this sense, he identifies some of the environmental challenges for practices of self-construction in relation to electronic media. If the psychoanalytic perspective poses the unpredictable force of individuated desire in the process of subject-formation, Baudrillard suggests a parallel instability driven by the 'viral' character of proliferating symbolic systems. Baudrillard's 'vanishing other', as the passage above indicates, is paradoxically supremely powerful as it draws in the subject so completely that one's own 'presence', to use Baudrillard's term, becomes effectively voided.

Fredric Jameson, whose understanding of the postmodern is perhaps the only rival to Baudrillard's in the breadth of its scholarly influence, adds another relevant aspect to the characterization of media culture-as-other. While avoiding the wild metaphysical claims so characteristic of the latter's work, Jameson nonetheless raises his own set of concerns regarding processes of self-formation and, although his orientation is a Marxist historicism, his arguments are quite compelling for the issue at hand. Jameson, as Fred Pfeil notes, draws a comparison between the postmodern, and particularly the increasing importance of surface at the expense of time, and Lacan's sense of schizophrenia (Pfeil, 1988, p. 385). Jameson specifically addresses this question in terms of an inability to develop a meaningful sense of the past – the historical dimension so important to Jameson's political framework – and thus to develop any coherency of identity. Jameson explains:

> If we are unable to unify the past, present, and future of the sentence [referring here to the 'linguistic malfunction' central to postmodern culture], then we are similarly unable to unify the past, present, and future of our own biographical experience or psychic life. With the breakdown of the signifying chain, therefore, the schizophrenic is reduced to an experience of pure material signifiers, or, in other words, a series of pure and unrelated presents in time ... (Jameson, 1991, p. 27)

This picture of the schizophrenic cultural subject is particularly critical to a hermeneutic perspective, and especially one informed by Mead, as Mead's theory of time explicitly ties the ability to construct a meaningful sense of past, present and future to the development of self-consciousness (Mead, 1938, pp. 455–457). Mead places a considerable stress on the importance of a reconstruction of the past as the basis for the understanding of the present (Cronk, 1987, pp. 55–58); along with Dewey, he argues for a future-directed consciousness tied to the aesthetic dimension of experience. Jameson thus suggests the profound difficulty of producing an internal dialogue – one, as noted, with clear autobiographical resonances – in a cultural environment characterized by a kind of semiotic chaos. In a sense, Jameson describes a perpetual present that provides no opportunity for the subject to escape the 'passage from attitude to attitude' through a kind of self-collection, which is the very process upon which Mead founded self-consciousness in his *The Philosophy of the Present*. One might say that while Baudrillard cancels out the other-directed self-consciousness of the role-playing process, Jameson does the same for the elements of self-consciousness built from the task of historical synthesis.

Jameson continues his description with an identification of the affective ambiguities of this process:

> ... thereby isolated, that [temporal] present suddenly engulfs the subject with undescribable vividness, a materiality of perception properly overwhelming, which effectively dramatizes the power of the material – or better still, the literal – signifier in isolation. This present of world or material signifier comes before the subject with heightened intensity, bearing a mysterious charge of affect, here [in the experience of an actual schizophrenic] described in the negative

terms of anxiety and loss of reality, but which one could just as well imagine in the positive terms of euphoria, a high, an intoxicatory or hallucinogenic intensity. (Jameson, 1991, pp. 27–28)

The recognition of this affective dimension, then, helps to fill out Jameson's notion of the perpetually present character of postmodern culture and it also unintentionally supports the supplementation of conventional hermeneutic models of subjectivity (e.g., Mead) with the more intense models of self-construction provided by post-Freudian, post-Lacanian psychoanalysis. The 'mysterious charge of affect' here could certainly be reconciled with the unstable sense of desire that permeates the imagination in Lacan's theory of semiotic self-formation. Baudrillard poses a postmodern culture that swallows up subjectivity in an act Baudrillard describes as 'the revenge of the crystal' – the reduction of the individual to informational. Jameson, on the other hand, describes a postmodern culture that renders the subject in a temporal and emotional daze, a mood-swinging perpetual present.

I should note that my deployment of both Baudrillard and Jameson is somewhat unusual and departs from the standard reading of their work. By containing their insights within the framework of a 'mediascape', I am explicitly resisting the notion that either provides a general social diagnosis (although that may be the intent of both) and instead arguing that they offer a particularly acute take on the subjective dimensions of the contemporary media experience. The 'other' that they describe, one characterized by a gripping intensity, a seductive fluidity and a chaotic symbolic structure, I think, is a fair picture of contemporary media culture. The issue is critical in that such a model of the mediascape is a particularly challenging one for practices of identity development, and yet, as the case studies that follow will demonstrate, it nonetheless serves in precisely that function. Indeed, much of the work of the contemporary media fan – an individual with very specific investments in these symbolic formations – involves the psychological and semiotic challenges of overcoming the Baudrillardian and Jamesonian barriers to self-construction.

The focus on fans in the analyses that follow demands some specific attention, though, as it reflects a particular region of the wider media experience and one marked by its own peculiarities. If all audience members are saturated – to use Gergen's term – by experiences with media, there are differing degrees and inflections to this saturation. Certainly, fans bear a more conscious and intense affective relationship to media objects; as numerous commentators have pointed out, 'fan' is derived from 'fanatic', a term with heavy connotations of extremism and irrationality (Grossberg, 1992, pp. 248–249). However, this is only one dimension of the fan experience and, as noted in the introduction, an emphasis on this sort of irrationality, whether presented as an amusing or dangerous obsession, tends to reduce fandom to a kind of pathology. What this almost always overlooks is a second characteristic involving the cultivation of a *hermeneutic* as well as an *affective* engagement with forms of mediated discourse. Without this second characteristic, it seems, media fans would inevitably resemble Baudrillard's victims of 'profuse otherness' and would find themselves dissolving entirely into their objects of attention and affection.

However, fans are almost always more than just affective investors (as Grossberg would put it) in a set of images, stories, icons and so forth. They are also often very intense interpreters and indeed have a profoundly aesthetic view of the objects of their engagement. This is an important point and one directly relevant to the issue of selfhood and the Meadian model, as Mead himself placed a considerable emphasis on the role of aesthetic practices – both creative and receptive – in the generation of forms of self-consciousness. For Mead, the 'aesthetic attitude' is one marked by the 'delight of consummation' and of a nearly utopian integration of self and other (Mead, 1938, p. 457). Indeed, Mead explicitly argues that the aesthetic experience offers a taste, so to speak, of a non-alienated, non-hierarchical model of self-fulfillment. This echoes a certain strain in classical Marxist aesthetics (e.g., Adorno, Bloch), but it also bears a strong resemblance to Appadurai's aforementioned 'protonarratives of possible lives' as an element within the mediascape. While this aesthetic dimension would obviously be present, to some degree, in a vast array of media experiences, the fan experience tends to place it front and center. The depth of the fan's connection with media objects, a depth that is registered in aesthetic as well as affective terms, would certainly increase the magnitude of commitment to this mediated other. As Tugendhat argues, there is always a degree of volition in the acceptance of an 'offer of meaning' and the fan's full embrace of this meaning offer often leads to similarly intensified practices of self-formation. The particularities of three such 'embraces' will be explored in the chapters that follow, but the uniqueness of this mode of experience is worth reiterating. I will argue, though, that the collective analysis of a variety of fan cultures can produce a kind of map of mediated self-construction and, through their particularly demonstrative character, provide a distilled version of a much wider array of practices connected with the intersection of media and social identity.

From Mead and in light of the German neo-Meadian tradition, then, I want to posit situated media experiences as symbolic engagements that act as an encounter with a 'generalized other' and, from a hermeneutic perspective, enable forms of self-understanding. In reference to the question of scale, I think that such encounters are enacted at a variety of levels: textual interpretations; wider events such as film festivals, television seasons, concerts or other strips of musical programming; and the still broader contexts of fandom, regional cultures, 'virtuality' and other super-textual elements. In this respect, any analysis of a 'generalized other' constituted by media practices needs to consider these wider contexts, wider regions in which self-perspectives can be generated. This does not mean that the more microscopic elements should be overlooked, analytically, but it does require a sense of context that may be wider than that implied by a traditional hermeneutic emphasis.

The best method for performing this kind of analysis, I will argue, is a hermeneutically-inclined ethnographic approach. In specifying a hermeneutic dimension to ethnographic practice, I am pointing to the need for the researcher to pay particular attention to the multi-leveled symbolic structures that are at the heart of media and especially fan cultures. It should be noted that this mode of ethnographic inquiry is not radically different from many other contemporary approaches. For example, Michael Burawoy describes his own 'extended case method' mode of ethnography as examining 'the interplay between system and lifeworld' as a means for understanding the generation of forms of social action (Burawoy, 1991, p. 285). What sets a hermeneutic approach apart, though, is the attention to the array of symbolic structures and interpretive practices that are entangled in a single research site, and the specific emphasis on the ways that such structures enable forms of self-construction and self-performance. While Burawoy's method places the final point of analysis in the examination of social practices, mine would place social identities in the same position.

More specifically, the case studies presented in the following chapters rely on a wide range of ethnographic methods throughout the research process. There is a strong emphasis on the examination of the secondary discourses produced within the respective fan cultures – fanzines, websites, works of fiction and visual art, critical discussions and other objects – as these offer particular access to the interpretive work central to the fan experience. Personal interviews, both formal and informal, and correspondence were also important methods for gathering material in all three of the studies, although these techniques were always approached with a good deal of caution. When examining an issue as potentially elusive as identity, the dangers of relying on 'leading questions' – questions designed to produce specific answers and to direct informants down fairly narrow paths of expression – are quite significant. Additionally, the setting of the formal interview can work to decontextualize the individual from the fan culture and can thus distort the responses that are elicited. Thus, I tended to rely on informal communications and conversations as the primary form of interpersonal exchange with informants. All three studies also involved a strong component of participant-observation research, including attending rituals, participating in critical and exegetical discussions, and, in the case of the study of 'Freaky' film culture, performing organizational and logistical duties related to three film festivals. While this always runs the risk of 'going native' and losing a critical perspective on the cultural under analysis, a strong measure of regular participation seemed absolutely necessary for cultivating an understanding of the unique and often obscure features of each fan formation. The hybrid nature of this approach – against, for example, a relatively fixed set of focus groups or a series of standardized questionnaires – stemmed from the often wildly heterogeneous nature of the cultures themselves. As the aforementioned theorists of the postmodern have argued, contemporary culture is marked by an extraordinary discursive complexity; this complexity is homologously evident even within the much narrower borders of a given fan culture, and thus necessitates a multipronged research strategy.

Indeed, one important prong, the critical analysis of primary media texts, would not even be considered 'ethnographic' in a standard sense and yet it is an absolutely crucial part of the strategy described above. If, as I have argued, fandom is a culture with a notably aesthetic character, then the objects of much of this aesthetic orientation – the films, songs, television programs, and other 'official' products – certainly merit careful and detailed analysis. In literary criticism and a number of other fields, of course, such a focus would arouse little controversy. Within the research tradition of media studies, and especially the 'cultural studies' subfield, though, textual analysis is often poorly regarded. As Charlotte Brundson argues, the automatic denigration of textual analysis and of the text as a crucial and irreducible object in the analysis of cultural practices of interpretation is certainly without justification (Brundson, 1990, pp. 68–69). In fact, textual analysis, as a part of a package of research strategies, is particularly critical in providing a strong sense of the semiotic contours of the fan's symbolic world. Recognizing that texts are the site of contestation and also of the imposition of socially determined and simultaneously individuated interpretive structures in fact increases the importance of subjecting them to an intense critical focus. Indeed, their status as a site of struggle is evidence of the important role they play within these cultures.

The larger goal of this hybrid approach is twofold – to test the analytical value of the model of social selfhood described above and secondly to provide exemplars of forms of self-construction within the world of media fandom. As noted in the introduction, the goal is not merely to offer a detailed demonstration of the particularities of a given fan culture but rather to provide, collectively, three very different ways that symbolic, self-constructive practices are realized in differing empirical contexts. In the final chapter of the book, I argue that each reflects a central strategic characteristic – hybridity, piety and irony, respectively – and that these qualities can then be understood as coordinates on a larger map of mediated modes of identity formation. While the cases are presented separately, all are offered under the umbrella of the larger theoretical argument that a rethinking of issues of media and subjectivity along the lines posed above will open a new horizon for both studies of mass media and for the larger question of culture and the self. With that in mind, my empirical journey begins close to home, firmly within the domain of the local, and moves outward to a final horizon of virtual culture.

2
Every Freak Needs a Show: Polyvalent Subjectivity and a Local Underground Film Scene

On Friday, 6 November 1998 at the Canopy Club, a former first-run movie house that had recently been converted into a bar and live music venue in Urbana, Illinois, in the American Midwest, the Second Annual Freaky Film Festival presented three programs of experimental and avant-garde films. The first two programs, entitled 'Love Sick Flix' and 'The Queer Experience', centered upon romantic and sexual relationships, and gay and lesbian themes, respectively. The final program, 'The Freaks Come Out at Night', ran until nearly 2 a.m. and did not have the thematic coherency of the previous two, instead featuring five films dealing with a variety of horrifying, aberrant and unusual aspects of contemporary life. The headlining attraction, *Affliction*, by Chicago filmmaker Mark Hejnar, is a controversial documentary dealing with several figures on the very margins of contemporary culture, including the late punk rock performance artist G.G. Allin, jailed cartoonist Mike Diana and fanzine writer Full Force Frank. Despite (or perhaps because of) advertising cautioning, 'WARNING!!! DO NOT ATTEND IF YOU HAVE A WEAK STOMACH!', the program attracted a sizable crowd. The material was strong enough to provoke a fainting episode in one audience member and vomiting in others; it had previously raised legal concerns for Hejnar when he took the film abroad, and had to be smuggled into certain European countries for fear of customs violations. Fainting and vomiting aside, the film seemed to succeed with the large crowd – there were relatively few walkouts – and Hejnar, who was present, was soon surrounded by a number of new fans eager to discuss his work.

I begin my discussion of a local 'underground' film scene with a discussion of *Affliction* because the film provides a rather nice distillation of the social and symbolic dynamics of such scenes. *Affliction* features a number of elements that are homologously present in the larger culture: punk rock (Allin, and Hejnar's band Pile of Cows), alternative comic books (Diana's work), body modification and s&m culture, fanzines (Full Force Frank) and even 'gut level' political commentary – in the film, Diana performs a stunt that involves vomiting on a Bible and a US flag. Rather than reflecting a distinct identity-political position in the way that, for example, an explicitly queer film might, Hejnar's film addresses the 'affliction' of a variety of cultural practices and identities at the very margins of the social order. Such positions are always tenuous, often politically ambiguous and usually analytically problematic. The 'underground', 'independent', 'avant-garde' or 'freaky' film scene – the latter name chosen by the festival founders to avoid some of the potential connotations of the previous three – is a similarly complex socio-symbolic formation, even when examined in a local manifestation, the purpose of the following chapter. In this chapter, I will offer an analysis of the newly resurgent 'freaky' film scene in Champaign-Urbana as a means of considering issues of identity formation within such subcultural practices and, related to this, the hermeneutic dimensions of such marginal cultural formations. After a brief description of the ethnographic work supporting this analysis, the chapter moves into a discussion of the peculiar contradictions that mark the modes of identity associated with the underground, an examination of the national and local historical context for an independent film culture and a discussion of the current local scene and especially the Freaky Film Festival. It will conclude with some theoretical speculation on the particular significance of this cultural formation in light of the model of hermeneutic subjectivity and media culture provided in the preceding chapter.

The material for this analysis is derived primarily from an ethnographic research project that I was engaged in for several years. I have an academic background in avant-garde film, as well as some experience in independent film production, but had not been actively involved in film-related activities for a number of years. My investigation of the local scene was initially focused on activities related to the presentation of the Second Annual Freaky Film Festival; I attended organizational meetings, helped with various logistical and promotional tasks, attended film screenings that were part of the selection process and performed a variety of other related functions. During the festival itself, I helped with projection, ushering, concessions, ticket sales and other similar duties; I also led a panel discussion concerning the state of current independent film production with several visiting filmmakers.

My work with the festival provided an entry into the local independent film culture. This ethnographic work was expanded to include aiding in the production of local independent films, as well as writing and photography for *Micro-Film*, a film journal founded in the wake of the Freaky Film Festival and designed to address issues of local, regional (e.g., Midwestern) and national independent cinema. This work continued through the third Freaky Film Festival, with a similarly varied set of activities related to the local film culture, through an ongoing involvement with *Micro-Film* and through providing production assistance on local independent film shoots. The length and depth of this ethnographic engagement has been personally rewarding and intellectually fruitful, as it has enabled the analysis of questions of subjectivity and symbolic environments that are central to my theoretical work, as described in the previous chapter. Without my own rather lengthy immersion in this culture, with all that such an immersion demands, I suspect that any real understanding of the culture would be quite elusive. As is the case with all three case studies, there is an aforementioned autobiographical element at work here, and I will move to this analysis with a recognition that much of it is directly applicable to my own participation and, ultimately 'myself', in the fullest sense of the term.

Ambivalent subjects and the avant-garde

The previous chapter provided an analytical framework for understanding the subjective dimensions of contemporary media experiences in their socio-hermeneutic fullness. Before moving directly to the analysis of a local film scene, I want to recap, briefly, a few critical aspects of this theoretical position, particularly as it is relevant to the material that follows. The primary issue at hand concerns the ways that the media formation – an entity that would include practices of text interpretation, social functions associated with the culture, the production of discourses concerning this culture and other related activities – serves as a mechanism for the generation and development of forms of social selfhood and identity. In neo-Meadian terminology, the media formation can be understood as a symbolic field, a 'generalized other', with which subjects form relations and upon which role positions are built and modes of self-relation are enabled. Along these lines, I begin this section with a rather broad description of the subjective dynamics of the culture of avant-garde, independent cinema.

As noted in the discussion of *Affliction*, this cultural world is not one of stable and easily defined subject positions, but rather one of hybridity and ambiguity; the (contingent) coherence one might recognize in common forms of gender, class or political identity is not present. Instead, one finds a diverse set of practices and modes of symbolic identification that often must be stitched together in a sometimes uneasy alignment. The generalized other offered by alternative film culture is, I will argue, a particularly complex symbolic body, one marked by a number of significant points of potential dissonance. This is most easily demonstrated by identifying four areas of potential socio-symbolic contradiction illustrative of this ambivalent character: the underground cinema as both popular and elite art; the cultural participant as simultaneous producer, consumer and critic; the tension between forms of identity politics and a hybrid culture; and lastly, the similar tension between the status of participants in this culture as aesthetes and as radicals.

Particularly in the early years of its cultural prominence, critics and artists associated with independent film, and especially those connected with the American experimental cinema, have taken great pains to emphasize the distance of this culture from mainstream film. P. Adams Sitney, arguably the most respected scholar of the avant-garde, exemplifies this approach, stating, 'the precise relationship of avant-garde cinema to American commercial film is one of radical otherness. They operate in different realms with next to no significant influence on each other' (Sitney, 1974, p. viii). While Sitney's approach has certainly influenced the critical understanding of such cinematic work – he was the best-known critic of avant-garde cinema for many years – it greatly oversimplifies the actual character of this relationship. As Lauren Rabinowitz points out, there has always been a substantial degree of dialogue between mass cultural forms and American underground cinema, one that has taken on a variety of forms, from direct critique to playful borrowing (Rabinowitz, 1991, pp. 15–19). As Rabinovitz mentions, some canonical figures of the avant-garde, most notably Kenneth Anger and Bruce Baillie (both venerated by Sitney, interestingly), have been particularly explicit in their engagement with mass cultural cinematic forms and popular culture in general (Rabinowitz, 1991, p. 19).

Nonetheless, Sitney's vision of the avant-garde cinema as a hermetic, elite culture is only a distortion, not a complete mischaracterization.

Certainly, key tendencies in the American underground cinema, particularly the more abstract tradition described, respectively, as 'structural' by Sitney and 'minimal' by fellow critic James Peterson (e.g., the work of Michael Snow and Ernie Gehr) as well as the 'mythopoeic' or 'poetic' tradition (e.g., the work of Stan Brakhage) are marked by a conscientious avoidance of virtually any formal aspects associated with classical Hollywood cinema. As Peterson notes, this is even expanded in Brakhage's work into a mode of film practice that 'rejects not only the norms of commercial filmmaking but all norms of aesthetics and perception' (Peterson, 1994, p. 4). This radically anti-commercial tenor has been buttressed by a critical discourse, largely grounded in Sitney's work but also including more recent writing by a variety of other notable scholars of American underground cinema including Peterson, William Wees and Regina Cornwell, that has served to support the 'radically other' model of this cinematic school. Additionally, the increasing relocation of avant-garde/underground film to academia and its relative withering in other public settings has tended to increase the appearance of cultural seclusion and aesthetic purity.

Ironically, this relative physical seclusion came at a time when the roughly concurrent rise of aesthetic postmodernism within a variety of art forms provoked, often intentionally, a challenge to the very divisions of mass and elite art noted above (see, for example, Jameson's *Postmodernism* and Hassan's *The Postmodern Turn*). The combination of a variety of styles from traditionally high and low cultural forms is remarkably common within elite art circles in the last few decades. Indeed, one of the most influential figures in the development of a postmodern sensibility in high art, Andy Warhol, was also a major figure in the development of an American avant-garde cinema. Ironically, Warhol's early film work was profoundly influential on one of the most militantly unconventional strains, the aforementioned 'structural' approach, within the early underground cinema (Sitney, 1974, pp. 411–412). In his later films and his other, better-known studio art works, though, Warhol explored the boundaries of high and low culture and was celebrated as an exemplar of the postmodern leveling – or at least scrambling – of norms of aesthetic and cultural value. For example, both Jameson and Baudrillard are particularly appreciative of this aspect of his work, citing it frequently in their own analyses of the postmodern (Jameson, 1991, pp. 6–12; Baudrillard, 1993, p. 157).

In addition to this rather direct influence, the American underground film scene is marked by the pervasive use of several aesthetic strategies associated with postmodernism, including a particularly frequent deployment of what Jameson calls 'pastiche'. This 'blank parody' involves a borrowing of older styles without the inevitable modernist return to an authentic personal voice (Jameson, 1991, p. 19). Indeed, this approach was an important element in some of the most influential fifties and sixties American avant-garde cinema, such as the work of George and Mike Kuchar (*Sins of the Fleshapoids, Hold Me While I'm Naked*), as well as Warhol's later films (*Lonesome Cowboys, Hedy*). Even today, it remains a prominent part of the underground film scene. Although the festival films will be discussed in greater detail later, it is worth noting that the 1998 Freaky Film Festival included Caleb Emerson's *Red's Breakfast III: Die You Zombie Bastards*, a pastiche of early sixties 'gore' films, and Dan Dinello's *Wheels of Fury*, which referenced the 'spaghetti western' genre of the same decade; the 1999 festival included *The Sore Losers* by John Michael McCarthy, a take on 'juvenile delinquent' films from the fifties and sixties, and Eric Landmark's satirical pseudo-newsreel *Golden Gate*. These are merely the most obvious examples, as numerous cases of other pastiche strategies are evident in a number of films in the festival.

Interestingly, the aesthetic source of the pastiche strategy evident in films such as *Red's Breakfast III* and *The Sore Losers* – low-budget, culturally marginal commercial cinematic work from a range of historical periods – has a substantial audience of its own, and one that is increasingly blended with the underground/avant-garde film community. Commonly dubbed 'psychotronic', a term coined by aficionado Michael Weldon, this culture encompasses a wide range of styles: kung-fu, low-budget horror and science fiction, 'blacksploitation' and a variety of other film genres. The culture that has emerged around such films, including websites, fanzines, video rental outlets, festivals and other events, enjoys a good deal of overlap with the existing underground film community. Indeed *Micro-Film*, the aforementioned local film journal, provides information on both areas of film culture; the debut issue includes a number of articles on independent and experimental filmmakers, and also an interview with Don May, co-owner of Synapse Films, a company that specializes in DVD reissues of a variety of psychotronic films. Here, the commingling of the putatively elite experimental scene and the kitschier, defiantly low-brow culture of marginal commercial cinemas is organizational and pragmatic as well as aesthetic. The overlap in audiences is evident in the media surrounding both cultures – *Micro-Film* is hardly exceptional in its blend of independent and psychotronic film coverage (see also the publications *Shock Cinema* and *Zombie's Movie Mania Magazine*) – and extends into commercial services such as video retailers. This certainly provides evidence that the dream of a hermetic, romantic modernist underground cinema in direct opposition to commercial production is just that, a fantasy that is rarely realized at aesthetic, critical or material levels.

There is a secondary kind of contamination that has grown more pronounced in recent years, and this involves the rise of the 'indie' film as a substantial part of the commercial cinema market. In this case, 'independent film' does not refer to the conglomeration of non-commercial, experimental and/or unconventional styles that it might have in earlier years. Rather, 'indie' is now used primarily to refer to rather conventional narrative feature films produced outside of the Hollywood production system. This type of cinematic production, sometimes referred to as the 'Sundance' film after the festival of the same name, has relatively little in common, aesthetically or commercially, with the earlier works of the American independent film. Rather, it serves both as a vehicle for aspiring Hollywood filmmakers attempting to attract attention through low-budget narrative cinema (e.g., Michael Lehman, director of *Heathers*) and for directors of more typical 'art films' such as Todd Haynes (*Happiness*). As critic and independent film scholar Emanuel Levy explains,

> Despite visionary claims, the indie cinema boasts few practitioners whose films are truly avant-garde or whose works are as eagerly anticipated as the films of Bresson, Godard, Ozu, Tarkovsky, and Cassavetes a generation ago. The absence of prominent followers of an early American avant-garde – Stan Brakhage, Robert Frank, Shirley Clarke, Ed Pincus, Jonas Mekas, Rick Leacock, and Andy Warhol, to mention a few – is highly evident in the new indies ... Indie films, as a whole, are not artistically groundbreaking or politically provocative. Despite offbeat characterizations, most indies lack the unusual stories, experimental pacing, fractured narratives, or kinetic editing, to mention a few radical devices. (Levy, 1999, pp. 54–55)

The rise of this middle ground, close to Hollywood in most aspects but retaining some of the aesthetic distinction and cultural cachet of avant-garde film, has further muddled the high/low culture, personal expression/commercial product and mainstream/marginal binaries that were an important part of the cultural and critical discourse surrounding the American underground cinema.

This somewhat ambivalent status is important for issues of hermeneutic subjectivity and questions of identity in that there is a kind of wavering instability in the ways that the symbolic fields associated with an underground film culture are constituted and the ways that these operate in conjunction with and in opposition to other practices of media reception. There are clearly some crucial distinctions between, for example, the modes of reception,[1] critical discourses, and socio-cultural status associated with elite art versus those associated with mainstream or even kitsch cultural production (even given the postmodern turn in high art), and these distinctions may have a real impact on the ways that such experiences might figure in the construction of a social identity.

The blurring of lines between fields of production, reception and criticism within the underground film scene is a similar and more materially significant instability. There is a long tradition in the history of the American underground film of communities structured upon this permeability of roles. Certainly, this was the case with the seminal New York scene of the fifties and sixties (Rosenbaum and Hoberman, 1991, pp. 39–76); David James' discussion of the career of filmmaker-critic-entrepreneur Jonas Mekas, a very important figure in the New York underground, points to the embodiment of such a diversity of activities in a single individual (James, 1989, pp. 100–119). There is also a strong tradition of 'indigenous' film theory – writing about the nature of cinematic experience and aspects of film production by filmmakers – that has emerged from the underground film scene (Sitney, 1978, pp. vii–xlv; Rabinovitz, 1991, p. 19). Through this confluence of practices, a relatively autonomous cultural community can be formed, one offering a measure of freedom, particularly in terms of role mobility, impossible in more conventional media formations.

This flexibility is certainly evident in the local film community I studied. For example, Jason Pankoke, who created a short film to serve as the trailer for the second Freaky Festival, also edits the aforementioned *Micro-Film*, a magazine offering critical and informational articles on local and national underground (or as Pankoke prefers, 'personal') film scenes, as well as serving as a key volunteer for the festival itself. Likewise, festival co-director Grace Giorgio is, simultaneously, a crucial figure in the organization of the festival, a filmmaker and an academic critic of film and popular culture. These are particularly prominent examples, but there are numerous similar cases: volunteers for the second festival included a number of film production and criticism students from the local University of Illinois, as well as the aforementioned Don May, who is involved professionally in the video industry. In my own ethnographic work within this community, I helped with the production of the festival trailer and with other film production projects, wrote a number of articles for *Micro-Film* and helped with more routine festival and screening duties (e.g., projection, venue maintenance, ticket sales).

One of the reasons for this flexibility of roles is the somewhat unconventional material economy of the underground cinema, one combining elements of conventional capitalist media industries, folkloric craft economies and patronage/philanthropic systems of artistic production. This economic organization is combined with a frequent commitment to the use of archaic technology, particularly super 8mm film, in the creative process, one that obviously limits costs but also precludes incorporation into larger mainstream media systems of distribution and reception. The fixity of economic roles encouraged by a more rigid material organization is not present, and the relatively small scale of the economy of underground film, particularly as it functions within local scenes, often demands an overlap of practices that would be separated in more conventional media economies.

The effacement of such practical boundaries suggests additional consequences for the status of the subject herself. The relative openness of the system of aesthetic production within this community and the tendency for individuals to be involved in a variety of diverse practices provides at least some access to the types of group activities that are particularly valued in the Meadian hermeneutic tradition (and also in Foucault's later work). The 'aesthetic attitude' and 'esprit de corps' that Mead finds in ideal social practices, those in which the roles of self and other become most comfortably intertwined, are certainly more likely to be present in situations permitting a mobility of practices. The filmmaker who is also a critic, an organizer and an avid audience member, all within the same local cultural community, operates within a milieu drastically different from that of the traditional audience member, the 'receiver' or 'decoder' of conventional media reception theory. The integration of multiple roles, each bearing a different relation to a symbolic field of texts and secondary discourses, cannot be easily squared with standard models of reception and interpretation.

This complexity does raise significant practical difficulties, though, for the rebirth of a cultural community, the specific focus of this case study. As the underground film community cannot be understood, as mentioned, as an 'audience' in the conventional sense, but instead as a collection of diverse symbolic practices, the reconstruction or rebirth of such a community involves particular challenges. This is true both in terms of the material resources needed to enable communal activities – venues, technology, and so on – as well as the development of less tangible symbolic fields in which the creative and interpretive practices central to this community might take hold. While the flexibility of practices of reception, criticism and production are an important factor in the hermeneutic power of the underground film scene, they can be quite difficult to maintain and even more difficult to rebuild after a period of dormancy.

The third area of cultural ambivalence central to the world of underground film revolves around the tension between a set of identity-political positions that have made a strong contribution to this cultural formation, and the need for such positions to be contained, however tentatively, within a broader array of political and aesthetic strategies. There has been a long tradition of the infusion of 'identity politics' into the American underground film community, particularly of the queer and feminist varieties. Many of the earliest and most important figures in the early American avant-garde created work that reflected an explicitly queer sensibility; the films of Kenneth Anger, Jack Smith and James Broughton are probably the best known examples of this approach, but the works of Andy Warhol and Gregory Markopoulos are also important here. These films ranged from explicit homoeroticism (e.g., Anger's *Fireworks* and *Scorpio Rising*) and celebrations of carnal excess and ambiguous sexualities (e.g., Smith's *Flaming Creatures*) to more subtle, psychologically 'queer' themes (e.g., Broughton's *Mother's Day*). There was a similar if less prominent, presence of feminist filmmaking within this culture, although it should be noted that the sexual politics of much of the early underground cinema, both in terms of film content and critical approaches, could be quite reactionary or at least regressive (Mellencamp, 1990, pp. 21–23; Rabinovitz, 1991, pp. 23–25). However, the status of Maya Deren as perhaps the most venerated of all American underground filmmakers and the subsequent work of Shirley Clarke, Marie Menken, Barbara Rubin, Carolee Schneemann and numerous others created a significant place for women filmmakers and in many cases feminist films within the avant-garde. As with 'queer' cinema, 'feminist' film necessarily covers a wide range of practices from the explicitly political (e.g., Schneemann's *Fuses*) to poetic meditations that reflect a more politically diffused feminist aesthetic (e.g., Deren's pathbreaking *Meshes of the Afternoon*). While the feminist and queer cultures were the most prominent formations of 'identity politics' within the underground film community, there were also important films produced from a polemically African-American perspective (e.g., the early work of Julie Dash), and an occasional example from other communities, but it is important to mention that such work has been notably sparse, particularly when compared to the voluminous body of queer and feminist underground films (James, 1989, p. 178).

The prominence of the aforementioned queer and feminist strains within the underground continues today, and the Freaky Festivals were no exceptions, as both positions were strongly represented. In the 1998 and 1999 festivals, there were specific programs of queer-themed films, respectively titled 'The Queer Experience' and 'Out and About'. The 1998 festival included 'Femme Fatale', a collection of films made by women and dealing with a variety of issues related to gender and women's experiences. While the 1999 festival did not have a specific program dedicated to feminist filmmaking, it did include a number of examples, including Jill Chamberlain's *The Tell-Tale Vibrator*, a short comedy concerning female sexuality, Jennifer and Amber Cluck's *Pigskin Orgasm*, a satirical film in the 'assemblage' tradition examining homoeroticism in the manly world of professional sports and Robert G. Banks *Jaded/Outlet*, which attempted to deconstruct mediated images of women.

The Freaky Festivals are interesting in this respect, as they require the location of such conventional identity-political strategies within a larger set of texts and positions, inevitably creating a symbolic tension. There is a useful contrast here with another local festival that preceded the 1998 Freaky Film Festival by a few months; the First Annual Reel Queer Festival was held at the University of Illinois Union in August of that year. When I discussed the aims of that festival with one of its organizers, he explained that the purpose was to provide an opportunity for filmmakers to screen work dealing with gay and lesbian issues and to give audiences an unusual opportunity to see such work. The films were extremely diverse aesthetically, ranging from a PBS television documentary, *Family Name* by Macky Alston, to more radical works such as *Cracker Barrel My Ass*, an avant-garde attack on the titular restaurant chain's homophobic company policies. However, all of the films included in the festival could be comfortably situated within a reasonably coherent politics involving a progressive assertion of queer identity and social justice, a position lacking the diversity and resultant potential contradiction that was an important part of the Freaky Festivals.

This sort of symbolic contradiction is particularly evident in the field of sexual politics. While the Freaky Festivals presented a number of films – like those mentioned above – providing at least marginally (and in some cases explicitly) progressive perspectives on issues of gender and sexuality, there were also some films, such as Greg Brooks' *Ribbed for Her Pleasure* and Evan Maderakis' *2 on You*, that harked back to the kinds of mythic masculinist versions of female sexuality evident in some of the foundational work of the American underground. While this sort of direct contradiction was relatively rare – and certainly the festival organizers made a conscious effort to avoid explicitly sexist or homophobic texts – the larger heterogeneity of the festival selections reflected the unique socio-cultural character of a 'big tent' model of the underground. Feminist and militant queer identities mixed with stoners (a number of films reflecting the weltanshuung of the pro-marijuana counterculture), punks, goths and the odd assemblage of marginal social formations reflected in *Affliction*. The conjoining of such culturally-constructed identities does not demand a surrender of the kind of subjective attachments they might demand, but it does leave the meta-identity of the 'freak' – as a kind of open-ended hybrid – in a contingent and perhaps precarious position.

This is compounded by a wider tension, with a similarly long history in the American underground, between a focus on radical politics and the concurrent demand for a high standard of aesthetic quality. Of course, the association of avant-garde cinema with radicalism predates any American underground film movement; it is particularly evident in the Soviet avant-garde of the twenties and thirties and European Surrealist films of roughly the same era, both key influences on the subsequent American scene and both closely linked with socialist politics. As a number of critics have pointed out, the politics of the American underground cinema have always been somewhat ambiguous (Polan, 1985, pp. 52–77). Early critics of the scene tended to emphasize a connection with radical, counter-cultural movements. Sheldon Renan, author of the first book-length study of the avant-garde, connects underground film with the post-war emergence of a 'new man':

> The new man and the underground film developed together. The climate of the new man, in which to be new is to be desirable, in which the individual is constantly re-forming his idea of the world, in which the personal point of view is all important, was one of the factors that produced the underground film. The underground film, with its conscious dissent from the standards and approaches of the commercial film, is the film equivalent of the new man and his dissent from society. (Renan, 1967, p. 46)

Parker Tyler, in another early (1969) and more whimsical history of this cinema, *Underground Film*, argues passionately – if somewhat incoherently – that the American underground is intrinsically radical:

> The forces in avant-garde films which have been named Underground conspicuously if tacitly support a code that would outlaw Establishments – that is, destroy forever the political validity of the

Establishment idea … Curiously enough, the Underground film movement, regarded in this light, can be identified as having traits of both Anarchist and Communist philosophy. The catch is that, considering its best predecessors in American avant-garde film, the movement has taken specifically *formal virtues* as the object of destruction, and has done so not autocratically, by rigidly excluding those virtues, but by using its universal-tolerance code. [italics in original] (Tyler, 1969, pp. 33–34)

Tyler goes on to point out that this 'universal-tolerance code' does tend to obscure the formal aesthetic achievements of some of the 'craft group', filmmakers who put a great deal of effort into artistic technique (Tyler, 1969, p. 34). The tension between the political virtues of a more open, anti-establishment sensibility and the emphasis on the artistic value of non-commercial cinema, with the latter retaining substantial elements of conventional and largely apolitical aesthetic hierarchies, has always posed problems for more univocal celebrations of the politics of the underground.

This tension is demonstrated most remarkably in a now-famous 1967 letter from Stan Brakhage, one of the best-known and most critically revered of all American underground filmmakers, to the aforementioned Jonas Mekas, an important filmmaker and the founder of Film-Makers' Cooperative, a crucial vehicle for the distribution of independent cinema in the era. The letter, explaining Brakhage's decision to withdraw his films from the cooperative, consists primarily of an extended comparison between the hippie counter-culture of the era and the forces in late twenties Germany that gave rise to Nazism (Brakhage, 1982, pp. 124–133). Brakhage uses six themes, 'Free Love'/'Sexual Freedom', 'Brotherhood', 'Nature Worship', 'Anti-(Academic)-Art', 'Drugs' and 'Peace', to provide the foundation for this comparison. Particularly notable are his critiques of Mekas' (and, by implication, the underground film culture's) use of 'the Establishment' – recall Tyler above – as an all-purpose scapegoat and the reduction of aesthetic concerns to a polemical insistence on an unqualified openness to all varieties of non-mainstream cinema (Brakhage, 1982, pp. 128–129). The letter is remarkable both for the historical detail and rhetorical vigor of its argumentation, but also because it provides a rather concise distillation of the tension between the linkage of underground film with a broad array of radical politics and its concurrent association with a fairly conventional and distinctly apolitical sense of cinematic work as high art.

This tension is important for the analysis at hand because it continues to operate within underground cinema culture and because – like the other ambivalences I have identified – it may have particular ramifications for the symbolic dynamics of this culture, and, subsequently the ways that this media formation might operate as a resource for identity construction. The explicit political drives lauded by Renan and Tyler and repudiated by Brakhage in the name of art, especially as they become shaped by the array of identity-political formations noted above, tend to posit a model of personal and social liberation through self-expression. This is evident, for instance, in the above quotations from Renan and Tyler. However, the Brakhagian disdain for 'propaganda' and emphasis on the aesthetic value of the underground has also continued as an important thread within the culture, particularly as certain segments of it – a canonical 'avant-garde' – became increasingly affiliated with academic institutions in the seventies. This point is crucial because it also implies a related distinction in the way that a subject's relation to the text and to the artistic community is understood. In the former, the communal, nearly utopian character of the underground film experience is foregrounded as a place for the operation of the 'new man' [sic]. In the latter, as Brakhage claims in the final sentence of his letter, the experience of art (in terms of both production and reception) is 'altogether an individual manner' (Brakhage, 1982, p. 133). This conflict between a socialized, politicized alternative culture and a hermetic and quite traditional model of artistic practice, this tension between an understanding of the participant within the culture as a radical and as an aesthete, is a final ambivalence that permeates the symbolic field of the underground.

All four of the points of ambivalence noted above, high/low culture, production/consumption, identity politics/cultural hybridity and aesthetics/radicalism, are further complicated by the peculiarly self-involved character of the underground cinema. I use the term 'self-involved' not in a pejorative sense, but rather in reference to the relentless emphasis on personal expression and individuality that continues to surround this culture. Interestingly, this is common to both the 'radical' and 'aesthete' models of the underground. Whether posed in terms of a utopian social liberation (e.g., 'new man') or the romantic individualism of the elite artist, there is always a return to the self as the center of practices of both production and reception. This sense is further reinforced at a number of levels: the formal and thematic character of films, privileged models of criticism and reception and in the ways that a relationship between the individual and a cultural formation is discursively situated. Of course, all of this rests upon a symbolic foundation betraying complexity and a significant set of internal tensions; in this regard, this implied self is necessarily of the 'protean' variety, to borrow Lifton's diagnostic term.

In formal terms, 'the self' has always been of paramount importance in many of the dominant aesthetic schools affiliated with the underground. Even the minimalist or structural films (e.g., Warhol, Snow, Gehr) reflecting an intentionally de-humanized and anti-psychological approach to cinematic creation, are most meaningful in their contrast with a dominant body of films heavily marked as personal. The strategies associated with this personalization, though, have been quite varied. Particularly prominent was the 'diary' film, a category that would include such canonical underground films as Jerome Hill's *Film Portrait* and Mekas' *Diaries, Notes, and Sketches*. These films provide a highly psychologistic, impressionistic account of the experiences of the filmmaker, offering an experimental cinematic equivalent to the conventional literary autobiography (Sitney, 1978, pp. 199–241). The rhetorical strategy is one of hyper-subjectivism; documentary images are sometimes present, but the material is often arranged to suggest the vicissitudes of memory rather than an objective chronicle of life events.

A related genre, sometimes called the 'hypnagogic film', raises the hermeneutic stakes in an attempt at a kind of physiological communion with the viewer, extending the subjective address of the diaristic mode by trying to replicate a variety of visual phenomena. This would include, as Peterson mentions in reference to Brakhage's work in this area, 'the pre-linguistic vision of childhood; phosphenes, those experiences of light triggered by pressing on the eyelid; the hypnagogic imagery one experiences in the twilight between wakefulness and sleep ...' (Peterson, 1994, p. 5). In this case, the viewer is placed precisely in the position of the filmmaker, replicating a visual experience directly, through what Brakhage describes as the 'adventure of perception' (Sitney, 1978, pp. 120–121). Rhetoric, in the conventional sense, vanishes in this strategy; there is an attempt to short-circuit the standard model of communication through the production of an onomatopoeic representation and thus to provide a kind of pure 'I'-experience. By avoiding the inevitable dilution of a symbolic medium such as language or visual imagery, the filmmaker seeks to create a nearly physiological form of intersubjectivity.

The irony here is that such strategies are comprehensible at least partly because they are discursively positioned – as 'hypnagogic', 'the untutored eye' and so forth – by a body of self-criticism and self-theory uniquely prevalent in underground cinema. Such work is another important element in the larger, culturally-connoted 'personal' character of this formation. As Sitney notes, there is a particularly strong tradition of self-theorizing within the experimental film movement, with filmmakers frequently providing a philosophical explanation of their cinematic practice (Sitney, 1978, p. viii). This is in addition to a more conventional body of autobiographical writing, interviews and personal presentations of films offering a similar emphasis on the authorial character of the work and building a particularly strong link between the filmmaker and the text. As mentioned, the overlap between filmmakers, critics and audience members helps to reinforce this emphasis at a material and organizational level. When one turns to 'external' criticism and theory – that is, material not produced by filmmakers – there tends to be a similar focus on the personally expressive character of the underground (Renan, 1967, p. 41). As Rabinowitz and Mellencamp point out, this is even true within academic criticism of the avant-garde, which has been very late to explore other critical paradigms, particularly when compared with a larger body of work on film and other media (Rabinowitz, 1991, pp. 17–18; Mellencamp, 1990, pp. 17–44). The intensity and persistence of this authorial discourse serves to increase the sense of a close relationship between the cultural producer and the text and thus to encourage a particularly intense affective self-investment on the part of individuals who participate in this culture in a variety of roles.

I will conclude this overview of the subjective dynamics, at least as they have emerged historically, of the American underground film scene by reiterating a few important points. First, the culture is inclined toward a kind of self-involvement, one built upon a symbolic framework marked by a notably ambivalent and/or contradictory character. Second, there is a tendency for the text to assume a particularly prominent status as the bearer of self-expression, a condition demanding both a careful analysis of such texts and an understanding that such a sense is culturally enabled through critical and personal discourses. Finally, the ability for such a sense of connectedness and self-involvement to develop is heavily dependent upon a community of supporting institutions, both symbolic and material. The functioning and emergence of the same will be the focus of the ethnographic analysis of one such community offered below. Understanding this specific and local example, though, requires a sense of broader context, and particularly of the tenuous state of the underground film culture in the eighties and nineties.

The historical context: national and local

Though it had roots in the aforementioned Soviet and European Surrealist film traditions, as well as the twenties French avant-garde and German expressionist schools, the American underground did not emerge as a significant force within the larger national film culture until the forties and fifties. There had been earlier films that would fit within the generous parameters of this genre, but these were largely isolated examples (Renan, 1967, pp. 75–83). San Francisco and especially New York saw the development of the first real underground film cultures, although the term 'underground' was not used to refer to this type of filmmaking until 1961, when filmmaker Stan Vanderbeek coined this usage (Rosenbaum and Hoberman, 1991, p. 40). The reasons for the emergence of such a culture are obviously complex, but some crucial factors include the following: the availability of affordable equipment, especially 16mm cameras (Renan, 1967, p. 41); the concurrent popularity of a variety of marginal cultural formations including, especially, beatnik culture – an early landmark of the underground cinema was Robert Frank and Alfred Leslie's *Pull My Daisy*, based on a play by Jack Kerouac and starring Allen Ginsberg and Gregory Corso; and the crisis in Hollywood filmmaking engendered by the 1948 Paramount decision and the rise of television as a serious competitor to Hollywood (James, 1989, pp. 25–28). Underground film culture also benefited from the fact that it offered access to sexually explicit material at a time when conventional pornography was difficult to obtain and carried a stronger social stigma (Tyler, 1969, pp. 20–23; Renan, 1967, p. 31). The underground culture peaked in the sixties, a generally prosperous period for a variety of experimental or alternative cultural practices and, like many other such practices, experienced a decline in following decades.

The general period of political reaction during the seventies, eighties and early nineties combined with a wider decline in both commercial and art cinemas in the period, contributed to the withering of the underground, particularly in the United States. In an ironic twist, as the scene itself became increasingly dormant, many of the formal techniques pioneered by avant-garde filmmakers were finding wider audiences, particularly within rock videos, advertising,[2] and even commercial television (e.g., *Twin Peaks, Wild Palms*) and mainstream film (e.g., *Natural Born Killers*). Of course, this follows somewhat naturally from the stylistic hybridity noted in the above discussion of cultural postmodernism; in this case, though, the stylistic borrowing is reversed, with popular texts imitating forms developed for more marginal and culturally exclusive genres. The rise of videotape as a major medium for film viewing was also a factor in the decline of an underground community by removing the necessity for communal organization to enable access to films; however, it also helped to introduce an expanded variety of films to the public, and thus may have created a more willing audience for marginal cinemas and therefore may have enabled a degree of rebound for the underground in recent years (Rosenbaum and Hoberman, 1991, p. 330). Even the rise of the aforementioned independent/'Sundance' film to greater prominence has had relatively little impact on the cultural position of a true underground. As mentioned, the former genre tends toward small-budget narrative films rather than the range of genres (e.g., non-narrative, abstract, animated) and formats (short films, super 8mm works, etc.) that was an important part of an earlier underground scene.

A final factor leading to a general decline in the prominence of underground cinema is the movement of a large part of this culture into academic institutions in the seventies and eighties. Many of the most prominent underground filmmakers – including Brakhage, Ken Jacobs, R. Bruce Elder and numerous others – assumed academic positions, and colleges and universities have become one of the few locations for the viewing of experimental cinematic work in the US, beyond a few non-academic venues located in major cities. This has led to a spate of aesthetic critiques of the 'institutional' state of underground filmmaking in the eighties, usually directed at a perceived lack of imagination among filmmakers (Camper, 1987, pp. 99–124), but it has also had a considerable impact on the broader cultural possibilities of an underground cinema. While the academic location of much experimental cinema production and reception has exposed a fairly large number of young people to this culture, at least through the relative coercion of university classes and officially sanctioned events, the context is radically different. Sitney once described the atmosphere at midnight screenings of underground films in New York in the sixties as refreshing in that the audience was 'purified by the absence of West side psychoanalysts and professors from Columbia' that were a part of the normal constituency for such films (Rosenbaum and Hoberman, 1991, p. 42). This largely academic element has come to dominate much of the remaining underground, as cinema retains relatively little of its counter-cultural cachet. The question of the academic domination of the avant-garde is particularly relevant here, in that the analysis that follows focuses on a community linked to a major university and a film culture with undeniable connections to this institution.

The specific case of Champaign-Urbana parallels the general trends in the history of the underground cinema noted above. The twin cities, with a combined population of about 100,000, are home to the main campus of the University of Illinois, with an enrollment of approximately 40,000 students. The community has never been a hotbed of alternative cinema culture, but had a reasonably lively scene in the sixties and early seventies, one with the usual ties to larger countercultural movements. In more recent years, though, this has declined significantly at both institutional and private levels. In a 1993 article decrying the collapse of extra-curricular film culture on college campuses, the New York-based *Village Voice* weekly newspaper singled out Champaign-Urbana as an example of a large university community lacking even a student film society as an illustration of the larger national decline. While the University, through its relatively small Cinema Studies Program, featured occasional screenings and guest filmmakers, and also sponsored festivals tied to specific constituencies or academic units (e.g., the Palestinian Film Festival, the Asian-American Film Festival), there was little in the way of an autonomous independent film culture. There was one venue featuring non-mainstream narrative films, The New Art Theater, but its programming tended towards fairly traditional art cinema – foreign films and the aforementioned 'Sundance' genre. The New Art would become an important resource for a resurgent underground in 1999 when it hosted the Third Annual Freaky Film Festival, but prior to that point was primarily involved in the presentation of more conventional cinematic work. There was a small community of cineastes and amateur filmmakers, certainly, but there was very little in the way of organizations, practices and publications that might unite the community, particularly at a distinctly local level. As noted, individuals associated with the university had access to institutional resources, though these were rather meager. Those without academic affiliations were largely dependent upon long-distance participation in national and international cultural organizations and a very small and informal local peer group.

Rebirthing the freak in the late nineties

As mentioned in the introduction to this chapter, much of the ethnographic work I performed within the local film community was related to the staging of the 1998 and 1999 Freaky Film Festivals, without question the most significant events within the local film culture in the decade. For the purposes of brevity and comparative juxtaposition,

I will present the analysis of both festivals together, examining the ways that the festival became a nodal point in a redeveloping film culture and, secondly, operated as a practical and symbolic resource for the generation of the complex alignments of identities noted in the analysis of an underground subject. I have decided to separate out an analysis of significant filmic texts from both festivals, as these are particularly rich and merit an extended discussion in themselves. Before moving to the films, though, I want to examine the context of their screening, concentrating on six salient aspects of the festivals: screening space, film selection, non-screening events, volunteers, financial support and printed materials/related discourse.

The First Freaky Film Festival took place in November 1997 and was held in the Channing-Murray Foundation, a meeting place run by the local United Church of Christ, and in a University auditorium. The festival was a considerable success and inspired the organizers to commit to making the Freaky Film Festival an annual local event. It was during the initial planning of the second Freaky Film Festival in the Summer of 1998 that I became a regular participant in organizational activities. The organizers, Eric Fisher and Grace Giorgio, secured the use of the Canopy Club, a local nightspot, for the festival. The club normally featured rock bands and occasional 'brew and view' film programs of traditional college favorites (e.g., *Caddyshack*, *The Blues Brothers*); thus, it offered the distinct advantage of having a very large movie screen and its own 35mm projection equipment. In other aspects, though, it was certainly not a typical venue for a film festival, as it permitted smoking, served alcohol and had only limited seating (primarily tables and chairs) on the main floor. As with the Channing-Murray hall, the use of such a venue recalls the earliest days of the underground cinema, when lofts, church basements and other unorthodox venues were pressed into service due to the lack of traditional screening facilities (Rosenbaum and Hoberman, 1991, p. 40). While the Canopy Club engendered a number of logistical hassles, including noise distractions from the lounge area adjacent to the theater and alcohol induced rowdiness, it did provide – through the lounge – a very convenient space for post-screening conversation and for meeting visiting filmmakers. By enabling a relatively seamless transition from spectatorial engagement to participation in a related dialogical community, the space was well suited to support the diversity of role-positions and a more general participatory atmosphere discussed above. The space was also valuable in that it was located in an area directly adjacent to the university campus, providing an incentive – along with the availability of alcohol, admittedly – for a higher level of participation by the university community and especially undergraduate students.

For the 1999 Freaky Film Festival, the management of the Canopy was unwilling to accommodate a longer festival – expanded from three days to six – so the festival was relocated to the aforementioned New Art Theater. In addition to offering a more conventional and less distraction-prone environment, the New Art was also a favorable venue in that it was a non-profit enterprise and would benefit financially, in the form of rental fees and concession sales, as well as from exposure to potential patrons; in this regard, the Freaky Film Festival could enter into a mutually sustaining relationship with one of the few other non-academic, non-commercial film resources in the community. Some work was required to allow for the exhibition of videotapes and 16mm films, but the construction of a projection platform in the rear of the auditorium was quickly completed. The lack of a bar/lounge area did mean that there would be little space for gathering before and after screenings; through the participation of local bars, a number of corollary events were organized. In some ways, the movement from a church-related meeting hall to a rock club and then to an actual movie theater provides a nice microcosm for a larger increase in prominence for the festival, as the last of these locations is certainly better integrated into the normal domain of cinema audiencehood. It also created a link with the culture of 'indie' films – as mentioned, a major part of the normal repertoire of the New Art – one with a significant following among students and the general public. In another sense, the movement also reflected a distancing, albeit largely unintentional, from the University, first through the move away from official University facilities for the 1998 festival and then from the 'campustown' area itself, as Champaign-Urbana has heavily marked campus and local (or 'townie') regions. As noted previously, one of the factors in the decreasing cultural relevance of the underground was its concurrently increasing incorporation within academic institutions and curricula, so this spatial relocation had an additional significance. This drift away from the campus area continued with a series of post-festival 'Happy Hour' presentations of various underground films – including selected highlights from previous festivals – at the High Dive, a bar/club located a few blocks from the New Art in Champaign's recently resurgent downtown.

The selection of venues was important, of course, but the selection and programming of films presented a more complex challenge. I was present at the meetings in which submissions were screened and films were selected for both the 1998 and 1999 festivals, and saw all of the submitted films. Film selection was accomplished through a process of screening and discussion, with some debate over the relative merits of each film. The selection committee consisted of various volunteers – a mixture of graduate and undergraduate students, local filmmakers and fans, and other interested individuals – as well as organizers Fisher and Giorgio; the committee's composition would shift depending on who was in attendance at a given meeting. There were no strict aesthetic criteria applied, and political value, ethnic origin or gender, while perhaps a factor in evaluation, were not used as formal criteria in the sense of having a quota for a certain type of film. The medium of a submission was an important criterion, though, as there was a clear desire on the part of the committee to maintain the 'Film' in Freaky Film Festival; selections that were to be presented on 16mm, 35mm or super 8mm film (as opposed to videotape) were thus particularly welcome. The screening procedure could be quite arduous, as hours and hours of films had to be viewed over the course of a few evenings, and many of the submissions were mediocre. The goal of a 'Freaky' character for the festival was both an aid and a challenge in the selection process. It allowed for a great deal of latitude without fear of violating a coherent theme, while at the same time offering very little, beyond having a personal sensibility and non-mainstream aesthetic or socio-political sensibility (or both), in terms of guidelines for inclusion. In this sense, it mirrors some of the tensions described above, which hold both an instability in their breadth and a power in their flexibility. Ironically, the term 'freaky' was the source of a good deal of confusion, particularly in relation to the promotion of the festival. Many potential audience members and journalists covering the festival assumed that 'freaky films' meant horror/gore films and other psychotronic works. Here, a term chosen to avoid the elitism of 'avant-garde', the dated 'underground' and the deceptive 'indie/independent' backfired by implying an even narrower and potentially more unappealing group of films.

Films were selected prior to the development of individual programs, and the construction of these programs offered an equally daunting task. The festivals, as mentioned, featured a number of thematic programs that grouped films around a central focal point. Dividing the selected films for programming was a challenge due to their wildly diverse character and the normal constraints of time, as the films ranged from less than a minute to nearly two hours. At this point, some of the socio-cultural components such as identity-political positions or lifestyle formations that are a part of the larger underground scene – and a part of 'the freak' – became useful as strategies for programming.

As noted, the 1998 festival featured programs of films addressing gender issues (*Femme Fatale*), queer themes (*The Queer Experience*) and the drug culture (*The Bong Show*), all important elements in the underground. The 1999 festival featured *Out and About* and *The New Bong Show*, addressing the latter two groups; feminist and other gender-themed films were numerous enough to warrant inclusion in two programs: *Love Comes in Spurtz* and *Oedipus Multiplex*, though neither was dedicated exclusively to this theme.

These programs, along with collections of animated films in each festival, were relatively easy to construct, as they were somewhat obvious groupings. A greater challenge was creating additional programs to organize films that could not be easily slotted into an existing social category or cinematic medium. Here, a number of strategies were used to produce coherent programs. Fairly conventional genres such as comedy (*Funny Shit*), action films (*Viva La Violence*) and the documentary (*The Truth is 'Out There'*) were particularly useful for the 1999 festival, in which these programs appeared. In another case, the music video format structured a program (*Freak TV*); in still another, the local origin of the films served as the organizing principle (*Who Are the Freaks in Your Neighborhood?*). Other programs were built around the kinds of hybrid identity positions discussed above, as in 1998's aforementioned *The Freaks Come Out at Night*, which presented films dealing with truly marginal social formations. In 1999, a similar strategy was used in the construction of *Punk Meets 'The Funk'*, a collection of films that engaged the both the punk rock and hippie subcultures, headlined by John Michael McCarthy's *The Sore Losers*, a feature length pastiche of fifties 'juvenile delinquent' films with a plot satirizing the hostile relations between punks and hippies. Finally, a few programs were designed thematically, drawing upon filmic content without recourse to the more obvious categories noted above. This was reflected in the *Planet of the Angst* (1999) and *Justice is Served* (1998) programs, centered around themes of social anxiety and cosmic justice, respectively.

The question of programming is important in that it is illustrative of the ways that the wider-ranging symbolic elements in an underground formation discussed above provide the framework for the practical task of festival organization. As mentioned, many of the criteria used in programming – identity politics, conventional genre categories, marginal social formations, unconventional media or formats – stem directly from the cultural composition of underground cinema. The difficulty and elusiveness of such categorical schemes, and the need for less explicitly coherent programs, though, provides evidence of the diversity and contingency of the same underground. The entire collection of films was only unified, therefore, around the generous, even ambiguous category of 'freaky', a definition that ended up functioning primarily in a negative sense, signifying a distance from both the economic and aesthetic mainstream, as well as from the pseudo-independent world of 'indies'.

A similar diversity is evident in the set of non-screening events (e.g., parties, workshops, music performances) that were planned as a part of the festival. The decision to include such events reflects an implicit recognition of the aforementioned breadth of an underground formation, drawing boundaries that extended beyond spectatorship. (On a more practical note, such activities were also designed to provide an inviting social environment for guest filmmakers and subsequently establish the desirability of the festival as a destination for artists and cineastes). For the 1998 festival, these events included a panel discussion with visiting filmmakers, a wine and cheese opening reception, a sake tasting featuring live jazz and a closing night party with local techno music performers. The 1999 festival also featured a wine and cheese opening, and, through the cooperation of local nightspots, two music events each night with free admission for festival guests. Both festivals also included less official, but festival-sponsored 'after hours' parties at local homes. The purpose of this body of events – beyond the pragmatic function noted above – was to create the kind of extra-filmic social community that had long been a part of underground cinema (Rabinowitz, 1991, pp. 2–3, for example, on the salon culture revolving around pioneering filmmaker Maya Deren). The events were a balanced group, representative of the diversity of the underground; highbrow wine and cheese, and sake and jazz, as well as the more stereotypically collegiate after hours keg parties and techno music. The music events reflected a connection with other media and a wider alternative cultural formation, and the 1998 panel discussion and *Work in Progress* screening honored the aforementioned blending of production and consumption roles common to the underground. More important than this cultural diversity, though, was the simple fact that such events facilitated an absolutely critical social proximity – between filmmakers, audience members and festival volunteers – and encouraged the exchange of discourse and the establishment of social bonds, however temporary. I will remember the success of this community-building enterprise most concretely through the image of Mark Hejnar – a relative superstar within the underground and an avid attendee at a number of the extra-filmic events in both 1998 and 1999 – helping several volunteers (including myself) in the rush to clear the theater of litter between programs. Such practices were not particularly unusual during the festivals, but they were dependent upon the establishment of a comfortable communal environment.

The aforementioned festival volunteers were a particularly heterogeneous group, a useful characteristic given the range of duties demanded of them. In addition to Fisher and Giorgio, the directors of the festival, there were about 20 core volunteers at each festival, with a fairly large degree of overlap between 1998 and 1999 staff. About half of the volunteers were students at the University of Illinois, mostly graduate students. The remainder came primarily from the more bohemian elements within the local community; like many college towns, Champaign-Urbana has a significant community of non-institutional artists and intellectuals. The age range was considerable – from 18 to 50, approximately – and there was a roughly even distribution of men and women. The demographic diversity, however, was less important than the diversity of skills the volunteers brought to the festival and were thus able to apply to organizational tasks. In addition to the aforementioned production of a trailer for the festival screenings that was made by a different filmmaker each year, the considerable graphic design and writing talents of several volunteers were used in the creation of festival programs and posters. An area potter fashioned three trophies – featuring the 'Freaky Guy' mascot featured in promotional materials – for award-winning films, and the website for the festival was constructed by a local Internet entrepreneur. Such contributions are particularly significant in that they reflect the integration of professional and personal creative practices into the larger framework of staging the festival and thus involve a meshing of individual and social functions, one homologously similar to the simultaneously individualistic and socialized milieu of the underground. Of course, any number of less artistic tasks were required, so that a given volunteer might also be involved in distributing programs, vacuuming the theater and selling popcorn, in addition to creative production work. As an example, I was involved in a vast array of practices, including distribution of materials, making promotional contacts in local media, collecting tickets, cleaning, projection and other technical work, and even the construction of the aforementioned projection platform. While I intentionally involved myself in a wide variety of tasks for ethnographic purposes, this diversity was rather common among volunteers, and helped to create a particularly strong sense of communal purpose. This can be linked back to the Meadian insistence that the 'aesthetic

LIVERPOOL JOHN MOORES UNIVERSITY
LEARNING SERVICES

attitude' is not limited to the experience of art in a strict sense, but is also accessed through the engagement in practices that work toward the dissolution of role as such and towards the realization of collective goals (Mead, 1938, p. 457).

Of course, as so many scholars would remind us, the material horizon always lurks beyond such practices, and a film festival is no exception. Indeed the diversity of festival-related events is more than the result of an intentional eclecticism in the programming; it is also the result of the willingness of businesses to contribute to the festival. All of the affiliated social events noted above were sponsored by local establishments and a number of local businesses (e.g., food and wine suppliers, a bed and breakfast) offered donations of services. There were additional general sponsors, ranging from bookstores, beer and soft drink companies and University departments and programs, to a fetish fashion store and local topless bar. This unusual coalition was reflective both of Fisher and Giorgio's formidable fundraising skills, as well as the odd conglomeration of material institutions – academic, corporate and marginal – willing to participate in exchange for publicity.

As might be expected, such a body of sponsors inevitably produced a certain degree of tension, particularly when both major corporate bodies and potentially offensive institutions (e.g., a topless bar) were a part of this group. As with many other aspects of the scene, this was hardly new to the underground. Major corporate philanthropic foundations, particularly the Ford Foundation, were heavily involved as patrons of the early American avant-garde film culture (Renan, 1967, pp. 112, 137, 141), and certainly a wide array of smaller organizations contributed as well. Obviously, the worldview of such organizations is often quite dissonant with the more politically-inclined elements within the underground. This can sometimes be reconciled through an understanding of the use of such funding as subversive, as undercutting the very goals of the sponsors; alternatively, a model of art as metaphysically separate from the domain of politics – the view, largely, of Sitney and Brakhage – can work to dissolve the tension entirely. In the case of the Freaky Film Festivals, the major concern was whether or not sponsorship might interfere with the autonomy of the festival, and there were some potential sponsors that chose not to participate due to festival content (or at least presumed festival content). However, the organizations that did sponsor the festival seemed uninterested in any control over content; the largest dispute with a sponsoring organization concerned the display of a banner bearing the sponsor's name and logo. In fact, the presence of the sponsors was felt primarily in such token symbolic gestures; in addition to the aforementioned banner, sponsors were recognized with a logo placed on the posters and programs for the festival.

The same promotional materials constituted a final important contextual element for audience practices engendered by the festivals. The printed festival programs, especially, are important in this regard, as they were a source of particular pride for the festival staff because of their striking design, and also because they served as the public face of the festival – several thousands were distributed throughout the region in the weeks preceding the festival. The program for the 1998 festival was designed to resemble a comic book and introduced the 'Freaky Guy' mascot, featuring him on the front cover and as a character in the rear cover comic strip. The link with comic books engaged another element of a larger alternative culture – the world of 'indie comics' – and one with considerable overlap with underground film.[2] For the 1999 program, the comic book theme was less prominent, but the 'Freaky Guy' returned, though his appearance was in this case linked to a larger motif – a parodic reference to the then-current independent film sensation *The Blair Witch Project*. That film, a very low-budget mock documentary horror film, was the subject of an enormous amount of mass media publicity and was a substantial box office hit that year, standing as the mainstream exemplar of 'independent film'. Thus, it gave the program designers a recognizable reference for defining 'freaky' cinema, although the use of *Blair Witch* as a program theme was much debated at volunteer meetings, and was actually somewhat less prominent than the design team had originally proposed. *Blair Witch* was referenced on the back cover with graphics mimicking the film and copy reading, 'There's more to indie film than stick figures and flannel shirts [icons of *Blair Witch*], and you'll find the proof right here at Central Illinois' premiere film festival.'

In an essay entitled 'Freaky Film 3: Season of the Witch' included in the program, the aforementioned festival volunteer and *Micro-Film* editor Jason Pankoke discussed the significance of *Blair Witch* for the festival and underground cinema:

> The heady implication [of the film's success] is that the average individuals possessing the proper dosages of guts, wits, desire, functioning equipment, and bare-bones can and will get off their butts out there and make that movie they've always dreamed of making, just as long as it doesn't involve something ridiculous like vast armies of dinosaurs or space bugs trampling the earth. Don't mull over what

you don't have; take the best of what you do have and go for it... the potential pitfall, though, is that the financial success of the Myrick/Sanchez effort will errantly send signals to these same bright-eyed-moguls-in-the-making that no-budget, shot-on-video, instant indie hits are a snap.

There is a telling ambivalence in the use of *Blair Witch* on the program back cover and in the above essay in that it serves as a kind of intro-duction to and inspiration for non-mainstream cinema, and at the same time, there is an attempt to distance the festival and its content from the mainstream media culture that adopted this film but could never accommodate the full spectrum of 'freaky' cinema. Such ambiva-lence, as I have indicated, is characteristic of underground film, but it is interesting to view its registration at the level of the discursive positioning of the festival.

While the program was the major promotional vehicle for the festi-vals, there were efforts to attain publicity through local media chan-nels. This is most evident and most symptomatically displayed in the use of radio for this purpose. Three local stations were important in this regard: WILL, a university-sponsored National Public Radio outlet; WWHP, 'The Whip', a local independent station staffed by volunteers and featuring 'roots' music; and WXPC, '93X X-treme radio', a rock station owned by a national radio conglomerate and also a festival sponsor. The contrast between stations is interesting, as it reflects, respectively, academic, bohemian and commercial threads in the local mediascape. The nature of festival-related material was similarly telling. The coverage on WILL for the 1999 Freaky Film Festival featured a reporter tracking the progress of the organization and staging of the fes-tival and interviewing volunteers (including myself) and viewing films for an extended piece on a program dedicated to local cultural activity. For the previous year's festival, 'The Whip' invited Fisher and Giorgio into the studio for a rambling discussion of the festival, interspersed with music and callers, that lasted for several hours. WXPC, on the other hand, aired a very brief interview with the two festival directors as well as a number of professionally-produced commercials (a part of the sponsorship package) that emphasized its 'freaky' aspects with a parody of older horror film advertising. The discursive styles of these three presentations reflected quite nicely elements of its character: a high cultural event, a remnant of an older counter-culture and an extension of the mass cultural obsession with the marginal evident in the hype surrounding *The Blair Witch Project* and prized by the 'main-stream alternative' culture exemplified by 'X-treme radio'.

All of the elements discussed above – the festival spaces, the selection process and programming, ancillary events, the festival volunteers, financial sponsors and the discursive positioning of the festival – are important in that they produce a context that enables the films themselves to attain a greater degree of symbolic purchase. One might think of these elements as a set of regions, roles and media flows with a high degree of permeability, that are in some sense unified by the underground film scene. As noted above, many of the spaces (e.g., the Canopy Club), individuals (e.g., the many volunteers who contributed in kind with their artistic/technical skills) and even extra-filmic media discourses (e.g., the references to *The Blair Witch Project*, the contrasting radio coverage) have only a partial affiliation with this culture. Their articulation – in the sense used by Grossberg and Hall – as a mechanism of community formation depends upon this flexibility, of course, but also upon the mutually developing willingness of individuals to support such a community.

Of course, this challenge is all the greater in a local setting lacking in substantive symbolic and material resources for individuals seeking to participate in the culture. The task of reconstructing such resources cannot be accomplished, paradoxically, without the simultaneous enabling of opportunities for affective and subjective connection with a cultural formation. This is evident, as noted, in the movement away from a strong geographic link with the University and a greater incorporation into a local 'townie' culture, and also in the expanded scale of successive festivals. It is also evident in the importance of social and cultural proximity in the entrenchment of the festival as an important element in the local cinema culture; the extra-filmic social events associated with each festival, particularly those that allowed interaction between filmmakers, organizers and festival attendees, were absolutely critical in attracting both volunteers and audiences for future festivals. Likewise, *Micro-Film*, the debut of which was preceded by a series of 'warning shot' flyers that included publicity for the 1999 festival, was itself a result of Pankoke being inspired by the 1997 festival. Additionally, a series of 'Freaky Film Screenings' at the Canopy Club, the New Art and later the High Dive, were scheduled throughout the year, to keep the festival name in circulation and to offer access to a range of nonmainstream films. These included a program of films by underground director Jon Moritsugu, Todd Solondz's controversial feature *Happiness* and Cass Paley's biography of porn star John Holmes, *Wadd*. These screenings were made possible, organizationally and in terms of attracting audiences, by the initial popularity of the festivals; thus, there was a mutually supportive relationship. The development of such activities helped to solidify the underground film community and provided the access to the extra-textual and text-based symbolic resources – in terms of both social practices and discursive materials – that allow for the self-investment of individuals within this cultural formation. The extra-textual elements have been discussed extensively above; the following section takes on the actual body of material presented at the Freaky Film Festivals, with a specific eye towards the hermeneutic significance of this cinematic work.

Reading the festival text – image and identity

As noted in Chapter 1, I am in agreement with calls by a number of scholars within media and cultural studies, including Charlotte Brundson and Elspeth Probyn, for a renewed interest in the significance and value of textual analysis within these fields. This is particularly important for the kind of social hermeneutic analysis at hand, as the texts associated with a given audience formation are particularly important in the development of modes of self-investment and self-reflection. This becomes amplified, as noted, in the world of underground film. First, there is the very prominent emphasis on the individual and authentic character of artistic expression within this culture – the 'personal cinema' angle – and the relentless attention to questions of the self through the deployment of autobiographical and psychodramatic genres. This emphasis is prominent at textual and critical levels and is promoted by practices of indigenous criticism and self-theorization. Secondly, the socio-cultural distinction attached to the viewing of associated texts creates an atmosphere of attentiveness and one that encourages interpretive effort; this is further emphasized by the relatively challenging aesthetic character and occasional incoherence of the same texts. The text-centered nature of the underground formation, a quality that is partly a critical construct – as in the authorial discourse surrounding the films – but is also intimately related to the socio-material circumstances of production and reception, thus demands a careful attention to these works. In the following analysis, I will proceed thematically through the programs of the 1998 and 1999 Freaky Film Festivals, with a specific concentration on texts having a special resonance both to issues of identity and to the multiple structuring binaries of an 'underground subject' noted above. Within this larger set, I have identified five areas of particular thematic concentration: interiority and the discursivity of the self, psychodramatic abstraction, fringe culture, daily life and meta-commentary on film and other media.

A number of films presented at the festivals directly engage the question of internal psychological states and the relationship of such states to environmental and discursive conditions. For example, Doug Wolens' *Happy Loving Couples* presents an internal monologue regarding the difficulties of life as a single woman in a big city, contrasted with a variety of images of urban locales, presumably the haunts of the narrator. Here, the rhetorical mode is specifically diaristic, although it should be noted that the narrator is not positioned, formally, as the filmmaker; Wolens is male and the narrator's voice is female. *Happy Loving Couples* is thus a 'personal film' enacted through a fictional narrator rather than a directly autobiographical work. The contrast between the blank character of the visuals and the intensely personal nature of the spoken audio track implies the inherent disjunction between the self and an environment, thematizing this alienation.

Janene Higgins' experimental video *We Hate You Little Boy* presents a somewhat different angle on the same theme of alienation; in this case, the estrangement is verbal rather than spatial. The video features black and white footage of a young boy playing in a yard juxtaposed with a variety of invective phrases – 'just go out and die', 'we hate you little boy' and so on – presumably directed at the titular figure. The video thus suggests the blindness of hate and the cruelty of the socialization process, implying that the boy is oblivious to the latent viciousness that surrounds him. The use of text to represent a hostile social world, the 'we' of the title, also poses the symbolic character of this faceless, pluralized menace. Alienation is figured here as a disjunction between the free, playful physical body and the harsh world of language, a hyper-Lacanian formulation in which the death drive appears as purely linguistic and in which symbolic containment becomes associated with personal violence.

A more abstracted, stream-of-consciousness variation on the social alienation presented in the films noted above appears in *Isolation*, a 1998 entry by the then-local filmmaker John May. The animated film uses expressionistic sets and stop-motion animation to present a vision of an internal world, one objectifying the anxieties of the protagonist. Rather than presenting the disconnection of two symbolic registers – the self and space and the self and discourse – as in the aforementioned films, *Isolation* turns fully inward, leaving only an expressionistic psychological landscape. It is thus fitting that *Isolation*, unlike the other works, uses no visuals with any claim to veridicality. Unlike the rather blank local imagery of *Happy Loving Couples* or the 'home movie' images of the title figure in *We Hate You Little Boy*, *Isolation* reflects a complete refusal of realism. The externalized psyche presented in the film is thus an amplification of the alienation present in the other films and simultaneously, through the absence of any gap between the psychological and the material, a more rhetorically open strategy, one creating a wider space for audience identification.

While these three films present self-centered, psychological ruminations of disjunction and alienation, a fourth film, Susan Rivo's *Amy*, explores an intensely personal form of symbolic affiliation from a somewhat sunnier perspective. The film consists primarily of a narrative exploring the filmmaker's personal attachment to a stuffed animal that began in her infancy and has continued through her life. The somewhat mundane quality of this very common bond is precisely the source of its expressive power, allowing the film to function in a highly diaristic mode – formally, it certainly fits within that genre of the underground – while providing an easy emotional connection for the viewer. The theme of the projection of the self onto an object is intriguing here in that it both references the paramount symbolic importance that such objects hold through one's life and uses the same object as a vehicle for communication, as the rhetorical ground for the sharing of an emotional experience. In addition to appearing at the Freaky Festival, the film has won a number of awards, providing evidence of the success of its warmhearted universalism.

While all of the above films operate within the long-established, aforementioned tradition of the personal film, a number of films from both 1998 and 1999 eschew even the rhetorical framework of a narrator/protagonist and instead attempt a kind of purely cognitive experience by offering a barrage of often provocative, emotionally charged images. This mirrors, of course, the hypnagogic and trance films of the classic American avant-garde, and through the frequent use of found footage, engage the similarly prominent assemblage strain (Peterson, 1994, pp. 126–144). In the case of films by Juan Carlos Garay Nietos and Mark Hejnar, such images are deployed to produce a particularly intense viewing experience, a practice suggested by *Isolation* but less evident in the other 'personal' films. Nietos' *Yuri Pentrado Al Maravilloso Mundo De Los Sunos* uses the framing device of a drug-induced nightmare to present a variety of unusual and somewhat disturbing images featuring heavily costumed individuals wearing bizarre makeup. In this case, the direct replication of a human mental experience – the nightmare – is offered, albeit through the somewhat conventional narrative device of the 'dream sequence'. There is a similarity here with *Isolation* in the attempt to visualize a psychological landscape, but in this case the visualization is not metaphorical or expressionistic, but rather posed as the replication of the physical act of dreaming.

Bible of Skin, one of a total of six films by Hejnar presented at the two festivals, lacks even the narrative anchor of the dream, as in *Yuri...* , to justify its stream of imagery. The film is a twelve minute collection of extremely graphic images, drawn from medical films, pornography, footage of war atrocities and other sources blended together in unusual juxtapositions. The impact of such images is profoundly disturbing, an effect increased by the disorienting nature of the editing style and the eerie, discordant soundtrack provided by Hejnar's band Pile of Cows (interestingly, the band itself was the subject of Hejnar's similar, if less abstract, *Herd Mentality*, a jury award-winner at the 1999 festival). *Bible of Skin* thus serves as a challenge to the audience member, dependent on the reaction to turn away as much as the films discussed above depended on a relative ease of identification. The traumatic character of the viewing experience has an extensive history in the many shocking films associated with the underground, although *Bible of Skin* intensifies the trauma both in its formal complexity – it is a dazzling visual spectacle – and in its unrelenting violation of representational taboos, particularly in the juxtaposition of sexually explicit and violent images. There is also a kind of secondary challenge for the viewer – beyond that of merely keeping one's eyes on the screen – to make sense of the visuals and to understand them in some form of logical sequence. Indeed, in a conversation with Hejnar following the screening of the film, he told me that while he considered the film quite linear in its organization, others who had seen the film dozens of times could not discern a firm structure. Through the hideousness of its visuals and the obscurity of its organization, *Bible of Skin* thus formally enacts the kind of alienation that was presented thematically in films such as *Isolation* and *Happy Loving Couples*, and reflects a typically avant-garde preference for a very direct visual rhetoric.

Two of Hejnar's other festival entries, *Jeff* and the aforementioned *Affliction*, are similar to *Bible of Skin* in that they feature shocking images and explore particularly aberrant aspects of human existence, but unlike the latter, they are not so much trance films but rather quasi-documentary explorations of figures and cultures at the very margins of contemporary social life. As noted in the introduction to this chapter, *Affliction* is a particularly rich text, as it includes a wide range of marginal and 'afflicted' cultural formations, from punk rock and fanzine writing to body modification and performance art. The film is a wide-ranging, 45-minute work utilizing a number of formal strategies, from completely blank cinematography very much in the minimalist tradition to heavily modified footage reminiscent of *Bible of Skin* to shaky, handheld camerawork associated with the cinema verité documentary tradition. *Jeff* is a much shorter film, four minutes, combining original material and found footage to create an expressionistic portrait of serial killer Jeffrey Dahmer. The pluralistic, non-judgmental and even celebratory character of *Affliction* is absent, replaced by a kind of monomaniacal obsession reflected in the use of Dahmer as an object of fascination. Dahmer's status is perhaps beyond 'marginality'; even with their various legal troubles, the figures documented in *Affliction* are essentially artistic in nature – writers, musicians, performance artists – and thus have an innate connection with the likely audience for underground film and especially the shock cinema genre. *Jeff*, however, raises the stakes by dedicating an elaborate and intense visual and sonic spectacle to a figure of nearly total abjection, one lacking even the perverse glamour of a figure such as musician-hippie-murderer Charles Manson. If *Bible of Skin* challenges one's physical ability to remain gazing at the screen, *Jeff* provokes a more subtle challenge to confront both the repulsion and the seduction of the anti-human.

The exploration of cultural extremes in both *Affliction* and *Jeff* provide an interesting counterweight to both the personal and hypnagogic films in that they enact a confrontation with a kind of otherness. Rather than representing the broken social integration characteristic of alienation or attempting a rhetorical morphing of consciousness, the films force the viewer to face individuals and acts that are not easily reconciled with the viewer's own subjectivity. There is a tension at work here that is not dissimilar from those evident in the social composition of an underground described above; this is particularly the case with *Affliction*, of course, given its mirroring of the component structure of this cultural alliance. However, by pushing the dissonant aspects to the forefront, the profound difficulty of any reconciliation with the other, any incorporation into a community (symbolic or otherwise) is highlighted and the sometimes jaded 'tolerance' of the audience is itself pulled into question. *Jeff*, as noted, takes this a step further, presenting a supreme alterity, but one couched within the formal terms of the avant-garde, thus articulating the extreme parameters of both social life and aesthetic presentation.

The third group of films, those roughly organized around issues of 'daily life' and the everyday, are interesting for nearly opposite reasons. Rather than fixating on the edges of contemporary experience, these films explore the phenomenological and social significance of mundane and routine social practices. *Next Station*, a one hour short feature by Chaker Ayadi, who had completed an MA degree in cinematography at the University of Illinois before relocating to Canada, presents the rambling path of a Vancouver office worker wandering about the city when he is given a day off from work. The film is a slow, understated piece, shot in a flat, documentary style. The narrative is relatively linear, but also undynamic; events just seem to occur, with relatively little dramatic tension. The coldness and alienation of urban life is certainly referenced, but unlike *Happy Loving Couples*, this is not achieved through a juxtaposition of the human and the environmental, but rather through a broader aura of emotional disconnection.

Lisa McElroy's *Job* also explores everyday life, but in this case, the focus is on the work experience itself rather than the day off. The film utilizes a visual style borrowed from twenties German expressionism and thirties Universal Studios' horror films in the presentation of a faceless protagonist in a business suit who performs trivial and typical office work. Interestingly, the film was shot at the actual site of the filmmaker's day employment (a fact included in the program notes), giving it an additional poignancy. Once again, the central theme is one of alienation, in this case compounded by the dehumanization suggested by the facelessness of the main character. In formal terms, *Job* is strikingly different from *Next Station*, given the former's pastiche of striking visual styles. Here, the effect is dialectical, creating a contrast between the mundane nature of the action and the flair of the formal construction. Thus with these films, one finds two vastly different strategies for the exploration of daily life: a symbiotic formal understatement in *Next Station* and a stylized aestheticization in *Job*.

The decision to focus on the unexceptional and everyday, though, unites the films and reflects the distance of both from the thematic conventions of Hollywood and mainstream international cinema. Both also reference a portion of social and economic life necessarily absent from the kinds of lives and practices that were the focus of fringe films such as Hejnar's. There is a corollary here both to the kinds of role-distance that Goffman locates within occupational situations (Goffman, 1961, pp. 85–132) – the day job as the site of artistic reflection in *Job* – and to the desire for communal integration that Tugendhat and others view as fundamental to self-realization. While a film like *Affliction* is, in an odd sense, a positive text in that it creates an aesthetic space for the recognition and even celebration of a multitude of 'afflicted' identities, the daily life-themed films suggest a negative, critical capacity generated by the respectively stifling and alienating milieu of the workplace and the city. Even *Jeff*, with its fascinated gaze at the monstrous, presents the individual as a kind of realized being, albeit one utterly divorced from the possibility of conventional social recognition; in *Job* and *Next Station*, there is only the recognition of an incompletion, of the dispossession of an integrated selfhood.

Job is a particularly interesting film because this theme is presented through a formal pastiche of earlier cinematic styles, a quality linking it with a final group of films, those offering a reflexive meta-commentary on film images and the mass media in general. Of course, this sort of reflexivity is quite common to any number of artistic media and genres and is frequently claimed as a hallmark of the postmodern aesthetic. Additionally, as mentioned, this aesthetic strategy has long been an important part of the American underground cinema and it continues as a very significant thread in the culture as a whole. In addition to *Wheels of Fury, Sore Losers, Red's Breakfast III* and *Golden Gate*, the festivals also featured Lisa Hammer's *Dance of Death*, which emulated the structure and look of silent-film 'cliffhangers' and *Roadkill Travelogue*, a parody of the 'investigative reporting' genre common to television news programs. In these cases, however, the pastiche strategy is fairly straightforward, featuring an imitation of a previous style, usually with some ironic or humorous twist (although the degree of comic intent varies greatly). These films are reflexive in their self-conscious engagement of historical or unusual styles, but this reflexivity is limited to a stylistic imitation, and not utilized in the service of a deeper philosophical argument.

There are a number of other films from the festivals, though, that attempt a more probing commentary on the nature of artistic production and the role of mediated images in society. Two films, Michael Kaplan's *Peoria Babylon* and Jon Moritsugu's *Fame Whore*, are feature-length comedies that ruminate upon the question of fame and fortune within the world of art and media. *Peoria Babylon*, set in the title city – about 80 miles from Champaign-Urbana – involves the misguided attempt of two art gallery owners to achieve fame within the international art world. *Fame Whore* offers three intertwining narratives concerning the lives of, respectively, a supremely bratty tennis star, a laughably untalented but ambitious fashion designer-actress-singer with a gigantic appetite for marijuana and a mild-mannered animal shelter manager with a foul-mouthed talking dog for a companion. Both films poke fun at the silly and shallow culture of celebrity with a broad comic approach, and the latter is particularly reminiscent of the early work of film legend John Waters, who started his career within the American underground scene (Rosenbaum and Hoberman, 1991, pp. 136–173). Such critiques of celebrity have a long history within popular and elite culture, particularly within more intellectually inclined segments of both cultures, but *Peoria Babylon* and *Fame Whore* are interesting in that both take aim at aspects of the cult of celebrity that have particular associations with avant-garde or 'alternative' cultures. *Peoria Babylon*, as noted, aims its satire at the world of high art and the peculiarities of the international art market, while *Fame Whore's* ambitious Sophie creates cutting edge fashions featuring the terms for regions of female genitalia (e.g., 'vulva') emblazoned on t-shirts. The films thus cast a reflexive gaze upon the same types of cultural activity that lend a degree of prestige and distinction to the underground, although the broad comic approach in both films adds a bit of distance and thus a degree of rhetorical security to the broadsides against the pretentious world of the avant-garde.

The festivals included other films, though, that look reflexively at the broader status of images within society and attempt, on more daring formal terms, a deconstruction of such images. Amy Talkington's *Number One Fan*, an award winning entry in the 1997 Hamptons International Film Festival and an audience favorite at the Freaky Film Festival, offers a grimly noirish tale of bored young people who photograph fake crime scenes for artistic purposes. The main character, a suburban teenager, becomes involved with the group and is sucked into a world of real criminal activity. The photography-as-death trope has been visited in earlier avant-garde texts – most famously Chris Marker's *La Jetee* – but here it is combined with a theme of suburban escape that lends it a particular poignancy for an audience of collegiate and post-collegiate bohemians, one never lacking in suburban refugees. The film also raises questions about the truth-value of the image and the line between representations and material reality, placing the viewer in the uncomfortable position of achieving a kind of vicarious thrill in identifying with the protagonist while simultaneously having the terms of that relationship called into question.

The filmic image and the implied symbolic complexity of the audience are also the subject of examination in Robert G. Banks' *Jaded/ Outlet* and *MPG: Motion Picture Genocide*, but in this case the strategy involves radical editing and imaging techniques, rather than the reflexivity of narrative and mise-en-scene evident in *Number One Fan*. Banks' films are similar to some of Hejnar's, especially the aforementioned *Bible of Skin*, in their visual virtuosity; in fact, both of Banks' films were produced in the 35mm format, a relatively rare practice in the underground, and benefit from the increased definition and luminescence of that medium. *Jaded/Outlet* is primarily concerned with media images of women, offering send-ups of fashion advertising, while *MPG* focuses on a variety of sensational images, particularly those involving sex and violence. As with *Bible of Skin*, there is an inherent contrast between the potentially objectionable content of the images and the striking aesthetics of their presentation, and a kind of challenge to the viewer. In this case, however, it is not a question of one's ability to physically accept the images, but instead of the interpretive challenge of making sense of them. The difficulty of Banks' films, the frustration that they engender in the viewer, works against the ease with which viewers have become accustomed to dealing with heavily commodified and fetishized images of sex and violence.

The issue of the seduction of media images and viewer passivity is the explicit theme of Hejnar's *TV Ministry*, an overwhelming audience favorite and winner of the 'Best of the Fest' award at the 1998 festival. The film presents a fictional congregation of individuals who worship television, the titular 'TV Ministry', located in the Chicago suburbs. The members of this congregation appear in interview segments discussing their love of television and appear completely dazed and utterly mindless; one member of the congregation links his passion for television with a love of getting stoned. Their comments are interspersed with stunning montages of found footage that provide an ironic commentary on the power of the television image. In a sense, the film offers a literalization of the Baudrillardian nightmare of 'profuse otherness', with the self entirely surrendered to the world of television, coupled with a dazzling display of the seductiveness of the televisual image. The film thus pushes the viewer into the somewhat uncomfortable position of both laughing at the zombiefied cultists while at the same time in symbiotic awe at the fascinating, viral power of the image. The hostility to television as a mind-rotting medium is a classic trope for intellectuals of all political persuasions, of course, but it has a specific resonance when contrasted with the collective, defiantly non-mainstream world of underground film. In a peculiar way, the film serves as a kind of esteem-boosting text for the avant-garde set (though Hejnar himself would likely loathe this interpretation), whose intellectual engagement presumably provides a stark contrast to the television zombies. This theme is intensified by use of a religious parallel, playing off of the hostility to conventional religion common to so many intellectual cultures. *TV Ministry* thus offers an implied positive identity – also present, as noted, in *Affliction* – to the more univocally critical themes of the previous films. However, this effect is tempered with the inevitable sense that whether one is a cineaste or a member of the 'TV congregation', she still remains firmly planted before the screen and the image. This rather unsettling reality lends *TV Ministry* an interesting tension and makes it a particularly resonant text for the culture of the underground, reflected in its notable popularity.

The 'media critique' strain in the festivals is thus a final important thematic locus in the corpus of films presented at the two festivals. This group of films is particularly interesting at three levels. Firstly, they are the most explicitly 'postmodern' group of films, a quality evident in their reflexive and meta-textual character, and thus reflect one response to some of the dilemmas that a postmodern aesthetic poses for an underground or avant-garde culture that were discussed above. At the same time, these films were also connected to an older modernist tradition of avant-garde filmmaking; *TV Ministry* bears a considerable resemblance to the seminal avant-garde films of Bruce Conner (e.g., *Cosmic Ray, A Movie*) while *Number One Fan*, as mentioned, thematically recalls Marker's *La Jetee*. Secondly, they tend to reflect a more explicit political position – roughly, a jeremiad against the all consuming power of the mass media – than the more insular 'personal' films. While this is also the case with some of the 'identity political' films that appeared at the festival and were not discussed above – such as overtly political films dealing with drug legalization (Kenya Winchell's *The Cannabis Conspiracy*), the environment/green politics (Doug Wolens' *Luna*) and other issues – the latter were more conventional documentaries and did not reflect the engagement with either an avant-garde tradition or with postmodern aesthetics. Finally, this group of films is significant in the attempt, thematically as well as formally, to create a distance from a mainstream media world through a critique of the latter in terms of passivity (*TV Ministry*), regressive imagery (*MPG, Jaded/Outlet*) and a meaningless cult of celebrity (*Fame Whore*). This position, of course, is not without a degree of ambivalence; there is an implicit celebration of the spectacular character of the same media products, and the avant-garde itself is not spared from a satirical critique (e.g., *Peoria Babylon, Fame Whore*).

When all five thematic loci – interiority, psycho-abstraction, fringe culture, everyday life and media critique – are taken together, one finds an interesting reflection of some of the broader super-textual dynamics described above. These would include an ambivalent relationship with popular culture, a relentless emphasis on the personal and the psychological as both areas of self-examination and as the sources of creative work, a multi-faceted collection and alignment of a variety of elements drawn from various alternative cultures and a tension between political critique and aesthetic elitism. In this sense, the films are homologous to the kinds of social practices bound up with their production and consumption; I would argue that they are also uniquely reflective of the composition of an underground subject, of a 'freak', that is engaged in the same practices. The cultural ramifications of such a subject, for film theory and for the understanding of media audiences in general, is the primary concern of the concluding section.

The freak as identity

In an analysis of the New York avant-garde cinema culture of the fifties and sixties, and more specifically the career of the aforementioned underground organizer and filmmaker Jonas Mekas, Particia Mellencamp uses Deleuze and Guattari's notion of the 'rhizome' as a means of understanding the composition of this cultural scene (Mellencamp, 1990, pp. 189–213). Mellencamp notes that, 'for D and G, like the avant-garde in the 1960s, the multiple must be made and it will be a rhizome, "absolutely distinct from roots and radicals"...The tree [or 'aborescent'] structure embodies order, hierarchy, a beginning and an end. The "rhizome can be connected to any other without radical separation... between regimes of signs"' (Mellencamp, 1990, pp. 190–191). Mellencamp finds that the comparison works at a textual as well as organizational level, arguing that 'D and G's emphasis on the middle reiterates many films' strategy – without titles or closing credits (usually taken as opposition to ownership and star authorship, the denial of either film or maker as commodities), without clearly demarked beginnings and often with only tails out endings' (Mellencamp, 1990, p. 192). For Mellencamp, the 'arrangement' of the New York avant-garde, including its logistical structure of production, its texts (or at least its exemplary texts) and even its politics (Mellencamp, 1990, pp. 195–197) is a distinctively Deleuzian one, offering an alternative to the conventional and hierarchical organization of mainstream media systems.

This analysis is particularly interesting because it shares a good deal with my own understanding of the local underground cinema culture described above. The organizational contingency, the emphasis on aesthetic inwardness and upon everyday practices and even the homology between the symbolic dynamics of the text and the larger character of the formation itself are all quite similar to the analysis of the local culture described above. The scene in Champaign-Urbana, though certainly lacking in the national cultural significance of the fifties and sixties New York avant-garde is one assembled out of elements drawn from a broad spectrum of cultural and material sources. As in Mellencamp's Bakthinian sense of the underground as 'heterology' – 'scenes of discovery and confrontation' and a 'celebratory dialogue' (Mellencamp, 1990, p. 188) – the local scene is marked by the collection of diverse voices, spaces and practices chronicled above. However, in the spirit of the previous chapter, I would argue that there is always another dimension to such arrangements – the subjective dimension.

I return here to the Deleuzian-Foucauldian sense of the 'folding' of such socio-cultural planes, a process that produces the self as a meaningful entity, one, as mentioned, quite consonant with Mead's concept of the social self. Mellencamp herself mentions the critique, in this case made by Meaghan Morris and Dana Polan, that the Deleuzian model may fall short in terms of producing a theory of the subject, and though she disagrees, she chooses not to elaborate further (p. 200). However, she does argue, quite intriguingly, that both the later Deleuze and Guattari and the early avant-garde, and specifically Mekas, rely on fundamentally internal models of radical change; that, '(quoting Mekas) "that the real work must be done inside; that others can be reached only through the beauty of your own self"' (Mellencamp, 1990, p. 194). Of course, this is compatible with the relentless psychologism of so much underground cinema production, historically and today, but it also points to the importance of a more substantive theorization of an 'underground subject'. In other words, it might be profitable to consider the underground in terms of an *engagement* as well as an *arrangement*, to look at the ways that a collection of texts, related discourses and practices becomes a site of self-investment and, ultimately, of self-construction. I would argue that the question should not be thought of in either/or terms; the analysis of concerns of identity is intended to supplement rather than replace a broader but also thinner model of cultural analysis, of which Mellencamp's work is an exemplary and intriguing example.

The nature of this hermeneutic engagement is evident in some of the ethnographic description and historical analysis provided above. Certainly, the multi-faceted character of the practices and texts associated with underground film in general and in its manifestation in a local scene provides some clues as to the ways in which individuals are able to gear into such a cultural formation. One might think of this in light of Goffman's sense of cultures as predicated upon a collection of 'roles' and the 'regions' that structure these roles, an analytic expansion of the basic premises of Mead's generalized other. While the variety of spaces and practices associated with a given culture provide both a set of regions and role-offerings, the assumption and adaptation of such roles demands a mode of self-relation. The variety of practices and the permeability of roles associated with the underground scene (e.g., the shifting producer-consumer-critic dynamic) gives this formation a peculiar complexity, of course. The subject here seems almost 'hetero-logical', to refer back to Mellencamp's Bakthinian language, in the odd combination of potential roles that can be quite easily assumed and in the kinds of ambivalent cultural positions – extensively characterized above – central to the underground cinema as a media formation. Of course, this immediately suggests a postmodern, perhaps 'multiphrenic' subject (to use Gergen's term), one marked by a severe instability and a hollow core. However, I think that there is consider-able evidence that this is not the case at all, and that beneath all of the contradictions and contingencies, one discovers a real cultural proteanism, used here as a counter term to multiphrenia, at work. Curiously, the aforementioned and seemingly silly 'new man' rhetoric characteristic of early underground critics such as Tyler and Renan might have an odd resonance here in that the underground – and here the term 'avant-garde' really does make sense – may indeed reflect an emergent model of the cultural subject, and perhaps a more optimistic rejoinder to the postmodern disappearance of the same.

There are two central mechanisms for the cultivation of this sort of protean self-consciousness in the underground: the assertion of a cul-tural autonomy in the face of varying symbolic demands, and the retention and development of deep-interpretive models of audience and critical practices. In the former, the very instabilities that give the scene a strong degree of cultural ambivalence (e.g., the binaries noted above) demand a greater degree of effort to produce the kind of separa-tion and, in some cases, cultural opposition that gives the 'under-ground' some meaning in relation to a dominant culture. Take for example the struggle with *Blair Witch Project* as a popular emblem of the underground and as a subsequent program theme for the third Freaky Festival; in this case, the status of this text becomes the locus of reflection concerning the relationship of underground film to a main-stream and the possible evangelistic effect the film might have by drawing new participants into the field of personal cinema. This sort of decision making is also evident in the textual ruminations – *TV Ministry*, the films by Robert Banks, *Fame Whore* – upon media culture and media audiences, and in the many attempts to incorporate more explicitly oppositional socio-political positions, such as feminism, queer politics and environmentalism, within the culture. A more light-hearted example from the actual staging of the third Freaky Festival also comes to mind. In the course of preparing The New Art Theater for the Festival (putting up posters, cleaning, etc), it was decided that a television in the theatre lobby, set up to provide entertainment for the ticket-taker during the show, should be wrapped in paper and used as a table for the ballot box used to collect votes that would determine awards for audience favorites. The decision, a source of joking for the staff, was simultaneously practical and symbolic. The location was ideal for the ballot box, but covering the television also served the purpose of negating a trace of mainstream culture and replacing it with a particularly didactic emblem of the participatory nature of the festival and the larger culture it represents. Rather sheepishly, though, it was later unwrapped at the request of the Theatre Manager, as it served as a relief from the tedium of working the concession stand or ticket booth during slow hours, one that I experienced (albeit briefly) when working at these positions.

In regard to the second mechanism for the process of 'folding' needed for self-reflection, the perseverance of discursive modes encouraging hermeneutic engagement is particularly important. In this sense, the polemic against formalist, authorial criticism common to traditional treatments of avant-garde cinema by contemporary scholars such as Rabinowitz and Mellencamp may be partially misplaced. While they are undoubtedly correct that such formalism should never be taken as a fully adequate approach to this cinema, the prominence of such critical paradigms is quite significant. I am reminded here of Baudrillard's comment that while the Althusserian-Foucauldian-Barthesian[4] anti-subjectivist line of theoretical work seems to enact its own 'disappearance', the more phenomenologically inclined theorists (e.g., Lefebvre, Sartre) 'survive better' by retaining a trace of the human (Baudrillard, 1990, pp. 160–161). The similarly persistent – if less philosophically inflected – critical discourses surrounding the underground seem to thrive at least partly because they too offer a trace of the self: film production as self-expression, meaning making as self-investment and criticism as hermeneutic work. 'Personal cinema', the organizing principle, as mentioned, for *Micro-Film* thus serves both as an aesthetic paradigm and a mode of relating to texts and systems of production.

This personal character is extended, of course, through the enabling of a multi-faceted involvement within the culture; as demonstrated, participation in a variety of associated practices is quite common, and this quality can be linked to the kinds of aesthetic self-realization associated by Mead with the communal engagement in tasks and the *esprit de corps* that emerges in such situations. Through an extension of the normal audience roles into productive positions in a system of artistic creation, critical interpretation and material organization, there is a furthering of the ways that this type of cultural system can assume an importance in terms of specific self-investments. This is acutely so in the local context; as mentioned in the ethnography above, one of the supreme challenges of resuscitating a local scene was the need to stage this reconstructive effort at several levels: accessibility to texts (the primary focus of a festival, of course), an enriched critical discourse (the impetus, at least partly, behind *Micro-Film*), social proximity and dialogue with filmmakers (the social events associated with the festivals) and the insistence on a local character and ties to a local culture (the programs dedicated to locally-produced films and the attempt to engage a wide variety of community organizations and resources). This is inscribed quite nicely in the language of a flyer distributed to promote the inaugural issue of *Micro-Film*: 'It's not just light and shadows anymore. This time, it's flesh and blood and lots and lots of ink... This is not just movies. It's your life.' In this passage, there is a remarkable distillation of the array of elements of that produce a cultural scene: the primary texts ('light and shadows'), critical discourses ('ink') and the location of the former within a larger ensemble of practices ('life'). The movement from light and shadows to life is precisely the foundation of a cultural hermeneutics, and in this case one linked to a symbolic foundation – a generalized other – that is complex and often ambivalent.

This process has some interesting implications for film studies and particularly the model(s) of subjectivity which operate within the discipline. A return to the Althusser-Thompson 'debate' noted in Chapter 1, and especially, the issue of the '*Screen* Althusserians' and the Thompsonian critique of the same is instructive here. In this critique, the hyper-textualist, psychoanalytic biases of the *Screen* school – based upon an 'unholy trinity' of Lacan, Althusser and semiotics – produces a criticism that is elitist, formalist and completely unable to account for any activity on the part of the audience. What is remarkable about the culture of underground film is that it validates some elements of this critique while simultaneously suggesting a new relevance for certain aspects of the interpellation paradigm. Certainly, any model of a doped, passive audience subjectivity fails here, as it is activity and engagement that allow for the construction of a meaningful culture and the linkage of a variety of related practices. However, the *Screen* model is not simply one of ideological entrapment, particularly in less orthodoxly Althusserian incarnations, but also one that places considerable emphasis on the centrality of the text and the subject-creating powers of this symbolic body. While the Thompsonians may be correct that one needs to look beyond the text and towards the audience and a wider array of life experiences, the symbolic – if not subjective – depth and hermeneutic grip implied in the neo-Lacanian model may in fact be quite relevant to this larger realm. Here, the aforementioned similarities between the Lacanian and Meadian positions (see Chapter 1) are particularly intriguing; the construction of a self from discursive foundations, when conjoined with an emphasis on practical intersubjectivity and the importance of communal practices, suggests that an either/or, Althusser/Thompson binary is theoretically and also empirically dubious.

Of course, one of the premises of the neo-Meadian model, particularly in its recent and more macro-social elucidations, is that the development of such intersubjective self-consciousness has a certain socio-political value or at least potential value; this is an important aspect of its contrast with the visions of a postmodern media culture in Jameson and Baudrillard. It is difficult, though, to measure such a progressive potential, as it rarely bears a direct connection to politics per se, and a recourse to dominant/popular binaries or theories of omnipresent 'subversion' are similarly problematic, as noted in Chapter 1. That said, I want to speculate on the ways that a formation that is largely cultural – and 'political' only in a fairly diffuse sense – nonetheless embodies certain political possibilities, possibilities that can be linked to the specifically hermeneutic, identity-creating qualities of this formation. The first involves the underground as the site of the mediation and potential unification of a diverse variety of political positions, many that could be classified as 'identity politics', with all the drawbacks and limitations that term can imply. As mentioned, feminism, gay and lesbian advocacy, anti-censorship movements, pacifism and even green ecological factions have all played an important role in the historical emergence of an underground, and all continue to hold a prominent place in the scene today, in a local as well as international context. However, 'underground', 'avant-garde' and 'freaky' cinemas are never reducible to a mere collection of such positions, and in fact are unified along a material axis of anti-commercialism and an aesthetic axis of non-traditionalism (from abstraction to postmodernism). This distinct symbolic space is thus open to more traditional politics without the barriers of organicism and/or absolutism which are so often critiqued in these positions. Of course, the aesthetic component here can also work to constrain such politics by limiting their articulation somewhat and certainly produces the sort of tension most pointedly evident in the Brakhage-Mekas dispute. Nonetheless, the continuing political openness is reason for some optimism in the potential political outreach of this culture; it certainly provides the opportunity for a good deal of cross-exposure among various political strands in the larger underground.

Secondly, in the similarly fluid distribution and alignment of roles in the process of producing and exhibiting films, there is the possibility for a critical perspective on the production and circulation of cultural commodities; this would be quite similar to the 'D.I.Y.' (do it yourself) ethos associated with punk and post-punk musical culture. This is compounded in both cases with the development of the aforementioned critical discourses (e.g., fanzines, manifestos, etc.). This echoes, of course, one of the hoariest chestnuts of Marxist utopianism, the communist (wo)man who is a fisherman in the morning and a poet in the afternoon, suggesting a utopian end to the alienation of producer-consumer dynamics. As mentioned, it also reflects the Meadian emphasis on the aesthetic character of practice, and especially practice producing a kind of consummation, as well as the more mystical countercultural ideal of a 'new man'. When combined with the aforementioned use of archaic and folkloric production techniques, there is an additional distanciation from the conventional social organization of mass media experiences. Again, there are absolutely no guarantees of concrete political effects – except perhaps in some of the micropolitical struggles with organizational barriers, censorship and other logistical constraints to production and exhibition. However, the fluidity of roles and the development of circuits of production and distribution does offer points of contact, however fleeting, with a utopian subjectivity offering more than a passive position within a media culture.

There is also the more explicitly political thematic content within many underground films, particularly within the local culture, and this content is certainly enriched by its articulation within the wider political and material frame described above. As an example, the somewhat routine if brilliantly executed critique of image-fetishism in Hejnar's aforementioned *TV Ministry* gains a good deal of ideological (and ironic) force through its dialectical placement within a culture bearing certain contrasts with this highly stereotypical model of television reception. This is similarly the case with McElroy's *Job*, which meditates upon the mundane, identity-stripping regimen of office work; the text itself, with its expressionist pastiche, is quite interesting, but its thematic force is reliant upon its engagement with an audience both frequently bound by the 'day job' routine and also immersed within a less alienated, pointedly self-centered culture. Here, the dystopian visions of both films, a Baudrillardian nightmare of a viral media in the former and a more conventional occupational alienation in the latter, provoke a dialectical contrast with the underground, at least in its idealized form.

In this instance, the issue of political effectivity, or at least the potential for it, would appear to revolve around the possibility for a kind of role-distance, for the development of a reflexivity – in this case towards media consumption and work, respectively – produced by a rhetorical-hermeneutic disjunction between symbolic fields. The framing of such political texts within a larger set of cultural practices is absolutely critical here as it is the source of this crucial dialogical tension. Isolating the text would fail to account for this potential, of course, but so would ignoring the critical ways that texts are positioned – as 'personal', as 'artistic' and so on – within the underground. In this sense, the significance of the text is most important in terms of the investment of interpretive effort and in its particular claims of both personal expression and intersubjective rhetorical force.

The larger point here is that the political potential of any aspect of the underground film community is closely related to the ability for individuals to cultivate the kinds of critical reflexivities that may emerge from the polyvalent collection of roles and significant texts offered by the formation. Understanding this larger range of practices is particularly critical for the case at hand, as the kinds of ambiguities and contradictions that surround the culture offer a complex and potentially confusing picture. It is at the level of practices and subjective investments that such surface tension becomes actively engaged and given a kind of coherence. Echoing Mellencamp, there may indeed be a kind of 'heterotopic' symbolic field here, as well as similarly complex subjects that operate within it. However, there is also the inevitable dialogue that emerges from this encounter, and it is in this dialogue that certain possibilities for political practices and forms of political awareness may emerge. Recalling Grossberg, a concrete political effectivity may indeed be reliant upon a larger alignment of material and social forces, but it seems foolish indeed to overlook the generative function of individually-rooted, intersubjective modes of ideological reflexivity and interrogation.

In the next chapter, I examine another audience formation, the world of Kiss fans, one bound up with its own set of meaningful practices and texts, and one implying a very different dynamic of symbolically mediated and culturally configured self-relation. The film culture described above, both local and 'underground', reflects a complex (particularly given its scale) and often loose arrangement, coherent primarily through a unified emphasis on personal expression and on the vitality of cinematic work. In this sense, it demonstrates at least some of the central tenets of the cultural postmodernist position, but it also provides evidence of a more optimistic view of the consequences of such cultural fragmentation and reconfiguration. This will be even more striking in light of the two case studies which follow, studies that if nothing else point to the singularity – logically enough – of the 'freak'.

3

'I Believe in Me': Self-Affirmation in the 'Kiss Army'

On 18 October 1998, The Canopy Club in Urbana, Illinois, site of the Second Annual Freaky Film Festival, hosted a very different sort of cultural event. A local FM radio station, WCKR, sponsored a release party for *Psychocircus*, the first album of new material by the recently reunited rock band Kiss. The party featured a screening of the band's unintentionally campy 1978 television film *Kiss Meets the Phantom of the Park*, performances by three local hard rock bands and the distribution of a variety of door prizes, including a grand prize trip to Los Angeles to attend the first concert of the forthcoming Kiss world tour. The event was generally well attended, attracting about 150 Kiss fans.

This crowd was quite different from the audience that would occupy the same space for the film festival just a few weeks later. It was clearly a local rather than student-dominated or mixed group (like the film festival), a very important distinction in a region – the twin cities of Champaign and Urbana – dominated by a major university. The overwhelmingly male crowd was also somewhat narrower in age range, and all but a handful of attendees appeared to be in their mid-twenties to mid-thirties, the prime demographic boundaries of the 'Kiss generation'. Most seemed to be working or lower-middle class, and a good number sported many of the fashion and grooming marks of the 'heavy metal' subculture, one that had returned to 'sub' status following a period of mainstream popularity in the eighties. The crowd was generally quite reverent during the screening of the film – the only heckling came from a Canopy employee – but was a bit livelier in response to the profanity-laden crowd-baiting of the WCKR deejay during prize presentations, mocking winners who were slow to claim their prizes and loudly critiquing the slow pace of the awards ceremony. There was a split sensibility evident at the event, with a respect for the band and its work; the crowd was particularly hushed when a complete collection of Kiss CDs was given away. At the same time, there was a rowdiness and irreverence displayed in regard to the event itself; when Kiss was not the specific focus of the event, as when the bands played or the radio station was promoted, the audience behaved much like a typical group of young adults in a crowded bar on a Saturday night.

This disjunction was particularly interesting, as I had conducted earlier research into the Kiss phenomenon and was quite struck by the intensity and seriousness of Kiss fans, who seemed able to maintain a real faith (and I choose the term deliberately) in a band that was so frequently derided both within a narrower rock music world as well as within the larger mainstream culture. The relationship between Kiss and its fans was quite striking and certainly resonated with my larger interests in the hermeneutic dimensions of mass media experiences. The claims on identity engendered by participation in the world of Kiss fandom were fascinating in this light and presented a real analytical challenge. Similarly, and mirrored in the mixed reaction of the Canopy crowd, the integration of such claims within a larger set of social-subjective demands, the management of an affective 'portfolio' described in Chapter 1, was a complex and sometimes contradictory process. Perhaps unsurprisingly, the Kiss fan formation exhibited dynamics that were very different from those associated with the underground film community. However, such distinctions were not always what one might expect, particularly when the analysis was extended into the areas of hermeneutic engagement and practices of self-construction that are the central focus of this book.

The subjective power of popular music

There is an initial temptation to explain such differences among fan cultures in terms of media, with a film audience simply not comparable to a music audience and perhaps especially a rock audience, and certainly these differences should not be ignored. Indeed, there is significant and worthwhile theoretical support for a view that accords a special status for the peculiarly subjective power of music, and especially popular music. Simon Frith summarizes his own position on the role of pop music in everyday life in the following:

> We all hear music we like as something special, as something that defies the mundane, takes us 'out of ourselves', puts us somewhere

else. 'Our music' is, from this perspective, special not just with reference to other music but, more important, to the rest of life. It is this sense of specialness (the way that music seems to make possible a new kind of self-recognition, to free us from everyday routines, from the social expectations with which we are encumbered) that is the key to our musical value judgments. 'Transcendence' is as much a part of popular as of the serious music aesthetic, but pop transcendence articulates not music's independence of social forces but a kind of alternative experience. (Frith, 1996, p. 275)

Here, one finds echoes of many of the most important themes explored by a critical/hermeneutic approach: self-recognition, a freedom from binding social conventions and a defamiliarizing experience of the everyday. That this is specifically ascribed to the popular music experience, though, is significant, as it can be connected with a long tradition, extending as far back as Plato, that links the experience of music with a particular intensity of affect. As Deena Weinstein points out, this tradition includes John Dewey, who in turn shares a view of the social importance of aesthetic experience with Mead (Weinstein, 1991, pp. 214–216). The combination of an intense emotional potency with a self-reflective 'transcendence' common to a variety of aesthetic experiences thus works to create a doubly powerful connection between the social subject and the musical discourses that she engages.

As Grossberg is so keen to remind us, such engagements are always already conditioned by a set of socio-material forces that structure any cultural experience. Still, he is willing to grant a unique status for the case of rock music, though his understanding is less dependent upon the formal specificity of the sonic experience and more concerned with broader cultural factors contributing to rock's specialness. Grossberg argues,

> Rock and roll removes signs, objects, sounds, styles, and so forth from their apparently meaningful existence within the dominant culture and relocates them within an affective alliance of differentiation and resistance. The resultant shock – of both the recognition and an undermining of meaning – produces a temporarily impassable boundary within the dominant culture, an encapsulation of the affective possibilities of rock and roll culture. Rock and roll is a particular form of bricolage, a uniquely capitalist and postmodern practice. (Grossberg, 1997, p. 36)

Here, some of Frith's points are echoed; the contextual resituation of elements of everyday experience and the sealing off of an autonomous

– or at least reconfigured – zone of aesthetic experience are similar, but Grossberg takes a less individualized approach to pop transcendence and also specifies a lack of real politics lurking behind such moments of shock. Grossberg continues, 'Because its resistance remains, however, within the political and economic space of capitalism, its revolution is only a "simulacrum"' (Grossberg, 1997, p. 37). One finds a microcosmic replay here of the kind of binaries described in Chapter 1, in this case upon the specific terrain of popular music. Although Frith is clearly aware of the limits of any rock and roll politics, his emphasis on the self-affirming aspects of popular music practices balances Grossberg's more cautious elucidation of the limits of the same.

Grossberg's more expansive perspective is valuable, however, in that it moves away from the formalist bent of many earlier theorists of music's affective power. While such formal qualities may be an important foundation for the unique status of rock and roll, they are clearly only a part of this 'encapsulated' culture. This is a particularly important issue for the analysis that follows, as the symbolic world of Kiss fans is among the most complex in popular music fandom and includes a large number of key extra-musical elements: the visual style of the band, folklore and legend surrounding them, material culture in the form of souvenirs and a variety of other significant elements. Although Kiss fans tend to posit the music as the ultimate and absolutely indissoluble threshold of appreciation and fandom – a position confirmed by the discourse of the fans themselves – the overall frame of engagement and interpretation is larger indeed.

The question of a larger musical culture is an important part of the analyses of the heavy metal subculture – in which Kiss is marginally included – offered by Weinstein and Robert Walser. While the two scholars have substantive disagreements, methodologically and analytically (Walser, 1993, pp. 23–24), both stress the ways that heavy metal offers a world that is very much sealed off, however tenuously, from the mainstream of both music and a general popular culture. Walser points to the means through which the music works as a form of world- and self-creation, how metal 'develop[s] new kinds of music and new models of identity, new articulations of community, alienation, affirmation, protest, rage, and transcendence by '"Running with the Devil" [a reference to a song by the heavy metal band Van Halen]' (Walser, 1993, p. 171). Weinstein, alternatively, describes the fans as self-identified 'proud pariahs' who consciously enjoy the negative social judgments that they perceive as heaped upon them (Weinstein, 1991, pp. 142–143). Unlike Walser, who focuses his analysis more narrowly on the musical attributes of the genre, Weinstein analyzes a variety of sociological and discursive elements (rituals, media, fashion, etc.) associated with this sub-culture in reaching the above conclusion. In his autobiography *Fargo Rock City* (the title is an homage to the Kiss song 'Detroit Rock City'), cultural critic Chuck Klosterman points to the deep personal impact heavy metal culture had on his rural upbringing and particularly the influence of Motley Crüe, a band deeply indebted to Kiss in both sound and visual image. For Klosterman, metal provided access to a rich and utterly tantalizing fantasy world, one in stark contrast to his austere surroundings in North Dakota farm country. In this respect, Klosterman provides a nicely personal and less systematically analytical reflection very much in line with the claims of both Walser and Weinstein.

In his social history of the electric guitar, Steve Waksman adds to the sense of heavy metal culture as a quasi-utopian formation through a discussion of the pioneering metal band The MC5. Waksman points to the particular power associated with extremely loud music and the ability for noise to create a kind of liberating atmosphere (Waksman, 1999, pp. 232–234). Waksman's analysis is intriguing in that it connects the technological practices associated with heavy metal with the symbolic ideals it seems to reflect. Not only does Kiss reflect a volume obsession common to heavy metal, boasting in 1982 that they were the loudest band in the world (Lendt, 1997, p. 264), they have extended such technological practices to the production of a visual as well as sonic spectacle. While Kiss' precise status within the heavy metal culture is debatable – although Walser, Weinstein and Klosterman include them – they certainly share many of the same audience characteristics, and there are some particularly interesting variations on the themes these authors describe within the culture of Kiss fans that will emerge in the following analysis. Most notably, the world of Kiss fandom is marked by a particularly intense set of 'self-esteem' discourses, an almost ecclesiastical and heavily mythologized relationship to the band and a strong rooting in a utopian fantasy of superhuman empowerment.

This chapter begins with some background information on the band, a general elucidation of some of the cultural connotations of Kiss fandom and a brief discussion of the autobiographical significance of this site. This is followed by an analysis of a number of significant and salient aspects of this audience formation, particularly as they relate to a theory of the social self and identity formation within a media-saturated culture. The conclusion attempts to fuse the kinds of social and subjective concerns evident in the Grossberg and Frith passages cited above, concerns that mirror the broader theoretical task at hand.

Why Kiss? the cultural significance of 'The hottest band in the world'

> When I woke up, mom and dad were rolling on the couch
> rolling numbers, rock and rolling, got my Kiss records out
> – 'Surrender' (R. Nielsen)

Kiss is a band that emerged from the 'glam rock' culture of the early seventies with a visual image and sound heavily indebted to both Alice Cooper and the New York Dolls, key pioneers in this scene. Backed by a relentless publicity machine headed by manager Bill Aucoin and Casablanca Records founder Neal Bogart, the group enjoyed a relatively fast rise to massive popularity (Dobrotovorskaia, 1993, pp. 43–44). By 1978, the band finished first in a Gallup poll of the most popular music groups in the U.S. (Swenson, 1978, p. 165), and was featured in the aforementioned television film, *Kiss Meets the Phantom of the Park* in October of the same year. Kiss released six Billboard Top Twenty albums – including the breakthrough *Alive* album that remained on the charts for 110 weeks – and five Top Twenty singles in the seventies. Kiss made frequent appearances in 'teen' rock magazines (as opposed to the more 'adult' *Rolling Stone*), such as *Creem, Rock Scene, Circus* and *Hit Parader*, and even finished fourth in a recent list of 'most appearances on the cover of *16* Magazine' (Marsh and Benard, 1994, p. 134). Kiss' success was particularly intriguing in that they were able to unite a variety of normally separate audience groups: 'teenyboppers' (the *16* demographic), a slightly older hard rock/heavy metal audience and a wider mainstream pop audience. This is due at least partly to the band's ability to create generic variety in the music, expanding their potential market; three of their largest chart hits were 'Beth' (a ballad), 'Hard Luck Woman' (gentle folk rock) and 'I Was Made For Lovin' You' (a disco song), while the bulk of the music was fairly conventional heavy rock.

Equal to this musical cunning, though, was the band's continuing ability to produce a memorable visual spectacle. Until 1983, when their popularity had greatly waned, the members refused to reveal the faces behind their Kabuki stage make-up, creating an aura of mystery that was extremely enticing to younger listeners. The band also created a spectacular concert experience, one that included fire breathing, blood spitting, guitar smashing and an enormous level of pyrotechnic flair, further attracting the interest of adolescent fans. Finally, Kiss offered an unparalleled variety of merchandise for the fan/consumer: lunchboxes, dolls, Halloween masks, board games, posters, trading cards and much, much more.

Partly because of this rather crass merchandising, and particularly because it was combined with instrumentally crude and sometimes lyrically juvenile and misogynistic songs, Kiss was the object of violent derision within some of the more elite factions of the rock audience in the seventies. There was a general loathing of the band by rock critics, who often denounced Kiss' music as 'unlistenable' (Milward, 1976, p. 70; Coleman, 1992, p. 403); a British critic described a greatest hits collection as 'the worst bunch of rubbish they've ever heaped on the rubbish-strewn heads of their fans' (Clark, 1982, p. 74). Kiss was also disliked by the more technically-inclined, 'progressive rock' segments of the popular music audience, who regarded the music as amateurish and the stage antics as embarrassing. When *Guitar Player* magazine, a leading periodical for rock guitarists, featured Kiss lead guitarist Ace Frehley on its January 1979 cover, the appearance generated enough feedback – overwhelmingly negative – to warrant an entire feature in the March issue ('Readers Respond', pp. 146–147). The reader's complaints echo the points noted above, and center upon a critique of the band's lack of musical skills and the gimmicky visual extravagance of their performance style. Nor was the band spared by the mainstream media, as evident in a January 1978 ABC television special, *The Land of Hype and Glory*, that presented the band as a canny business enterprise with little connection to serious musical expression. This reaction is not unusual for groups popular with younger fans, of course, but the level of attention directed at Kiss was particularly intense.

Both the positive and negative attention to the band did not last beyond the early eighties, particularly in the United States and Europe. By 1982, two of the four original members had left the band, Kiss' U.S. record sales had dropped to about one-third their previous level, and concert attendance fell significantly (see Lendt, 1997, especially Chapters 8 and 9). The band continued through the eighties and early nineties as a middle-level heavy metal band, enjoying modest popularity and continuing to tour and record regularly. Until the 1996 reunion of the original band members, though, Kiss was certainly a shadow of its former, culturally ubiquitous self.

This ubiquity is clear from a brief look at a number on interesting cultural texts both from the initial seventies period of popularity and from the lower profile years that followed. The quote introducing this section comes from 'Surrender', a 1978 hit by Cheap Trick, another popular hard rock band from the seventies. The song, a brilliantly acute take on seventies midwestern American adolescence, ends with the narrator finding himself in the above scenario, a comic reflection on the horror of parents trying to be teenagers; here, 'Kiss' serves as the emblem for a larger culture of juvenile vulgarity. Similarly, in Richard Linklater's wonderful 1993 film *Dazed and Confused*, a tale of seventies suburban adolescence in Texas, several high school students deface statues of American Revolutionary War heroes by covering them with Kiss make-up; the defiant substitution of icons illustrates quite well the potency of Kiss' symbolic association with an entire generation of rock fans. The release of *Detroit Rock City* in 2000, a mainstream film dealing with the trials and tribulations of attending a Kiss concert in the seventies further mythologizes this relationship, presenting it as a kind of existential youth quest.

There are less dramatic examples as well. Rock critic Chuck Eddy remembers 'several sleazy Harlots in my high school's "Designated Cigarette Area"' painting their faces in imitation of Kiss' stage makeup (Eddy, 1989, p. 122). Courtney Love, leader of the popular band Hole and a film star, was arrested for stealing a Kiss t-shirt from a Woolworth's store at age 12, a biographical detail frequently repeated in publicity surrounding Love ('The 1994 Spy 100,' 1994, p. 55). Recently, while battling insomnia, I tuned into a late night talk radio program dealing with listeners' favorite concerts; the topic soon turned into a forum for a discussion, primarily by age 25 to 40 males, of their Kiss concert experiences. All of this was of special interest to me, as I have focused my research primarily on 'first generation' (i.e., seventies) Kiss fans that have retained an interest in the band. In their case, of course, the engagement goes well beyond this sort of mild nostalgia, but the broader dissemination of this discourse is evidence of a commonality of experience that is striking indeed.

My own life is not without its 'Kisstory', to use the term employed by fans to refer to such autobiographies. Born in 1967, white, male, suburban and middle-class, I fit ideally into the 'Kiss Generation'. My first Kiss record, a 45 of 'Beth' b/w 'Detroit Rock City', was a Christmas gift received when I was nine. I soon became a fan of the group, though never particularly intense in my passion, and owned a few other albums. I was also involved in a neighborhood plan to put on a lip-synched imitation Kiss show in a garage, though this never came to fruition. This period was brief, though, and I soon regarded my earlier enthusiasm for the band as an embarrassment, particularly from my incipient 'punk rock' perspective. More interesting than this very common experience is an incident from my elementary school years. As a demonstration of the functioning of electoral democracy, members of the fourth and fifth grades voted to choose music that would be played through the school's (very low fidelity) public address system before class each morning for a week. The female vote was split between Shaun Cassidy and the Bay City Rollers, so with a unified male vote, Kiss won, and students were treated to scratchy renditions of 'I Stole Your Love' and 'Christine 16' at 9:00 A.M. It would be tempting to deploy this anecdote to demonstrate, in the spirit of Toby Miller, a harnessing of the unique power of popular music for the purposes of creating citizen subjects (and perhaps it is), but I will use it only as an especially peculiar and memorable example of the ways the music of Kiss becomes bound up with a set of youthful experiences, as well as additional, anecdotal evidence of their overwhelming popularity in the late seventies.

As mentioned, the fans that comprise the strongest element in the 'Kiss Army' – the official name of the Kiss fan organization and the informal self-identification of many devout Kiss fans – and those most deeply involved in the various rituals associated with fandom tend to share much of my general demographic background. There is a significant number of women in this group, but they are vastly out-numbered by male fans. There is considerable international representa-tion within the Kiss community, a quality greatly enabled by the use of the Internet as a major tool for the maintenance of a fan community, although US fans are still dominant. The vast majority are white, and most have working- or middle-class backgrounds. There is an important split between my perspective, though, and those of the fans I am ana-lyzing. I gave up my Kiss fandom early on and returned to interest in the band as an academic scholar of popular culture rather than as a fan (though I did find myself enjoying the music and even the spectacle more than I had expected) – an undeniably significant distinction. For the fans under examination, there was no similar 'loss of faith', or in the rare case of one, a return of the 'prodigal fan', so to speak.

Long-term appreciation of a band is not unusual, but there are sever-al facets of Kiss fandom that make this feature distinctive. The first is the tendency toward an extremely young onset of fandom. Many Kiss fans and particularly those seriously involved with fan culture became interested in the band at a very early age. Most of the fans I interviewed, as well as those who offering their 'Kisstories' in various publications, gave ages between five and eleven for the onset of their love for the group, and even younger ages occasionally appear. Thus, the maintenance of Kiss fandom involves retaining what is often a pre-adolescent passion, a particularly unusual characteristic for music fans, a wider culture that tends to be hold music beloved by children in extremely low regard (witness the treatment of most teen idols only a few years after their peak success). In addition to the contempt hurled at the band by elements of both the rock world and a wider mainstream culture, Kiss fans stand in dedication to a group that has a distinctly artificial image, and one in direct contrast to the authenticity commonly associated with rock's emotional potency. As a number of scholars have pointed out, audience evaluations of the aesthetic value of rock tend to be based on the apparent expression of real experiences and passions, of speaking 'from the heart' (Belz, 1973, p. 6; Frith, 1988, p. 136; Grossberg, 1992, p. 206). Kiss departs strongly from this standard iconography, and also lacks the 'genius behind the mask' connotations of figures such as David Bowie and Madonna who employ theatrics but retain an impression of artistic credibility. Kiss members themselves have actively subverted such an image; while they are careful in interviews to insist on the musical quality of their work, they have also compared it to McDonald's hamburgers. More recently, bassist-leader Gene Simmons has suggested that Kiss was harmless and that the group was comparable to the circus. Thus, Kiss lacks many of the trappings of artistry common to other performers with strong and/or cultic followings. As shall be evident, this lack of external (and even self-proclaimed) credibility does little to diminish the interpretive intensity of the fans or their interest in potentially profound messages within the music itself. Before moving to the question of interpretation, though, a very significant change in the field of Kiss fandom needs to be analyzed, as the world of these fans was drastically altered by the 1996 reunion of the original band members and their return to a much greater degree of mainstream attention.

'The Second Coming' is the title given to a video documentary chronicling Kiss' 1996 reunion and the vastly successful world tour that followed. The religious pun is intentional, of course, and is extended in Simmons' description, within the film itself, of the Kiss reunion as 'Phoenix rising from the ashes... very Christian... a rebirth'. Indeed, the success of the band's return was quite amazing, if only as a marketing phenomenon. As mentioned, they had settled into a fairly low profile existence as a moderately popular heavy metal band, a steep drop in symbolic and commercial stature from their earlier career. In 1995, the band appeared on an *MTV Unplugged* special, a regular program on the channel featuring performers playing selections from their career with only acoustic instrumental accompaniment. The last four songs featured guest appearances by Peter Criss and Ace Frehley, the original drummer and lead guitarist, who had been absent from the band for fifteen and thirteen years, respectively. The program attracted considerable attention that grew with the appearance of the band – in original makeup and stage costumes – as presenters at the 1996 Grammy Awards. In April of the same year, the band held a press conference on the aircraft carrier USS Intrepid in New York to announce a reunion tour. The tour continued for over a year, attracting crowds that exceeded those of the late seventies tours, generating more than forty million dollars in ticket sales and making Kiss the top-grossing concert attraction that year (Lendt, 1997, p. 341). This was followed by the release of a new album by the reunited band, the aforementioned *Psychocircus*, in October 1998, and another world tour.[1]

I was fortunate to have conducted a good deal of research on Kiss fans before the reunion was announced; indeed, I completed the first written version of this research in the weeks immediately prior to this event. Largely by luck, I was thus able to gain a 'before and after' view of Kiss fandom, particularly in terms of the discursive character of this community. Prior to the reunion, the 'Kiss World', while considerably smaller, was still quite significant in relation to other, similar fan groups. There were fan clubs, regular 'Kiss Conventions' throughout the US and a number of other countries, at least a dozen paper fanzines and at least fifty Internet sites dedicated to the band as well as a very active market for Kiss collectibles, such as vintage Kiss comic books and action figures. Additionally, there were a number of 'tribute bands' performing a simulation of the late seventies Kiss show; I saw one such band, 'Strutter', perform to a sell out crowd of over seven hundred in Champaign, Illinois in 1995, several months before reunion plans were announced. There was little mainstream attention in rock music journalism or general media channels to the band, but it would be inaccurate to describe the fan formation as low profile.

Nonetheless, many of the fans I was involved with in the initial research perceived a real uniqueness, a kind of personal distinction, in being a Kiss fan, one suggestive both of Weinstein's sense of heavy metal fans as 'proud pariahs' and of a wider cultural tradition of macho individualism. As informants told me at the time, being a Kiss fan meant:

> Not taking bullshit from anyone... Being able to love myself no matter if anyone else does or not and being able to just let my hair down and 'rock and roll all nite'.

Being part of an elite force where everyone is welcome but only few survive. True Kiss fans are like no other fan to a person or a group. What other groups have fans so dedicated that they volunteer their efforts in establishing KISS conventions for no other benefit other than to their fellow comrades to show their dying [sic] love for the band.

... that you can overcome the odds and make it. Also, standing up for what you believe in... even if it's not the popular thing to do.

Being a Kiss fan – I really do not care if anyone else likes their music or not. It is akin to having a real neat secret that no one else knows.

It means believing in something, even when everyone thinks you're nuts. It means almost as much as my family means to me. Since, I've loved them ever since I've had memories, they're like members of my family.

It means being special because you see and feel something that a lot of people will never feel or understand... it means being set apart from a good majority of people... because you know or understand something that maybe a lot of people... even people who think that they are fans will not understand. Knowing that I am one of these ppl. [people] that have this gift... its kinda cool...

Kiss fans stick together as a community even when the rest of the world, peers included, shun them and their heroes. Its kinda like being a Harley owner/rider (someday I will be both!). Although you are millions strong, you always feel like the outsider. People always slam you for loving Kiss, but you say 'Fuck 'em! There [sic] the ones missing out'. And you've got plenty of support from others. It is, and I've never though of it this way before, a unique position.

The repeated appearance of this theme among fans is particularly interesting as it is evidence of the residual power of the constant invective cast at the band – and by implication its fans – in the initial period of popularity, as well as a clear awareness of the considerable drop in popularity in the intervening years. Recalling Frith's and Grossberg's respective discussions of the 'specialness' and 'differentiation' associated with music audience cultures, one finds these themes undeniably present in the discourse of the fans cited above and of Kiss fans in general. Of course, this was enabled both by the aforementioned drop in popularity and earlier media disdain, qualities that serve to increase the sense of 'encapsulation', to use Grossberg's term, around this culture. In this vein, 'an elite force', 'a real neat secret', a 'gift' and so forth evoke a self-identification that might seem puzzling as it involves dedication to a once popular and at the time still moderately successful rock band, as well as a commercial venture, as the last informant implicitly notes in his comparison with Harley-Davidson motorcycle owners. I will later argue that such contradictions may actually increase the symbolic potency of the discourse surrounding Kiss, one actively encouraging a self-directed fantasy of autonomy and distinction. However, it is first essential to examine the drastic shifts in the symbolic world of such fans engendered by the 1996 reunion.

The return of Kiss to a general cultural prominence certainly exceeded the expectations of many of the fans – there had been rumors of a reunion for some time – even those optimistic about the success of the reunion. The most notable aspect of this return was a tremendous increase in the band's mass media profile. There was the aforementioned Grammy appearance, a performance at the 1999 Super Bowl pre-game show, guest shots (in dramatic roles and as themselves) on Fox's science-fiction television series *Millennium* and on Fox's 1998 Halloween special, appearances on the covers of *Fortune, Playboy, Spin* (four different 'collector's covers' featuring each member of the band) and *Entertainment Weekly*, as well as in numerous heavy metal and general interest music magazines. Kiss also appeared in the popular 'got milk' advertising campaign, as well as making a number of network television appearances, including utterly mainstream fare such as NBC's *Today* show. Strangest of all may have been the 'Kiss Nites' staged by a minor league baseball team from California, the Rancho Cucamonga Quakes, that included (in addition to a baseball game, of course) tribute bands, players in special 'Kiss Uniforms' and even a Kiss wedding, with bride and groom in Kiss makeup. Even the release party at the Canopy Club would have been highly unlikely without a reunion, a return to the stage makeup, and an increased public profile; pre-reunion Kiss simply did not merit such treatment, even from the hard rock media, of which WCKR is certainly a part.

These changes in the level and nature of Kiss' prominence in the media might be thought of as a microcosmic variation on the 'detraditionalization' of a lifeworld posed by Habermas in his aforementioned discussion of Mead. I am not suggesting, of course, that the kind of deep social ramifications – the collapse of forms of belief, drastic alterations in everyday practice and other impacts – that are a part of this process come into play here, but the internal dynamics are quite similar. The stability of a close-knit world of self-identified Kiss fans sharing this 'secret' is undeniably shaken by the expansion and diffusion of discourses concerning the band and its fans throughout a media-saturated culture. This would thus also mirror the kinds of symbolic fragmentation, dispersion of discourse and relative emptying of signification suggested by postmodern theory. The stability of 'Kiss' as a social signifier is certainly undermined by this diffusion, particularly as the band is symbolically repositioned within a set of cultural contexts often far removed from the narrower fields, primarily tied to music and especially heavy metal/hard rock, in which it had previously circulated. One of the most important aspects of this self-identification – the sense of being an outsider, of turning against the crowd and taking a stand for one's personal cultural icon – becomes a somewhat different task when the same icon is selling out stadiums and advertising milk. This is compounded by a contradiction stemming from a satisfaction in seeing the band return to prominence – the fans were overwhelmingly excited by the speed and intensity of the comeback – while at the same time wanting to retain an exclusive communal fantasy at the heart of the 'Kiss Army'.

This situation thus demands greater work by the individual, particularly the more committed fans. The sense of encapsulation is considerably more difficult to maintain when the materials from which such a sense of autonomy and self-containment can be derived become so widely scattered and symbolically diffused. The work of bricolage is thus more challenging, with a need to separate 'real fans', the real members of the Kiss Army, from the merely nostalgic thrill seekers or those interested in Kiss as a form of camp, as a weakly ironic foray into bad taste. Certainly, Kiss has always attracted a following among self-conscious aficionados of 'cheese'; one fan, a graduate student, told me that being a Kiss fan simply meant that 'youthful bad taste is hard to overcome', and attendance at tribute band performances and the release party revealed a small but noticeable participation by individuals who clearly regarded the band (as opposed to the event, as noted above) as essentially a joke. The presence of such attitudes has always served to reinforce the need to build an authentic Kiss community, but is certainly exacerbated by the band's heightened public profile. One way that such a process occurs is through an increasingly intense dedication to more obscure fan practices: archival work on the band's history, exegetical explorations of associated texts, the related production of fan texts (e.g., fiction, poetry, artwork) and an attachment to lesser-known aspects of the band's career, as in the discourse surrounding *(Music From) The Elder* discussed below. When the criteria for being a 'true fan' can no longer be satisfied with concert attendance, or even a more-than-passing familiarity with the band – as it had before the reunion – alternative practices and even alternative modes of relating to all of the materials that are conglomerated as 'Kiss' must be developed.

There is an interestingly comparable cultural phenomenon, involving the 1999 release of the fourth installment of the *Star Wars* film series, *The Phantom Menace*, an event briefly discussed in the introductory section. Clearly, the *Star Wars* saga has enjoyed a cultural ubiquity that exceeded Kiss, even at the band's popular peak, and this high profile was retained to a greater degree in the 16 years between the third and fourth installments of the series, particularly when compared to Kiss' fall in popularity. However, the return of *Star Wars* shares a good deal with the roughly concurrent revival of Kiss. The demographic and chronological similarities are quite striking: the first *Star Wars* film was released in 1977, the time of Kiss' peak popularity; *Star Wars* fandom was especially intense among eight to fifteen-year-old males, but the film also demonstrated a high degree of general mainstream appeal; a strong element in the appeal of the films was its technical spectacle, also the case with the Kiss stage show; finally, the large number of toys and other merchandise associated with *Star Wars* mirrors the similar proliferation of Kiss souvenirs.

Beyond these significant similarities, though, is a deeper connection, one that involves the rhetorical-hermeneutic power of both cultures, a power explicable at least partly by the ways that both engage heavily mythologized, quasi-religious symbolic structures, producing a form of pop-cultural discipleship. With *Star Wars*, this may be more obvious, with an explicit narrative struggle between good and evil, the importance of 'The Force' as a mystical source of power and other elements. Kiss, on the other hand, is a rock and roll band, albeit a very theatrical one, making such immediate connotations much subtler. The styles of narratives, and even the kind of generalized mythological significance attached to the band require a more extensive degree of personal and social bricolage, of dedicated and self-involving interpretation. The band certainly worked to reinforce many aspects of this fan piety in artistic productions as well as in interviews and other extra-textual discourse, but, as noted in an earlier section, there was a simultaneous stepping away from excessive claims of deeper meaning, as in the aforementioned comparison with the circus. The latter seems to have little effect on the fans, though, as they are often quite concerned with a set of deeper meanings associated with the band and its work. The following sections examine some of these meanings, particularly as they are bound up with issues of self-relation and symbolic self-construction.

'God(s) of thunder and rock and roll': Kiss and the search for self

In a self-interview on the *KissWorld* website, an increasingly popular feature in which fans download questions and submit answers to the site, 'Ron' provides the following answer to a question about how he became interested in the band:

> It was everything about the band. Everything they stood for. Freedom, being yourself and doing your own thing. I liked it all. Even though I was only 11, my parents had instilled a strong sence [sic] of individuality in my upbringing. Plus they really had it going on with their look. I really thought they didn't wear any makeup for a while.

Here, Ron echoes some of the themes that were referenced in the previous section concerning the distinction and uniqueness that appear to stem from Kiss fandom. Ron takes this further, as did many of the fans I interviewed, viewing Kiss fandom as symbolic of personal freedom and autonomy, of 'doing your own thing'. Of course, this sort of self-esteem discourse and individualist ethos is quite common throughout the history of rock music. For example, it is a centerpiece of counter-culture ideology, and certainly persists in the post-punk tradition; the work of musician-poet Henry Rollins, for instance, offers a particularly explicit discourse of self-love and self-reliance. Thus, it is certainly not unusual that Kiss would reflect this attitude. However, in the case of Kiss and its fans, the symbolic dynamics are distinctive in that the discourse is not merely connected to a performer and a set of aesthetic texts. It includes an expanded symbolic world in which fantasy personas, elaborate related narratives, a body of folklore and even mass-produced material objects (beyond the texts) play a significant role in producing the ground – the 'other' – from which a sense of self can be derived.

The issue of fantasy personas demands some explanation for the uninitiated, as it is an absolutely integral part of Kiss' appeal and its rhetorical power. From the very beginning of the band's career, the members were positioned as distinct fantasy personas, though, importantly, these were never posed as separate in any real way from the band members; there were not distinct stage names, and the band members, as mentioned, were never photographed without their stage makeup. Unlike David Bowie, who assumed the persona of 'Ziggy Stardust' in the early seventies, or even Alice Cooper, there was very little of the actor/character distinction, though I do not want to suggest that Kiss fans – at least those beyond the age of ten – really believed in these personas. Rather, the personas were discursively positioned to encourage a mode of identification that would certainly be lessened by a glimpse 'behind the curtain'.

The four personas – 'the Demon' (bassist Gene Simmons), 'the Starchild' (lead singer Paul Stanley), 'the Alien' (lead guitarist Ace Frehley) and 'the Cat' (drummer Peter Criss) – were initially developed through stage costumes, the fabled makeup and to some degree in live performance, in terms of bodily demeanor and theatrical embellishment. However, when the group started to gain mass popularity in 1975–76, the personas began to be referenced more explicitly in the music and packaging. For example, the gatefold cover of the breakthrough 1975 *Alive!* album included 'letters' from the band members that played off of these fantasy roles:

> Dear Victims... I Love to do all those deliciously painful things to you that make you writhe and groan in ecstasy... (from Simmons)

> My Dear Lovers, Nothing arouses me more than seeing you getting off on me... my body is yours, yours is mine. We explode together. (from Stanley)

> Dear Earthlings, The gravity on earth isn't quite the same as it is on my home planet, but I'm slowly getting used to it. (from Frehley)

> Dear Cat People, Well you should get your claws into this album! I know it will make your tails stand straight up... (from Criss)

At this point in the band's career, there was little in the music itself that suggested these personas; the lyrical content featured a fairly standard set of themes regarding sex, teenage frustration and partying, all quite common among seventies hard rock bands. While the sexual emphasis is obviously present in these letters and would continue to be a huge part of the band's appeal, the deployment of characters was emerging more explicitly in this era, a period when, not coincidentally, the median age of the band's following was dropping quickly.

The following album, 1976's *Destroyer*, Kiss' first release as established stars, played directly off of the fantasy personas and marked the first serious musical enactment of them; in fact, it won modest but unusual recognition from critics for this apparent conceptual orientation, and it remains an overwhelming fan favorite. Through lyrics to songs such as 'God of Thunder', 'Do You Love Me' and even the hit ballad 'Beth', as well as a variety of sonic production techniques, the album created a set of associations with each persona. There was the all-powerful and menacing 'Demon', the super-sexualized ultra-stud 'Starchild', the cosmic, futuristic 'Alien' and the mysterious, introspective 'Cat'. These were presented, in a sense, as facets of a larger, super-human fantasy persona; as a later song asserts, 'We are one'. Of course, all of these qualities, except perhaps those of the 'Cat', would have a particularly strong appeal for adolescent males and certainly echo the content one might find in comic books, science fiction novels, action and horror films and other elements of teen culture. Again, the strangeness here is that they are simultaneously fantasies and yet many of the marks of fiction are quite blurry, a quality that the band and its promotional machine certainly took great pains to preserve.

The sense of the band as a complementary set of archetypes then becomes entangled in a narrative that directly references a 'coming to self' that would certainly have a strong appeal for adolescents. This first appears in a number of *Destroyer*'s songs, such as 'God of Thunder', the source of this section's title and a paean to rock and roll rebellion, and more deeply in 'Flaming Youth' in which the narrator proclaims, 'my power is my age, I'm gettin' it together to break out of my cage'. There are also numerous references to parental authority and rock and roll as an escape; again, this is not an unusual theme for rock lyrics, but here it is conjoined with a fantastic symbolic dimension. Kiss would continue to touch upon these themes in the music, albeit usually less explicitly, throughout their career, and certainly the publicity materials surrounding the band extended this, with frequently circulated tales of sexual prowess as well as a curiously old-fashioned 'you can make it if you try' rhetoric.

The linkage of fantasy personas with actual band members was seriously weakened with the departure of 'the Alien' and 'the Cat'; a brief attempt was made with replacement drummer Eric Carr featured as 'the Fox', but this lasted only three years. After the makeup was dropped in 1983, there was little or no reference to the earlier personas. However, with the reunion and return to costumes, the mythology was revived, albeit with a far greater degree of self-consciousness. Rather than a kind of liminal blend of fantastic fiction and material reality, the personas now appeared as explicitly symbolic. However, many of the most dedicated fans became attached to the band in the earlier period, so the revival of the personas certainly touched upon a deep-rooted sense of identification, even if its ontological status may have shifted somewhat.

A good example of this revival can be found in the *Psychocircus* comic book series. There was an original Kiss comic series launched in 1977 by Marvel Comics, but it had long since ceased publication. In August 1998, a *Psychocircus* comic book was published by McFarlane productions, a popular comic book company and creator of the wildly successful *Spawn* series. The narrative of the comic book touches upon many of the themes of personal quest and self-creation through heroic identification noted above. In the first story, spread over the issues #1 and #2, 'Adam', an adolescent outcast living in a dismal small town in West Virginia and regarded by his abusive alcoholic father as a 'worthless little maggot', attends a sleazy traveling circus. At the circus, Adam has a mystical encounter with a fortune teller, who informs him that he must choose his destiny and harness his hunger. After initially claiming that what he wants is 'a hot chick and a cool buzz? A family life that doesn't completely suck? A Nirvana reunion...', Adam is confronted by all the demons that have held back his life. After going home and being beaten by his father, Adam returns to the fortune teller and makes contact with the four Kiss personas, who appear as God-like figures; in the comic book series, they are known as 'Demon', 'Star Bearer', 'Celestial' and 'King of Beasts'. After fantasizing about his father's death, Adam realizes, 'I chose not to be like **him**. I want to be like **me** and I guess I have to start learning what that is [boldface in original]', and leaves home.

In the course of this narrative, there are encounters and victories over a number of very typical icons of adolescent frustration and social control. In addition to the abusive father, there is 'Father McGowan', a priest and a 'hypocrite', who curses when his church is destroyed by Celestial; 'Mr. Delgado', a bullying teacher, is mauled by the King of Beasts and sent to a 'special trauma center, like on that tv show'; finally, there is 'Kerner', a mean-spirited police officer, who affronts Adam and his pals' masculinity, calling them 'girls', 'ladies' and 'sweeties', before he is vanquished by the Demon. In this brief narrative, the creators – who provide brief 'Kisstories' in the biographical blurbs featured on the cover of the first book-length collection of the series – offer a remarkable condensation of the narratives of self-empowerment that have been associated with Kiss since their original rise to popularity. Certainly, Adam's troubled life has a particular resonance for the audience of a band that, in the words of a former business manager, attracted those escaping from the 'drudgery and dreariness' and 'crashing boredom and paralyzing monotony' of teenage life (Lendt, 1997, pp. 69–70).

The comic books are an official product, licensed and approved by the band and its management. However, much of the narrative is similar to the tales of life transformation that have circulated among the Kiss fan community for many years. Some of this is evident in the self-descriptions noted earlier, in which fans discussed the uniqueness that comes from being a Kiss fan and the powers that one derives from the same. Additionally, though, many fans articulate a more specifically mythological connection with the band, as for example, 'Jeremy', who told me, 'my first Kiss concert was almost a religious experience for me. I was so excited I could barely breathe. To this day I still think of that concert as a defining moment in my life'. Earlier, he had told me '[being a Kiss fan] means listening to the music. For me there is no special endowment in being a Kiss fan', suggesting that investment in the Kiss mythos is not necessarily an either/or proposition, or at least is not without its evident contradictions. Quasi-religious implications are additionally present in many of the publicly available 'Kisstories'; a particularly fascinating example comes from a Native American fan, whose father burned one of her albums, saying 'they were demonic and that they let evil spirits in the house'. Later in the narrative, she compares the Kiss concert experience with Native American religious practices,

> We have a yearly pow wow there [the arena which also hosted a Kiss concert] every June and when you are there you can feel the emotion as our Native American elders dance in the arena and when you leave and then come back for another event you still feel the emotion and the spirit there! It's the same feeling every year when I walk into that arena for the pow wow I can feel the emotion from that Kiss concert! ... So when I walk across the arena floor in a few weeks for our pow wow, I will not only be listening to sounds and celebrations [from] my ancestors but I will also be listening to sounds from the hottest band in the land KISS!

Notice the parallels here with comic book plot both in the familial obstacles to fandom – an extremely common motif in such tales – and the powerful, ritualized qualities that are in this case directly analogous to more traditional spiritual practices.

In another web-based Kisstory, 'Domino', a fan from New Zealand, echoes the comic book narrative (as well as the conceptual premise behind *Destroyer*) in a somewhat different fashion, again claiming religious significance for the band, but in this case utilizing the four-dimensional structure of the band's fantasy personas as an important element in this 'faith'.

> Ask who my favorite member of the band is and I'm afraid that I could not choose. To me, they are all gods, with each one having individual traits of which I both respect and adore and I think that Gene sums it up nicely when he said the Kiss fans religion is Kisstianity. So, come take my hand and I will lead you into the temple of the Kiss Asylum where together we can worship Kiss... the gods of rock and roll [ellipses in original]

Domino refers here to Simmons' often-repeated remark that the level of dedication displayed by Kiss fans would qualify as a religion – hence 'Kisstianity' – and apparently rejects the aforementioned disclaimers of significance that Simmons simultaneously offers. It should be noted that Domino's comments, while particularly poetic, are not unusual in their explicit deification of the band.

'J.D.', for example, explains in his Kisstory that he initially hated the band, but after a friend played *Alive II* (a 1978 album), 'a new Kiss fan was born. I have loved Kiss ever since and feel their music is my religion. I have always tried to live my life like a Kiss song and I think I turned out pretty good'. 'Parasite' (name taken from an early Kiss song) describes a first encounter in terms of the realization that 'KISS is a powerful thing... it shaped my life from that day on' [caps and ellipses in original]. Another fan, the 'Goddess of Thunder', claims, 'They're in my soul! I collect, go to conventions, I still have a lot of my original KISS items. My condo is a shrine to KISS! People never did really "understand", but I know you all can relate and understand'. Again, there are parallels with both the comic book and a more general set of Kiss-related narratives; finding people who understand becomes a very important aspect of fan practices and complements the more internal self-narrative that structures many such 'Kisstories'. Although most the fans cited above identify themselves as 'first generation' Kiss fans, new fans can also display a similar fervor; take for example, 15 year old 'Jon', a fan since 1996, who claims that following his first concert, 'ever since then I've been a different person'.

Other fans provide a more specific description of the struggles that sometimes follow an initial conversion to Kiss fandom. Certainly, Kiss has always served to divide listeners, particularly younger listeners – witness the aforementioned grade school election – and Kiss fans often describe resistance not only from family, but also from peers. As several of my informants noted above, being a Kiss fan was perceived as requiring the ability to 'stand up' for yourself, 'even when its not the popular thing to do' and 'everyone thinks you're nuts'. Other 'Kisstories' offer more concrete tales of adolescent persecution and tests of courage related to their status as a Kiss fan,

> [In response to the question, 'Did you ever get into a fight because of being a KISS fan?'] All of the time! I won most of them, being kind of big for my age (I was 6ft from 6th to 8th grade). It usually started by someone busting on one of my many KISS shirts and saying: 'Dude, you like KISS, they suck. You must be a pussy...' It would go down hill from there with my kicking the shit out of them.

> that [hearing the *Revenge* album] was a momentous event in my life, for it was to change the way I looked at pop music (down the barrel of a gun!!) and set me off down the road to metaldom, and persecution from my fellow 'classmates' (bastards!! Hated EVERY ONE of those c#@ksuckers!!) I nevertheless stuck by my beliefs and never swayed from what I adored the most, and as cheesy as this may sound, Kiss music helped me through those tough times, and got me where I am today!!!

In this case, the oppressive societal forces are not linked to the police, the church, the school or the family, but from a social circle less obviously connected to concrete forms of regulation. Fidelity to oneself is fidelity to the Kiss army and this can require action, though it is always couched in terms of self-defense (literally and figuratively) rather than attack. One fan even told me that being a Kiss fan meant, 'do(ing) anything you want as long as you don't hurt or kill anyone else', a kind of golden rule, and one reflective of the kind of self-directed – or is that Kiss-directed? – ethos that has apparently placed other fans in the position of physically defending their 'Kisstianity'.

Perhaps the most remarkable tale of life-changes through Kiss fandom, though, was in response to a question about Kiss' significance that I posed to a number of fans. One fan, 'Brad', who is visually impaired and communicates through a voice activated computer system, provided this narrative [I have retained the original spellings]:

> Most people that I run into don't know that Kiss is still rockin as they did in the seventies. [this interview was conducted electronically in early 1996]. Then they ask me what do I know about the group. I know that they will always be special to me because when I was six I was run over by a UPS truck and I was in a comma for 6 weeks. on Easter Sunday my mom left my bed side to go pray in the chapil. She left this tape player beside my bed and it had Kiss Alive II playing. Then the doctor came and knocked on the door of the chapil and said Miss Lovern, it's your son. She didn't wit to find out what he was talking about, she went to my room, opened the door. And there I was tapping my leg keeping time to Kiss. So that's way they are special to me.

There are some interesting implications to this narrative: first, that the music served to awaken him from a coma and, second, that Kiss served as the first memory after an enormous personal trauma. 'Brad', it should be noted, never actually assigns credit for his recovery to Kiss, and the simultaneity of his mother's praying and his awakening is somewhat ambiguous. The juxtaposition with conventional religion can be interpreted as suggesting a complementary relationship with the power of the music, as in the earlier comparison with Native American spirituality or, conversely, as evidence of the superior power of the rock and roll, as in the comic book destruction of 'Father McGowan'. What is clear, however, is the richness of this mythology, particularly when the concrete anecdotes cited above are combined with the musical and visual texts associated with the band. This will be further evident in the forthcoming discussion of *(Music From) The Elder*, perhaps the most 'theological' of all Kiss-related texts and one with particular resonance to the issue of a quest for selfhood. First, though, I want to examine an important secondary element in the mythology surrounding the band.

Kings In Satan's Service: Kiss-lore and the 'fear factor'

There is a distinctive body of lore and legend surrounding Kiss, one with few parallels in the world of popular music. With the notable exception of the similarly theatrical Alice Cooper and, more recently, Marilyn Manson, few rock performers have been surrounded by such an extensive set of narratives related to behaviors so bizarre and stereo-typically evil. Of course, there have always been legends surrounding the sexual and material excesses of rock stars – from Elvis Presley to the Gallagher brothers – but these have tended to depict rather routine celebrity decadence: trashing hotel rooms, exploits with groupies, drug and alcohol binges and so forth. Kiss, particularly in its heyday, has been surrounded by a rather different set of folklore, a body of material with a peculiar relation to the religiosity noted above.

My initial interest in this area of Kiss fandom was spurred by my own childhood experiences with these legends. For example, a young neighbor told me that he would never listen to Kiss because he heard that they would stop in the middle of a concert and demonstrate how to shoot heroin for the young, presumably impressionable crowd. Initial conversations with academic colleagues produced even stranger tales. One, who had been a hardcore fan, told me that he had heard that the band would lock the doors of the arena and drag a randomly selected audience member onstage to be beheaded. Another colleague and former fan remembers hearing that before the concert, the stage would be covered with live puppies; Gene Simmons ('the Demon') would then crush them under his famous dragon boots.

When I raised the issue with informants, a number of similar tales emerged. One had heard that 'Kiss would sacrifice a virgin backstage before every show and Gene would use her blood to spit on stage while praising the devil', referring to Simmons' onstage blood-drooling rou-tine, a highlight of the Kiss visual spectacle. Others added rumors that Kiss was 'this huge Satanic cult'; that they 'puked and pissed on the audience'; that 'Gene Simmons is a devil worshipper'; that 'Gene's [famously long] tongue was a cow's tongue and the band ate feces on stage'. There were also two very bizarre tales of Kiss' attacking teen idols of the seventies (recall the earlier male-female conflict surrounding the 'election'): 'all four ganged up on Leif Garrett and beat the snot out of him'; 'Gene Simmons bit Shaun Cassidy on the neck'. One fan added that, 'there were many more stories I've forgotten for good measure (I was brought up in Pentecostalism. Enough said.)' Nearly every Kiss fan I have encountered had heard the rumor, referenced in the title of this section, that 'Kiss' was an acronym for 'Kings/Knights In Satan's Service' or 'Kids In Service to Satan'. This particular piece of folklore even appeared in literature from anti-rock activists on the Christian right back in the seventies and early eighties, suggesting that it has enjoyed an unusually extensive circulation both within and external to the world of Kiss fans.

Indeed, much of the folklore surrounding Kiss, like the similar tales regarding Cooper and Manson, describe violations of common social taboos with a particular tendency toward occultic and/or satanic activity. Not incidentally, many of the same behaviors associated with Kiss – cruelty to animals, human sacrifice, devil worship – also appear in the 'repressed memory' accounts of satanism so common to talk show culture. Interestingly, Kiss, along with Manson, continues to be a target for the aforementioned religious activists. Both were subject to protests and a prayer service organized by the American Family Association, a right-wing cultural organization, in Wheeling, West Virginia in 1997, and Kiss faced similar protests the same year in Elvis Presley's hometown of Tupelo, Mississippi. Indeed, Kiss is the topic of an extended discussion – including repetition of the 'Kings in Satan's Service' legend – in Jeff Godwin's *The Devil's Disciples*, a fundamentalist Christian analysis of satanism in rock and roll (Godwin, 1985, pp. 115–118). While few of the old seventies folktales continue to circulate, even among the most extreme critics of the band, a general reputation as both satanic and more broadly deviant continues to follow the band.

There is an intriguing ambivalence in the reaction of many fans to this mythology. Some deny having ever believed any of it, such as the fans that told me that they had always regarded it as 'crap', 'a bunch of hooey' and that 'I was not susceptible to such lies'. However, some did indicate that this reputation increased their enjoyment of the band. As a fan told me, 'However as a kid it [the satanic mythology] made it even more fun to like the band because people attached such negative connotations to the name. It made being rebellious more fun'. Another fan shared a narrative that touches both upon his youthful inculcation into Kiss fandom, and the band's fearsome reputation,

> Well initially it [what attracted me to Kiss] was the makeup and the outfits. I remember seeing the first album cover in a store while I was with my mother. I'll never forget her reaction – 'Get away from there!!!' That was in 1974, I was 10. What really hooked me though was the first time I actually remember hearing them and it was Alive's 'Rock and Roll All Nite' that did it. I hung out at my local community center and the jukebox had the 45. I was soon banned from putting in more than 1 quarter at a time – I played that thing over and over again.

Here, the mythology surrounding Kiss provides a mechanism for separating oneself from those who are deterred or disturbed by the discourse surrounding the band, echoing an earlier comment about he sense of Kiss fans as an 'elite force' where 'few survive'. The religious basis of at least some of this fear – the satanic angle – both serves to pit Kiss and its fans against an established theological tradition as well as amplifying the quasi-religious relationship that is central to this community. Certainly, accusations of deviance in general and satanism in particular have been launched at rock and roll, and especially heavy metal, for decades (see Weinstein, 1991, pp. 258–263, for example, and Godwin's book), but rarely are these supported with the kinds of graphic legends connected with the Kiss mythology. The fantasy personas so critical to the marketing and ultimate success of Kiss provided a perfect venue for such stories, as they helped to create a predisposition to these hysterical narratives.

In the above examples, Kiss appeared as frightening to the 'outside world', to parents, clergy and anyone else willing to accept these legends. However, many fans also couched their coming-to-fandom in terms of a conquest of their own fears of the band. Certainly, fear and attraction are commingled in any number of popular cultural phenomena; the success of horror films, thrill rides and 'extreme sports' for example, clearly depends upon this mix of emotions, but this is an unusual position for a rock band. For example, an academic colleague remembers Kiss 'scaring the hell out of me' when they appeared on a mid-seventies television variety show, and similar tales appear in a number of 'Kisstories', as in this story of a first encounter with Kiss,

> I was getting off the school bus one fall afternoon, walking home through my front yard. Something near the street caught my eye, and being a typical eight year old, I went to investigate. It seems there was this discarded 8-track cartridge laying face down in the grass, with much of the tape strung out of it blowing in the breeze. Something compelled me to pick up the case and turn it over to check out the label, and there it was... My eyes scanned the picture of these four faces and almost instantly locked on this evil, demonic looking one glaring up at me! I froze for a moment, then quickly threw down the tape and ran straight home! It was KISS, the first album. If I ever get a chance to meet Gene, I would like to say, 'Thanks for scaring the crap out of a little kid. You have been frightening me ever since!'

Another fan, '5Card Stud', provided a similar story, in this case involving fans in Kiss costumes:

> Well, my earliest memory of Kiss was when I was about 3 years old. I was at my grandmother's house, when two teenagers from across

the street came over dressed as Gene and Paul for Halloween. I ended up hiding under the dining room table until they left.

In an interesting twist, another fan, calling herself 'HotterThanHell' after the title track of Kiss' second album, describes a similar encounter, but her response is quite different,

> It all started when I was 5 (1978) in Pa [Pennsylvania]. My older cousins were into kiss and they thought hey lets get our little cousin we will scare the crap outta her. So they called me upstairs and on the way I heard this really cool music. I got upstairs and they (Chris and Dwayne) said 'this music is Devil music and these pictures are all the faces of the devil'. Well me being only 5 but said 'no there [sic] not the devil is red with pointed horns and pointed tail'. I was a demented child I think LOL [internet abbreviation for 'laugh out loud']. Anyway I wanted to know who is it really was and they told me it was a band called KISS. I was in love from that day forward. Thank you Chris and Dwayne...

All of these narratives describe a particularly important facet of the Kiss fan experience and particularly the mythological status that gets assigned to one's relationship with the band. Much of this discourse echoes the earlier claims regarding being a Kiss fan within a social context in which it is not appreciated and the sense that declaring one's fandom is a kind of accomplishment. Of course, amid rumors of onstage killing and satan worship, this accomplishment takes on more grandiose connotations. Whether this is posed as overcoming a general social rejection of Kiss – as deviant and/or satanic – or a personal fear of Kiss, being a Kiss fan becomes attached to ideals of personal courage and individualism that are intertwined with the quasi-religious dedication expressed in the earlier comments and writings of fans. The most intense version of this sense of a quest to achieve a self, though, is discussed in the following section.

The strange career of Kiss' *(Music From) The Elder*

In November 1981, Kiss released *(Music From) The Elder*, the last album to feature original lead guitarist Ace Frehley, and the first with new drummer Eric Carr. The album was produced by Bob Ezrin, who had also worked with the band on *Destroyer*, and reflected a striking change of musical direction. While the previous Kiss albums had consisted primarily of mainstream, pop-oriented hard rock with occasional ballads and a few disco-influenced songs, *The Elder* featured an instrumental prelude played by the American Symphony Orchestra, a background vocal chorus supplied by the St. Robert's Choir, and narration by actors Robert Christie, Anthony Parr and Christopher Makepeace. Three songs were co-written by art-rock legend Lou Reed, a performer whose audience, critical status and music were far removed from the cultural milieu associated with Kiss. The album was organized, lyrically and musically, around a single narrative. The plot follows the journey of 'the boy' who must prove himself to Morpheus, 'the caretaker', so that he may be deemed worthy of 'the Order of the Rose', a sacred group of warriors fighting evil under the aegis of the titular 'council of the Elder'.

The album was a colossal failure, selling dramatically fewer copies than any previous Kiss album; it would eventually become the lowest selling album in the entire Kiss catalog. It was released as the band's popularity had already started to plummet rather rapidly and 'was the nail that sealed the coffin' (Lendt, 1997, p. 241). The parenthetical '(Music from)' was chosen because it was originally assumed that the musical narrative would serve as the basis for a theatrical film (Lendt, 1997, pp. 237–238), but these plans were shelved when the album failed to sell. Even the band members themselves – never known for their modesty – have been highly critical of the album in subsequent interviews. Asked to evaluate the album in a feature in *Goldmine* magazine that had group members rate the band's records on a scale of one to five stars, Gene Simmons responded that, 'as a Kiss record I would give it a zero. As a bad Genesis [English art-rock band] record I'd give it a two' (Marsh and Benard, 1994, pp. 380–381). The album has thus become an emblem of Kiss' decline in popularity and of the most pretentious excesses of overambitious rock musicians, the musical equivalent of a big-budget cinematic flop.

However, the reaction among a significant number of the most devout Kiss fans was and continues to be dramatically different. The album is prized as one of the band's most ambitious efforts and as an artistic masterpiece. There was even a campaign, proposed within some Kiss fan organizations, to encourage members to buy the album, as it was the only album in the Kiss catalog that had not been certified gold in the U.S. (sales of 500,000 copies) and was thus perceived as an embarrassment. Of course, the lack of popularity only increases the cultic aura surrounding the album, and serves as a means of delineating true Kiss fans from dilettantes; this dynamic is quite common within rock fandom in general, a culture in which appreciation for obscure and especially less commercially successful recordings is often a significant measure of audience allegiance. However, *(Music from) The Elder* was not merely a commercial failure and simultaneous fan favorite. It was also, through its textual content and the ways that it had become a vehicle for fan discourse – fiction and artwork as well as critical exegesis – a particularly crucial text and a potent allegory for the place of the fans themselves. In this section, I will examine the ways that the album has become an object of this kind of engagement, but first it is useful to take a closer look at the album itself.

As mentioned, *(Music from) The Elder* was presented as Kiss' attempt at a serious artistic achievement. Not surprisingly, then, it utilizes many of the musical strategies associated with the art-rock tradition, one inaugurated by the Beatles' *Sgt. Pepper's Lonely Hearts Club Band* and continuing through the sixties and seventies work of bands such as Yes, the Moody Blues and Emerson, Lake, and Palmer. These include a lyrical narrative, complex arrangements, unorthodox rock instrumentation, longer song lengths and an emphasis on instrumental virtuosity. The production is similarly grandiose; Ezrin had just completed work on Pink Floyd's *The Wall*, a hugely popular and critical success and an album firmly within the art-rock genre, and *(Music from) The Elder* deploys a similarly elaborate sonic strategy. The liner notes for the album elucidate the basic premises of the narrative, thus providing an easier entry into the plot, which would otherwise be quite obscure. The notes describe a group, 'the Elder', that watch over the Earth and its dwellers. They are also responsible for 'train(ing) a warrior' who will fight the evil that inevitably inhabits this world, and the notes end with a description of the Elder sitting at their 'ancient table', waiting to hear from the aforementioned 'Morpheus' as to the fitness of 'the boy' to join the sacred 'Order of the Rose'. The notes are illustrated with a rather luminous photo of seven intricately carved chairs gathered around a large wooden table topped with a single candle. This is presumably the interior of the space referenced on the cover with a photo of a hand reaching out to a brass knocker attached to an elaborately carved door, suggesting the boy preparing to face his judgment.

The album begins with a brief orchestral instrumental entitled 'fanfare', followed by the first full song, 'Just a Boy'. The latter, a rather delicate ballad, is written from the perspective of the titular character, 'frightened of failing' and wary of those looking to him for guidance. The following track, 'Odyssey', continues along these lines, utilizing an instrumental and vocal style highly reminiscent of contemporary musical theater[2] and describing an 'odyssey through the realms of time and space'. This is followed by 'Only You', a song using a dialogic structure in which Paul Stanley's voice is used to play the role of the boy, and Gene Simmons' serves in the role of an omniscient narrator. The lyrics posit the self as the origin of truth and when the voice of the boy asks 'Why am I still afraid', he is told that only he can ever overcome his own weaknesses and find the answer.

The narrative shifts a bit with the next track, 'Under the Rose', which features a prominent use of the choir and a dirge-like tempo. Here, the lyrics are written solely from the perspective of the Elder, describing the challenges that the boy will face on his 'odyssey'; it will require 'sacrifice', 'loneliness', and a long quest to find 'your destiny' if the boy wishes to take the oath and join the Order of the Rose. 'Under the Rose' is followed by 'Dark Light', which uses the voice of guitarist and very occasional vocalist Ace Frehley to provide a warning about a 'darkness never ending' and to tell the boy that, 'for all the things you believe in, you're gonna be attacked'. The song plays upon Frehley's 'alien' persona, deploying his voice in a mystical, oracular mode, somewhere between Stanley's innocent boy and Simmons' God-like narrator. This is followed by another ballad, 'A World Without Heroes', offering a rather sappy and self-serving description of the titular condition, a place in which 'there's nothing to be'. Penned jointly by two very different rock heroes – Lou Reed and Gene Simmons – the song is both a naked plea for the value of celebrities and in the context of *(Music from) The Elder*, a rather somber turn in the narrative, with the title referring to the possible fate of the world if the boy should fail.

This condition is quickly reversed, though, with the following song, 'The Oath'. The track serves as the climax of the narrative, in which 'a boy goes in and suddenly a man returns'. The boy, again voiced by Stanley, has now come to an understanding of his destiny, though he still wonders 'is this really me?' The track is particularly intense musically, using a guitar-driven approach that would later gain favor in the mid- and late-eighties heavy metal renaissance, and reflects a shift from the more lugubrious sound of the previous two tracks. The harder sound continues into the next song, 'Mr. Blackwell', which introduces a final character to the plot, one representing all of the evil in this 'virgin world'. The Blackwell character is never really developed – though he will be in *Elder*-inspired fan fiction – and is depicted primarily in vaguely poetic terms as 'rotten to the core', 'a real disgrace' and 'cold and mean'. The most intriguing lyric, though, describes Blackwell as 'the truth about this crummy hole, there's nothing here that can't be bought or sold', somewhat ironic given the remarkable merchandising empire surrounding Kiss. In any case, though, the Blackwell character makes his only appearance (on the album) in this song, followed by a second instrumental, 'Escape From The Island', that is primarily a vehicle for displaying Frehley's guitar playing.

The denouement comes with the final track, titled simply 'I'. The song stands out on the album in that it marks a return, at least partially, to the instrumental sound of the 'old Kiss'; 'I' is quite catchy and features a simple melodic hook, shouted vocals and a thundering, guitar-dominated arrangement. The lyrics, though, reflect a logical conclusion to the narrative. The vocals are split, line by line, between Simmons and Stanley, presumably to suggest a union of the boy and the Order. The lyrics provide a particularly concise variation on the kind of 'self-esteem' discourse described in the previous sections, as well as depicting the ultimate victory of the boy over the series of challenges structuring the narrative. There is the repeated chant, complete with choral backing, of 'I believe in me'; the lyrics also make reference to standing up to social pressures ('they said I didn't stand a chance'), refusing drugs and alcohol ('don't need to get wasted')[3] and 'need(ing) a will of my own'. The song is thus the culmination of the album's lyrical theme, bringing the message of 'finding yourself' to an undeniably anthemic finale. The album then closes with a very brief spoken postscript in which Morpheus informs the Elder that the boy is 'worthy of the Fellowship'.

As evident from the above description, the commercial failure of *(Music from) The Elder* is not particularly puzzling, given its departure from the band's prior work. Indeed much of the album is laughably pompous and unlistenably bombastic to me, particularly in its artier moments. My personal reaction is not completely unusual, even among veteran Kiss fans; for some, much of the album simply did not sound like 'Kiss' (see, for example, 'Lynn's' review on her *Kiss Dominion* website). However, for many fans, the album is held in very high esteem, and it has certainly inspired some of the most interesting related discourse.

An example of this *Elder*-related material would be the poetry of Melissa LaRose, a fan who also calls herself 'Midnight Queen'. Inspired by the album, LaRose has written a three-part poem entitled 'Ode to the Elder'. Each section also has an individual title: 'A Look Ahead', 'On My Way' and 'Reflections', respectively. The poem follows the same narrative line as the album itself, describing a journey into the Order of the Rose. Similarly, LaRose retains much of the emphasis on self-conquest evident in the original; a couplet in the third section reads, 'With my soul's knife, my inner demons have been slayed, My pain is now a mere reflection, Forever trapped in its blade'. The poem also pays homage to the sequence of songs on the album by working the title of each song, sometimes quite cleverly, into the poetic flow of the piece. LaRose's poem is indicative of the peculiar status of *(Music from) The Elder* within the Kiss catalog as it is virtually inconceivable that any other album, even the marginally conceptual *Destroyer*, could serve as the narrative and thematic basis for such literary work. The album demands a level of interpretive effort and reflects a singular thematic breadth that lends it a particularly prophetic quality. While the discourses associated with fantasy personas, the critical and social resistance to the band and the folklore surrounding Kiss may imply a model of self-realization and self-esteem, *(Music from) The Elder* engages these concerns directly.

The most remarkable literary work inspired by the album, though, is Dale Sherman's 'Kiss Novel', *A World Without Heroes*, that takes its title from the aforementioned song. Sections of the novel first appeared in a 1984 issue of *Strange Ways*, a short-lived Kiss fanzine, but it was not completed until 1997 when the final chapters appeared on the *Kiss Asylum* website. The novel is a full length fantasy narrative (about 200 pages) using the band as central characters. It should be mentioned that Sherman has published other material related to Kiss. He is the author of *Black Diamond 1 & 2*, commercially published (and widely distributed) books about the band; the first is an 'unauthorized biography', and the second is a guide to collectible Kiss merchandise. However, the novel is categorically different from these more conventional works, as it reflects a very unique combination of three narratives associated with the band interwoven into a single coherent plot.

Sherman uses much of the basic structure of *(Music from) The Elder*: Morpheus, Mr. Blackwell, and the Elder are all present in roughly the same roles they play in the album's narrative. In this case, the band members collectively serve in the role of 'the boy' and are being tested as potential members of the 'Order of the Rose'. However, Sherman also adds elements taken from the plot of the Kiss's aforementioned television film, *Kiss Meets the Phantom of the Park*; the film features the band as cosmic superheroes battling an evil puppet maker in a California amusement park. These elements include a set of mystical talisman – one for each member of the band – that gives them magical powers (e.g., time travel, super strength, lasers that shoot from an eye), as well as the character of Mr. Deveraux, the puppet maker and robotics expert that tries to destroy the band. In a particularly reflexive twist, their encounter with Deveraux is set during the making of the same television film, and the coincidence is mentioned within the plot itself

(Sherman, no date, chapter 10, p. 2). This coincidence is enabled by the use of a third strand in the narrative, which is the real-life story of the band, covering its rise to popularity, the defection of Frehley and Criss and the subsequent use of replacement members Eric Carr, Vinnie Vincent and Bruce Kulick in the eighties. Sherman includes a number of significant events in the band's career as pivotal moments within the narrative: the recording of the *Alive!* album in Detroit in 1975, the production of the television movie and the band's troubled 1982 *Creatures of the Night* tour (Kiss' last in makeup and costume). Sherman even makes a sly reference to 1991 rumors appearing in the tabloid press that Criss had become homeless and was living under a pier in Los Angeles, rumors that drove Criss to appear on the *Donahue* television talk show to reassure the public that he was not a vagrant.

The final chapter of *A World Without Heroes* finds the band defeating Blackwell and assuming membership in the Order. However, they are also given the surprising news that their struggles were really being waged against their own weaknesses and that,

> Heroes are not born out of individuals that merely pick up a weapon or throw a punch. Any toddler can do that. Power for power's sake is nothing – the ability to use power wisely and constructively is what really matters. Your battles were not about winning against others, but about those things inside of you that hamper your ability to be more than just animals running around on a planet. (Sherman, no date, chapter 25, p. 2)

Then, in a twist ending, all of the magical talismans merge into one and are left by Morpheus in the hands of Stanley, who is told that he will become the guardian of these powers; this may be a reference to his increasingly dominant role in leading the band in the eighties. Thus, the novel ends up in much the same thematic territory as the album and LaRose's poem, with a union of elder and acolyte and an affirmation of the power of self-esteem. Unlike the aforementioned 'Ode', though, *A World Without Heroes* does this through an odd mixture of factual and fictional material; it is not a work of fantasy in quite the same sense as the other objects, even if Sherman offers a standard disclaimer concerning its fictional status at the beginning of the novel.

Media audiences have long been engaged in the practice of taking fictional characters and narrative threads and incorporating them within their own fictional work; indeed, 'fan fiction' has inspired a considerable body of critical work, including Henry Jenkins' landmark *Textual*

Poachers. Jenkins analyzes the use of television programs as fodder for such fiction, identifying ten strategies (e.g., moral realignment, genre shifting) used by fans to rework television texts (Jenkins, 1992, pp. 162–176), and points to such practices as examples of the ways that audiences transform media objects, 'so that potentially significant materials can better speak to the audience's cultural interests and more fully address their desires' (Jenkins, 1992, p. 279). While such strategies are certainly evident in the fictional/poetic works inspired by *(Music from) The Elder*, Sherman's novel reflects a step beyond the far commoner fan fiction inspired by television. While the novel displays some of the attributes of Jenkins' sixth strategy, the 'cross over', in which normally discrete fictional worlds become mixed together within the narrative (Jenkins, 1992, pp. 168–169), *A World Without Heroes* extends this process by merging fictional and actual worlds, blurring boundaries that are generally impermeable. In fact, the very genre of Sherman's novel, musical fan fiction, is rather anomalous.[4] For obvious reasons, television and filmic texts, which tend to offer fairly complete fictional worlds, are more likely to inspire fan fiction than popular music. Both the unique mixture of narrative elements within the novel and its place in the relatively minuscule genre of rock and roll fan fiction can be attributed, of course, to the peculiar status of Kiss as both a group of rock musicians and, simultaneously, the center of a rich mythology, complete with fantasy personas, folk and official narratives and a doctrine of personal empowerment and communal solidarity.

The extended life of *(Music from) The Elder* is not limited to the literary work discussed above. The tradition of 'fan fiction' was extended into the field of performance with the transformation of the album into a stage musical by a group of students at Athens High School in Athens, Wisconsin, a small town in the central part of the state. The musical was staged in 1996 and received considerable attention within the Kiss fan media, and was later performed by the original cast at the Tennessee Performing Arts Center in June of 1997. This musical theatre version featured the basic plot line and all of the songs from the original album. However, as students involved in the production of the musical mentioned to 'Kiss Asylum', a Kiss fanzine, a number of changes had to be made to render *The Elder* suitable for the theatrical stage. Songs were added to flesh out the narrative and extend its length. 'The boy' was named 'Aerick' after the deceased drummer Eric Carr, and as the students explained, 'in order to give more opportunity to female members of the cast, characters were created to fill out a predominantly male perspective'. The students were assisted by director Donley Niskanen, a local rock musician and vocal teacher at the school who, along with fellow members of his band Cruz, were 'lifelong Kiss fans, veterans of tours since *Alive II* and owners of all things Kiss'. Niskanen, along with bandmates Joey Nelson and Dag Bystrom also composed new material for the adaptation, with some help with lyrical additions and revisions from the high school crew. In addition to reaction within the Kiss fan community, the musical also attracted a bit of general media attention as well; the producers report 'five newspaper stories, 3 radio interviews, 2 television pieces, contact from *MTV Unfiltered* [a program featuring "local color" segments], and several other print media'. Most of these likely stem from the sheer novelty of the adaptation; despite the suitability of the album, with its narrative structure, for theatrical adaptation, its relative obscurity and the distinctly low brow culture associated with Kiss make the production strange enough to merit a degree of public notice. Furthermore, the production team, along with Niskanen and Athens High School Principal Lance Alwin, was honored with an official commendation from the State of Wisconsin (proudly displayed on the Cruz website) for their efforts.

While the musical version of *The Elder* may be less aesthetically adventurous than Sherman's novelization, as it remains completely faithful to the original storyline, it is certainly an impressive logistical accomplishment, and one reflective of a fairly significant dedication to the material. This was already noted in regard to 'lifelong fan' Niskanen, but publicity surrounding the presentation of the musical also confirmed the fan status of the eight member student production team. Interestingly, all four female members list older siblings as the source of their initial attraction to the band, while the male students all mentioned textual encounters – seeing videos or hearing songs – to explain their journey into fandom. Niskanen characterizes the decision to adapt *The Elder* in the following terms,

> A classic in most KISS fan's eyes, an aberration in others, we saw 'The Elder' as an epic tale of good vs. evil, obstacles to be overcome, and ultimately a tale of belief in yourself and the people you call friends. KISS' music is so powerful in any context, here it is equal to the tale of a hero and a champion... Everyone has images of what 'The Elder' means to them, we hope our vision is worthy of a small place in the hearts of fans and Kisstory, and musical theater in general... we hope Kiss would be proud.

Niskanen's comments are fascinating in that they imply a nearly irresistible analogy between the textual narrative of the *The Elder* – the coming to self-understanding of a young boy – and the act of staging the musical itself, one dependent upon the interpretation of the wisdom offered by the band, and the subsequent expansion of the narrative beyond 'the eleven tracks and mystic paragraphs of the original'. Niskanen mentions, 'being told we couldn't accomplish this fueled the fire all the more', while the crew offers 'a HUGE thanks to Gene, Paul, Ace, and Peter, for inspiration to do things you dream of...;' there is a nice convergence here between the discourse of the album itself and the accomplishments of such devout fans.

I would argue that it is precisely such a convergence that has given *(Music from) The Elder* its prominent status – again, notable given its commercial failure – within the Kiss fan community. The narrative enacts a struggle with inner demons, one with an undeniable appeal to audience members struggling with issues of identity and the frustrations associated with restrictive social situations. Earlier in this chapter, I mentioned the media frenzy surrounding the resumption of the *Star Wars* saga and a general similarity between Kiss and the *Star Wars* films as cultural phenomena. There is a second, more specific similarity between the *Elder* narratives, at least those of the original album and the stage musical, and the narrative of both the first and fourth *Star Wars* films, one that may help to explain the peculiar 'grip' of *The Elder* upon Kiss fans. Both narratives are centered on a naïve boy/adolescent chosen for membership in a sacred order (Jedi Knights/Order of the Rose), guided by a spiritual guru (Obi-Wan Kenobi/Morpheus), battling evil (Darth Vader/Mr. Blackwell) and ultimately learning that 'the force' comes from within rather than from anyone or anything else. Of course, such narratives have an extraordinarily long history, and I do not mean to suggest that there is a particular novelty to such tales, nor to imply any plagiarism, unintentional or otherwise, in the creation of *(Music from) The Elder*. What is interesting, though, is that this narrative can be so comfortably situated within a larger framework of spectacle and a tradition of mainstream entertainment, in this case popular cinema and/or rock music, enabling a real rhetorical potency.

Of course, *Star Wars* was and continues to be an incredible commercial success while *(Music from) The Elder* was the 'nail in the coffin' of Kiss' initial popularity, a difference with significant implications. In a sense, the exclusive character of *The Elder*, noted by Niskanen and by numerous other fans as well, fits nicely with the theme of an elite and the need to stand apart and 'believe in me'; as mentioned, for many fans, the album seems to serve as a filter separating less devout Kiss fans from those willing to take on the interpretive challenges, musical and thematic, of *The Elder*. The narrative of *The Elder* is also oddly homologous to its reception and activation within the Kiss fan community in that it references, through the use of both the Morpheus character and the 'World Without Heroes' theme, the importance of fantastic modes of identification in the journey to self-confidence. Even when, as the lyrics tell you, 'you're gonna be attacked' for the things you believe in (like a much maligned flop album), the true fan stands her ground, and accepts the challenges of the elite.

The comparison between the respective symbolic worlds engendered by Kiss and the *Star Wars* films also involves a second distinction regarding the ontological status of the producers in relation to the text. Sherman's novel, for example, places the band within the text itself – as a pluralization of 'the boy' – while Niskanen and his student production team regard the band as the Elder, as the conduits for wisdom regarding one's self-affirmation. 'Kiss', unlike 'George Lucas' (who would be most commonly identified as the creator of *Star Wars*), reflects a symbolic liminality, standing both for the fantasies embodied in their personas and in a mythic narrative, and also for the artistic and commercial producers who create the same. I am not suggesting here that Kiss fans believe that the members of Kiss battle evil or have superpowered talisman, but rather that there is symbolic permeability that is unusual both for rock music and for popular culture as a whole. In this light, one might surmise that *(Music from) The Elder* is of particular value to Kiss fans at least partly because it epitomizes this merger of worlds, standing as the most intense and fully developed version of the self-esteem message so central to Kiss fandom and as the band's most ambitious aesthetic work.

Scapegoats and martyrs in the Kiss world

As mentioned, one of the modifications of *The Elder* made in the Athens High stage musical version was the choice of 'Aerick' as a name for 'the boy'. The name, the crew explained, was chosen in homage to Kiss drummer Eric Carr, who played on the album and died of cancer at age 41 in 1991. Carr is a unique figure in the Kiss community, one who plays a particularly interesting role in the symbolic structure of this world, serving both as a deified martyr and simultaneously as a uniquely human figure. Carr joined the band in 1980 and was not well-known at the time; he was chosen at least partly because he had not been in the public eye and thus could retain the mystery associated with the band's hidden faces. After being introduced to fans on a 1980 episode of the children's television program *Kids Are People Too* (indicative of Kiss' fan base at the time), Carr recorded and toured with the band until health problems forced him to step down in 1990; at that time, he was replaced by veteran rock drummer Eric Singer.

Carr is often regarded as the finest musician to play in the band – he was certainly an excellent rock drummer – lending him particularly strong appeal among the more musicianly segments of the Kiss Army, a significant minority in the larger fan group. For these fans, Carr helped to vindicate the band from charges of musical incompetence, and pushed the band further along instrumentally. However, as mentioned, Carr is also the first replacement member of the band, and his tenure is generally regarded by fans as their weakest in terms of overall quality (with the notable exception of *(Music from) The Elder*). While Carr was given the persona and costume of 'the Fox', this was never developed in any detail, and after only two albums, the makeup and costumes were dropped. Thus, Carr was never included in the initial spate of folklore surrounding the band, nor did he achieve the mythologized status associated with other members.

What, then, makes Carr such a important figure in the 'Kiss World'? Obviously, his tragic death lends a certain poignancy to his time with the group, but this is not the whole story. A careful look at some of the discourse surrounding Carr as well as the attempts to integrate him within a larger symbolic formation can help to answer this question. Part of Carr's status within the fan community can be attributed to some of the qualities noted above, as he exists as a liminal figure, a part of the final days of 'classic Kiss' but never fully integrated into the symbolic aura surrounding this incarnation of the band, and simultaneously achieving a kind of natural mythos through his undeniably tragic death. Within fan discourse, Carr is often posed as 'one of us', as a normal guy lucky and talented enough to wind up in Kiss. As one fan put it on his internet shrine to Carr, '... he was so down-to-earth, he never really considered himself a star or any better than any of us'. In the same vein, much of Carr's appeal seems to be rooted in the sense of identification fans have with his position. As another fan explains on his tribute website,

> My recent defeat of skin cancer makes me feel I have a sort of special connection with him. Eric should be an inspiration to all of us to live life to the fullest and experience every moment. His life should show us that if we have a talent or a dream, that we should follow it. Eric is an example to us all that we should never take anything for granted, and always let our creative spirits fly.

Although there is a similarity with much of the self-esteem discourse in previous sections, the key difference is that it is not derived from a sense of the band as 'Elders' or 'Gods of Thunder' offering wisdom, but rather from the very human struggles of one member.

That said, one of the most interesting developments in the fan community has been the attempts to include Carr in a revamped Kiss mythology, creating a place for him that was never really present during his lifetime. This is evident in the decision to include a cameo appearance by Carr, in full Fox regalia, in recent issues of the *Psychocircus* comic. In an interview, Todd McFarlane, the founder and head of the publishing company responsible for the comic, mentioned that he had received a number of letters asking that Carr be included, and in issue #10, Carr makes his first appearance. In issue #15, the Carr character appears for the last time, eulogized with the following:

> On the day he died, all the nation mourned, and his name was given a place of honor in the pages of history. And the Elder gods looked down on him with pride, and wrote his name in the stars, so that he should never be forgotten. And so it was from that day to now... and till the end of the world. [ellipses in original]

While the inclusion of Carr in the comic book reflects an official acknowledgment of his role in the group, there had already been similar efforts made within the non-commercial fan media. As mentioned, he appears in Sherman's *A World Without Heroes* and serves along with the original members of the group in their war against Blackwell and their pursuit of membership in the Council of the Rose. Carr is also present in a number of other pieces of fan fiction, such as 'Val Kyrie's' short story 'Twist of Shadows'; here, he appears as 'a person who possessed the magics that had been lost (with the departure of original drummer Criss), but a darkness claimed him for itself and took his life'. In 'Kisstory 2''s Creatures of the Night', another piece of short fiction, Carr battles with former Kiss replacement members Vinnie Vincent and Mark St. John and is saved by Ace Frehley, who 'use(s) his teleportation powers to zap Eric into another Universe'. Later, he returns from 'the anti-matter universe' to recruit the rest of the band into his cosmic battle, and with their help banishes Vincent and St. John forever. In both of these examples, Carr is given the kind of magical powers that had been conferred upon the original four members of the band in the comic books and the television film, and is thus integrated within this fantastic dimension.

The most interesting example of the attempt to situate Carr within a 'Kiss mythology', though, was the campaign to have McFarlane toys (a subsidiary of the comic publisher) create an action figure modeled after Carr's 'Fox' persona. An original series of Kiss action figures were issued in the late seventies and are prized by collectors, and in honor of the band's reunion, two sets of new action figures were created in 1996 and 1998. These sets include a figure for each of the band's four original members, thus excluding Carr. In an attempt to rectify this apparent oversight, Kiss fan 'Essex Dog' launched 'The Eric Carr Action Figure Campaign' to try to convince McFarlane Toys to create a Carr figure. In his campaign literature, Essex offers some suggestions for the figure: that it featured his original 1980 costume, that he should be supplied with magical drumsticks and that proceeds from sales of the figure be donated to a cancer charity. This literature also includes a 'plan for getting an Eric Carr action figure made' and suggestions for fans writing letters in support of the campaign (e.g., 'keep it nice!', and 'don't mention the campaign'). Interestingly, some fans had already created homemade Eric Carr action figures using commercially available figures and modifying them to look like Carr; one, created by fans Chris and Cherie Legg, is displayed on their web site, along with other examples of Kiss-inspired art work.

The desire to have Carr's status recognized in an action figure reflects the peculiar significance that merchandising and material artifacts hold among Kiss fans, most of whom collect Kiss-related objects. Honoring Carr with an action figure thus serves as a means of incorporation within the symbolic field of Kiss, as a way of acknowledging his role in the group's career, and as a dramatization of his ascension from regular guy to tragic hero. Here, the action figure serves as an icon in the narrow sense of the term, as a material representation of a larger set of spiritual beliefs, and while it may seem quite odd that such meaning should be attached to a plastic toy, one needs to consider the absolutely paramount role merchandising has played in the career of Kiss, and especially in attracting fans. While rare, it is not unknown for fans to have a primary interest in the merchandise and only a minor interest in the music. Secondly, such merchandise, and especially the action figures, is crucial to the dissemination of the mythology described throughout this section.[5]

While Carr is the subject of numerous tributes as well as the aforementioned action figure campaign, the Kiss community is marked by the simultaneous presence of a figure serving in nearly the opposite role. I had mentioned Carr's fictional battle with former Kiss members

Vinnie Vincent and Mark St. John, and it is Vincent who has become a kind of pariah for Kiss fans, epitomizing a set of personal attributes – disloyalty, 'suspect' sexuality, whininess, self-destructiveness – that stand in direct contrast to the values permeating the discourse surrounding the band. Vincent was only a member of Kiss for a few years, from late 1982 until 1985, a period that included the last year of the band's makeup era, and one generally held in low esteem by fans. There was little about Vincent's time with Kiss that would seem likely to explain the reaction he now provokes among many fans; his sins, it seems, came after his dismissal from the band.

Vincent sued the band for non-payment of royalties in the late eighties, an act viewed by some fans as a form of betrayal. For example, Rick Faidley, a longtime fan who describes Kiss as 'a driving force in my life', told a Kiss fan organization '... as for Vinnie Vincent, he can kiss my ass. No real Kiss member would of done [sic] what he did to the boys'. Additionally, Vincent has been critical of the band in interviews (not particularly surprising given his firing in 1985), another factor in raising the ire of fans already angered by Vincent's replacement of the very popular Ace Frehley. The members of Kiss have also fueled the animosity toward Vincent with their own public criticism, as in Simmons' attack on Vincent as ungrateful and self-destructive in the popular *Kisstory* video released in 1992. Even before the resurgence of Kiss as a major act in 1996–97, criticism of Vincent had become a major element in fan discourse; in early 1996, fanzine editor and moderator of a web-based Kiss mailing list Chris Dessing was forced to bar 'Vinnie bashers' from the list, as their complaints were simply occupying too much space.

Most of the criticism directed at Vincent centers around the themes noted above: his ingratitude (financial and personal) to the band and its fans; his lack of talent, particularly when compared to his replacement Bruce Kulick and especially his predecessor Frehley; his erratic, seemingly self-destructive personal behavior measured against the anti-alcohol, anti-drug ethos of Simmons and Stanley; his apparent lack of macho credentials and the subsequent questioning of his professed heterosexuality. As Walser notes in his wider analysis of the heavy metal genre, the last critique is common among fans confronted with apparent deviations from the hyper-masculine gender norms of the genre (Walser, 1993, pp. 130–131). In the specific case of Vincent, such complaints are often particularly ugly and unabashedly homophobic, although a number of fans explicitly distance themselves from this line of criticism. Others, however, justify it in terms of a question of honesty, with a concern that if Vincent were not heterosexual, then the songs he wrote for the band – largely standard hard-rock heterosexual fantasies – would somehow be 'lies'. This standard, however, certainly seems odd when applied to a band that has always embraced the fantastic, and is not applied to other Kiss songwriters. Similarly, Vincent is often referred to by his real name, 'Vincent Cusano', though this mode of address is not used for other band members, all of whom use altered names. The impetus here seems to be toward an unmasking of Vincent, one involving more than just the literal disconnection from a fantasy persona – after all, the band as a whole made this move in the eighties – and turns upon an attack on Vincent's suitability for participation within a community unified around the model of self-assertion described above.

In this sense, particularly, Carr and Vincent serve in truly complementary roles as figures of identification and abjection, respectively. Both are humanized: Carr through his modesty, accessibility, and ultimately his mortality, a positive gesture; Vincent through a highly negative process of debunking, in which he appears as down-to-earth in the worst ways, as a caricature of selfishness and weakness. This humanization is significant because it gives both figures a peculiar connection with the fans in that they are not – and Vincent will presumably never be – accorded status as full members of 'Kiss', but rather exist as aspirants to this higher level. In this light, the aforementioned decision by the crew of the Athens High School production of *The Elder* to name 'the boy' after Carr makes sense as more than just a nominal tribute; Carr's place in the group itself has been discursively positioned as that of an acolyte to an Elder, the same position reflected in many of the fans' remarks about themselves. In this sense, the aforementioned fictional fates of both Carr and Vincent are telling, with Carr returning from the dead and Vincent banished to 'the prison of Venus where (his) powers could not harm anyone'. In yet another piece of fan fiction, 'Unity' by Jeffrey Baker, Carr makes a similar return from the afterlife when his talisman is reactivated in the band's battle with 'Dr. Doom'. In these examples, the religious overtones that run through a good deal of the lore surrounding the band become explicit, with Carr's dutiful sacrifice rewarded accordingly. Through a kind of mediated piety and iconic identification, Kiss fans are invited to follow a similar if rather less fantastic path in the service of the Kiss Army. In the following sections, I will examine some of the implications of this symbolic world and its participants, particularly as they reflect upon the larger core issues of media and identity.

'Fractured mirror': Kiss fans, identity and media culture

In the analysis that follows, I will make a claim that Kiss fandom, and the various discourses and practices upon which it is based, involves a unique and particularly intense form of symbolic self-construction. However, before moving directly to some of the dynamics of this process, I want to consider an alternative understanding of the Kiss phenomenon that may be analytically tempting but ultimately fails to comprehend the depth, in a subjective sense, of this culture. Such an approach would regard the culture of the Kiss Army as a kind of carnivalization of social norms, and as a grotesque parody of respectable culture. There is certainly a good deal of support for such an understanding; think, for example, of the monstrous spectacle of the Kiss concert experience with its fire-breathing, blood-drooling excesses and the folklore of taboo-smashing degeneracy that surrounded the band, with its tales of sexual exploits, satanism and animal cruelty. Likewise, the lyrical content of much of Kiss' music features a similarly excessive celebration of the earthiest aspects of youth cultural fantasies, with heavy doses of sex, drinking and violence. Even the makeup itself is reminiscent of clowns, masked professional wrestlers and other figures of cultural liminality. All of this is quite consonant with a Carnivalesque tradition, and the academic analysis inspired by the same that has extended from Bakhtin's groundbreaking work on Rabelais to John Fiske's more recent analysis of television's *Rock'n'Wrestling*. Indeed, much of Fiske's analysis of that entertainment spectacle would appear to be applicable to Kiss as well, with its mocking of authority, celebration of cartoonishly excessive masculinity and intensely participative audience (Fiske, 1989, pp. 82–104). These qualities are certainly a large part of the appeal of Kiss' reunion tours, particularly for audience members whose interest in the band is primarily nostalgic or campy. Likewise, Fiske's conclusion that, 'traces of the carnivalesque remaining in today's popular culture are unlikely to have any direct politically transformative effects...', would also seem appropriate to an understanding of any such effects related to Kiss fandom. However, in addition to these political limits, Fiske's analysis tends to draw other, more subtle boundaries around his analysis, boundaries closely related to some of the concerns regarding Fiske's work raised in Chapter 1.

Fiske's scholarship on the carnivalesque elements of *Rock'n'Wrestling* is based primarily on textual analysis – albeit a carefully historicized and very thorough one – with some additional attention to audience practices. What is absent, though, is a sense of the symbolic engagement that is an important dimension of the audience experience and one that may not register, with any obviousness, in immediate audience practices and certainly cannot be deduced wholly from a text itself. While this analytical thinness was discussed in earlier sections, I risk repeating myself here because it is in precisely this area that the reading of Kiss-as-carnivalesque becomes problematic and thus provides a nice demonstration of the importance of a more deeply hermeneutic approach. Kiss fandom, it seems, involves more than just a set of texts and the practices they may engender. It also involves processes of self-development, or what I will characterize as a kind of gradual symbolic inhabitation.

I want to return here to Ernst Tugendhat's discussion of the ways that the Meadian I/me structure becomes engaged in a kind of quest for a generalized other, Mead's 'higher sort of community', that might enable self-realization and reconcile the demands of the 'I' from the inevitably normative and conventional structure of the 'me'. It is important to remember that, as Kögler reminds us, such a process can only proceed symbolically; the act of generating a relation to self involves a relation to symbols, and it is this process that one finds in the self-identifications and self-reflexive practices (e.g., aesthetic productions, autobiographical 'Kisstories') so prevalent in the symbolic universe of the Kiss Army. While the connection between the kind of communities Mead had in mind – from children's baseball teams to the League of Nations – and the mass mediated, consumer-driven world of rock fans may seem absurdly remote, the case of Kiss fan culture suggests that self-generating practices need not be limited to a predictable collection of institutions.

Take for example the discourse that has emerged in response to *(Music from) The Elder*, a work that explicitly dramatized the quest for self-knowledge and self-realization, a likely reason why it is held in such esteem within the fan community. As important as this textual theme may be, *The Elder* itself becomes additionally significant as an important resource for a similar, if less dramatic, self-identification on the part of many fans. Recall the words of the Athens High School crew that produced *The Elder* musical, who found analogies to their own struggle to realize the production in a 'tale of belief in yourself'. LaRose's recasting of the narrative in the form of an epic poem highlighting the themes of purging fears that might contaminate the self, and of becoming aware of one's own autonomous will is another example. The aesthetic re-production of *The Elder*, even in Dale Sherman's more fragmented, bricolaged version, is evidence both of the power of this primary text for fans and for its oddly homologous status as fertile ground for exegetical labor and resultant site of self-identification.

Perhaps *The Elder* seems like a slightly unfair example, almost too tempting in its parallels with the fan experience; this appearance of singularity, though, is diminished when one considers many of the other attributes of Kiss culture noted above. The narratives of overcoming resistance from non-fans or even Kiss-haters, the fearsome reputation and associated folklore surrounding the band and the continual emphasis upon the unique, proudly deviant status of the Kiss fan within a larger culture all point to the centrality of experiences directly connected to issues of identity construction in this symbolic world. That these activities so often depend upon a fragmented practice of pulling a variety of sometimes disparate semiotic threads together recalls both Foucault's pre-Christian subject and more generally the postmodern self of contemporary social psychology (e.g., Gergen and Lifton). As eclectic as these practices may seem, they are aimed at constructing a symbolic space that would allow for the generation of a fulfilled and in some sense unified identity, the goal, however contingent, of the process described by both Mead and Tugendhat.

Of course, the very concept of this kind of happy destination for the self, the site of I/me convergence, is at heart a utopian one, and I will argue that this distinctly utopian dynamic is particularly evident in three notable aspects of the Kiss universe: the construction of self and community histories, the role of commodified material objects and the hyper-masculine gender dynamics. Here again, I would return to an earlier theme regarding both Foucault's and Mead's sense of the importance of the aesthetic attitude (to use the Meadian term) in self-construction, as well as Mead's additional analysis of the aesthetic dimension within social experience as one reflective of the possibility of a future perfection. I would argue that one finds instances of the fleeting and intermediate 'delight of consummation' continually referenced within the Kiss fan culture, and that these instances are inextricably related to the symbolic quest described above.

This kind of future-directed attitude, as Mead additionally reminds us, is nevertheless always dependent upon a kind of historical reconstruction, one using materials 'drawn from the storehouses and quarries of the past' (Mead, 1938, p. 456). The 'Kisstory', as evident in the examples discussed above, works in precisely this manner, as in Brad's miraculous awakening from his coma and in the self-descriptions of individuals who engaged in physical fights to defend their honor as Kiss fans. Such narratives may have a somewhat nostalgic cast – particularly the many that deal with childhood experiences – but they are almost always posed in terms of the present reality of maintaining one's devotion to the band. This becomes keenly important in light of the resurgence of the band's mainstream popularity, in which maintaining a distinct fan identity becomes imperiled. In this case, it may be useful to draw a distinction between the *nostalgic* attitude, one that involves the often ironic production of a historical gestalt out of present materials, with the aforementioned *aesthetic* attitude, one that is centered upon the nearly opposite task of the imaginative construction of a future out of historical materials. While the former, through an ironic and temporal distancing, tends not to involve any substantive degree of self-commitment, the latter depends precisely upon the ability for a deeper inhabitation of a symbolic community, upon what dramaturgical sociologists might describe as the 'organismic involvement' and subsequent 'preemptiveness' of this role position. Such a distinction is critical, then, in understanding the ways that Kiss fans are able to retain a sense of distinction and deploy narratives of self-development to reinforce this in the face on an increasingly diffused symbolic status for the band and a similarly unstable larger cultural economy. The 'Kisstory' thus serves both as an explanatory mechanism – explaining the generation of one's current status – and as a potent mythological narrative. These narratives are often accounts of a symbolic consummation, of one's journey to full participation within the Kiss Army, a process predicated on a union of the individual and the community.

While the 'Kisstories' reflect the use of personal experiences to fashion narratives of selfhood, material objects related to the band are also implicated in a similarly utopian-aesthetic discourse. Recalling Joas' point that the Meadian role-play is not limited to one's position in relation to an other in purely human terms but also involves the perspectival relationship with inanimate objects, one finds a particularly interesting relationship with such objects within the world of Kiss fans. Take for example the campaign to have an action figure created in the image of Eric Carr, in which symbolic inclusion within the Kiss mythology becomes registered through the creation of a commodity. Here, Carr's death achieves an additional significance, as a material icon is thus allowed to serve as a substitute presence, occupying the symbolic slot that Carr can no longer hold; while homemade Carr figures can be and are constructed, these lack the universality and breadth of circulation of a commercial figure and thus do not possess the generalized recognition that is an important aim of the campaign itself. In this light, the suggestion that any proceeds from the figure be donated to a cancer charity becomes particularly important as it allows the action figure to be situated both as part of a larger economy of exchange, thus enjoying the universality of the mass produced object, and as benevolent. This positioning is significant as it works to mitigate the potential impression of greed associated with the enormous marketing apparatus connected to Kiss; even hardcore fans will often admit that they find the level of merchandising excessive.[6] The proposed Carr action figure, then, would serve as a mechanism for Carr's symbolic inclusion but would not violate his memory with another cheap cash-in.

The tendency to be suspicious of the profit motive may be relatively unusual in regard to official products offered by the band, but it is common among fans exchanging various personal materials. This is evident in a series of messages posted to the Kiss Army mailing list in 1996; among other functions, the list serves as a marketplace for fans selling Kiss items (especially bootleg audio and video tapes). One fan offered a particularly desirable live performance video for sale at $20, and received a number of angry responses regarding the price, which was perceived as excessive. One member even itemized the approximate cost of producing such a tape (e.g., duplication, tape cost, postage) and came to the conclusion that the seller was making a considerable profit – about $12. This was considered inappropriate behavior among fellow fans, a violation of the type of economic egalitarianism quite common among many music fan communities, including Kiss fans. The latter are somewhat unique, however, in that such egalitarianism is combined with a particularly iconic attachment to material objects and a willingness to dedicate considerable economic resources toward the collection of materials, and in some cases the construction of a merchandise 'shrine'. Thus, the objection in this case stems purely from the fact that this was an intra-fan economic exchange; some profit would be both expected and accepted if it were an official product, but among fans such a practice is considered unethical, reinforcing the sense that within the Kiss Army, all are equals. The exceptions to this rule, of course, are the band and its official organs, a contradiction that will be explored more thoroughly below.

First, though, I want to move to the third dimension of this utopian dynamic, one involving the linkage of Kiss fan identities with a hypermasculine sexuality. The band, as mentioned, has continually utilized sexual themes – usually male heterosexual fantasies – in song lyrics, videos and promotional materials. In addition to the satanic lore described above, there are numerous sexual legends surrounding the band, particularly Simmons. The most notorious and widely disseminated of these legends concerns his collection of pornographic photos of various groupies and other sexual partners, alleged to number in the thousands (Lendt, 1997, p. 45). The band has always worked hard to maintain this super-stud image; recently, reporters were told the band carried 5,000 condoms on tour, in addition to the usual gear. For some of the most devoted fans, an intense attachment to a similarly hyperbolic sexuality assumes an important part of this identity. In a particularly striking variant of the Kisstory, 'Ray' offered the following tale of a kind of sexual communion with the band,

> this is funny... I once met a stripper/dancer that appeared on the last tour for the song 'Take it Off' (they had strippers on stage, ya know). Anyway we got to talkin and I found out that she had given Gene a blow job and fucked him one of the nights she was on stage. 'Movin' along, comin on strong, I was getting drunk!' (Ace-Wiped Out) [this is a reference to the lyrics of a song on Frehley's 1978 solo album] and the next thing I know, I fucked her later that night! So I can say that I fucked someone that Gene Simmons has! (as a sidenote, the condom worked, I've been tested and all is well! Hehe!) [parenthetical comments in original.]

This tale is quite remarkable for several reasons. First, the homoerotic implications of the story are quite transparent – essentially, second-hand sex with a member of the band through the 'medium' of the stripper – and interesting given its mixture with masculine braggadocio and the band's relentlessly heterosexual aura. Beyond this, though, there is the very interesting incorporation of song lyrics within the narrative, rendering the episode a mixture of personal recollection and intertextual reference. Stereotypically postmodern of course, but also of interest for the ways that the lyrical content is given a direct personal significance. Not only is Ray taking the place of Gene Simmons (in the 'fucking') but he is also expressing himself through the voice of Ace Frehley, and thus he experiences a kind of double integration, physical and discursive, within the symbolic milieu of the band. In an almost literal sense, Ray occupies the (symbolic) place of the other, and thus achieves, however fleetingly, the kind of unification dramatized in both the self-esteem discourses surrounding texts like *The Elder* and in the coming-to-selfhood narratives of personal Kisstories, fan fiction and the *Psychocircus* comic book series.

Of course, all of this fantastic hyper-masculinity raises the issue of women fans and their relationship with this aspect of Kiss culture;

while, as mentioned, they are greatly outnumbered by men, there are certainly many female fans. Obviously, the kind of jubilant identification one finds with a fan like Ray would be much more difficult, culturally, for the female fan. In some cases, female members of the Kiss Army simply take the band members as objects of sexual desire; Stanley, playing the role of the erotically-charged 'Starchild' and the most conventionally handsome member of the band, seems to inspire the greatest following in this respect. However, this rather standard rock and roll fan-performer dynamic is actually less prevalent than might be expected given the sexual emphasis of much of the music. More commonly, women fans, and particularly those with a fairly deep involvement with the culture surrounding the band, tend to focus on other aspects of this culture. As evident from the above analysis, there is a symbolic richness to the world of Kiss fans that is wide enough to enable an affective investment not dependent upon an engagement with all of its major components. However, there is a sense that such fans are denied a full integration within the symbolic milieu of the band, a key aspect in the utopian dimension of Kiss fandom. The homophobic aspersions cast at Vinnie Vincent certainly support this assessment by utilizing doubts about Vincent's heterosexuality – and particularly a resultant contradiction with his songwriting – as one criterion for banishing him from full status as a member of the band. So perhaps it is not surprising, then, that the final verse of the final song on *(Music from) The Elder*, the aforementioned 'I', concludes with the line 'I just need a will of my own/and the balls to stand alone'. While a 'will' can be made available to any fan and is certainly an important part of much of the discourse described previously, the requirement of 'balls' creates a difficulty for many female fans. The strategies emerging in response to this situation, collusion through a rechanneling of sexual desire toward the group, or more commonly a simple avoidance of sexuality as a major component of fandom, offer a way around this dilemma but it remains nonetheless. While one should not overlook the importance of masculinity (and a particularly narrow variant of it) as a component in the culture surrounding Kiss, I would point out that it may actually be less so here than with any number of other major rock acts. Despite the textual and folkoric evidence that this is a highly gendered discursive formation, the overall framework nonetheless revolves around a more generic fantasy of fully realized, empowered and autonomous selfhood.

This fantasy, which I have described as both aesthetic and utopian, is also shrouded in a religiosity that would initially seem unusual for a band more commonly associated with a culture of low brow commercial vulgarity. There are the obvious nods to the spiritual, of course, in song titles like 'God of Thunder' and 'God Gave Rock and Roll to You', Simmons' references to the 'Kisstianity' of fans and the voluminous discourse surrounding *(Music from) The Elder*. Also, in a much publicized media stunt and wacky twist on the Eucharist, vials of blood collected from the band members were poured into the ink used for the first printing of the original 1977 Marvel Kiss comic book (Swenson, 1978, p. 34). Even Ray's tale of shared sexual experiences suggests a kind of bodily communion with one's idol. Beyond these rather obvious, and in the case of the former, calculated nods to the sacred, there is a second, more subtle connection involving the ways in that a deep, hermeneutic – used here with its original Biblical inflection – engagement with Kiss culture mirrors religious discourses, and this involves the negotiation of a number of particularly intense symbolic and material contradictions.

The first is the obvious and aforementioned disparity between the band's mainstream popularity and the fans' sense of uniqueness, individualism and social risk. Of course, this can be mitigated with a deeper appreciation of the band and a thorough involvement in more obscure fan activities, but these passions cannot completely erase a certain discrepancy here. Secondly, there is the rather striking material contradiction of fans dedicating themselves to a relentlessly profiteering commercial organization while simultaneously taking a stand against intra-fan economic exploitation. Lastly, there is the dilemma of taking what were often childhood fantasies accepted as truth – regarding the band's supernatural personas, the folklore surrounding them, and so on – and converting these into a more distant and explicitly symbolic mythology. The last of these disparities is particularly unique to Kiss fans, while the others have a greater general applicability to serious fans of a variety of rock bands. I would argue that, in a parallel to the functioning of a good deal of religious discourse, Kiss fandom is particularly intense *because of* (rather than *in spite of*) these contradictions. Although there are certainly some attempts made to overcome these contradictions through a process of rationalization, as in the attempts to separate true fans from 'wannabes', there is little evidence of much effort in this regard. Rather, such contradictions seem to be largely overwhelmed by the affective intensity and symbolic plenitude associated with Kiss fandom. Interestingly, Lifton points out that particularly intense religious orientations tend to flourish in the face of encroaching identity fragmentation and that such orientations restore, at least temporarily, a stability to the self (Lifton, 1993, pp. 202–205). I think that a similar, albeit less dramatic process is at work with Kiss fans, who must cope with the difficulty of managing the type of contradictions noted above.

Here, recent work by Zizek can shed some light on the ideological ramifications of such seemingly paradoxical self-identifications. Zizek notes that rather than being frustrated by inconsistency and contradiction, ideological interpellation is actually enabled by what he calls a 'pre-ideological kernel of enjoyment' that acts as 'the last support of ideology' (Zizek, 1989, p. 124). He later supplements this with an analysis of what he terms 'symbolic efficiency', the degree to which a merely existent or shared object becomes registered with 'the big other' and thus attains a level of performative power (Zizek, 1999, pp. 322–334). In this analysis, Zizek makes the point that a certain gap between reality and the symbolic is actually critical to such a process of registration, noting that the gap can serve to intensify identification, as long as it remains largely if ineffectively hidden and not acknowledged overtly (Zizek, 1999, p. 331). In this scenario, subjectification is not predicated upon a sort of perfect identification with the symbolic, but instead on an always incomplete process in which aspects of the real – in the Lacanian sense – seep through; this instability thus creates a level of tension necessary for the intensification of symbolic attachments.

Zizek additionally argues that this process of attachment is increasingly difficult, not just because the subject is postmodernistically dispersed or drifting, but also because the symbolic stability of the 'big other' – the symbolic field that allows an identity to achieve meaning – has become greatly undermined (Zizek, 1999, p. 330). There can be very little of the tension needed for intense symbolic attachment without this kind of symbolic grounding, as it provides a unity against which the more chaotic real can operate. On this point, Zizek is certainly in accord with Mead's aforementioned sense of the 'me' as the foundation upon which any 'I', which can only be accessed as a 'me', could possibly function. The relevance of this point to the often intense symbolic attachments evident among Kiss fans is that the task of producing a symbolic other upon which such tensions might take hold becomes one of considerable effort, in intellectual, emotional and logistical terms. It is only at that point that any enabling contradictions can even appear – the aforementioned question of profiteering is moot without the sense of an egalitarian Kiss Army – and that the kind of defiant self-affirmation characteristic of this symbolic formation attains an affective potency.

Zizek, concentrating on the psychoanalytical and philosophical implications of this apparent shift in processes of symbolic attachment, has relatively less to say about the linkages of these changes to wider social formations. However, some of the same premises are picked up by theorists more directly concerned with the social dimensions of mass media, which will allow for the resituation of the present analysis of the 'Kiss world' within the context of a media culture. Baudrillard's aforementioned work on these developments provides such an analysis, albeit with the limitations noted in Chapter 1, and one that shares a good deal with Zizek. In a recent interview, Baudrillard raises the stakes on Zizek's more modest claims, arguing that the impossibility of a meaningful sense of subjectivity leaves only a 'pathetic dream' of identity as the site of subjective investment (Baudrillard, 1998, p. 49). The reasoning here is similar to Zizek's – a demise in the ability to produce some distance from a symbolic other – but with the additional specification that such a shift is largely the result of media saturation (Baudrillard, 1998, p. 50); this point logically follows his earlier work on 'profuse otherness' and hyper-reality. For Baudrillard, there is no mirror in which a self might be recognized, not even the 'shattered mirror' of alienation (Baudrillard, 1998, p. 50). While there is undoubtedly a certain resonance in this rather drastic claim, I chose to title this section 'Fractured Mirror' both in reference to the title of a song by Kiss guitarist Ace Frehley and, more significantly, because such a process of other-derived self-construction is indeed evident in the case at hand.

As with the earlier theoretical work, Baudrillard is useful here as pole marking a limit-point of contemporary forms of subjectification as opposed to a factual diagnosis of cultural conditions. In this light, three aspects of the hermeneutic practices evident in the culture of Kiss fans – all tied to the question of media – reflect an attempted evasion of the grim Baudrillardian fate. The first involves the creation of symbolic distance through the production of secondary discourses and objects, such as the aforementioned poems, novels and even handmade action figures. In this case, individuals can reshape the symbolic contours of the field of self-identification – as Zizek notes, this region is always subject to contestation (Zizek, 1999, p. 332) – in ways that preclude its reduction to Baudrillard's 'video-stage' (Baudrillard, 1998, p. 50). If fandom demanded a complete and unmodified immersion within the symbolic positioning offered by official discourses, then the result would be the sort of 'profuse otherness', akin to perfect Althusserian interpellation, described above. However, this is clearly not the case; there is a process of selection and modification of discourses at work here that demands a deeper sense of subjective engagement as well as an inevitable friction in the hermeneutic engagement.

Secondly, shifts in the ways that Kiss is positioned within a larger popular culture, most notably those associated with the recent reunion, frustrate the kind of affective ubiquity that Baudrillard identifies, and break the uniformity of otherness. As noted above, different practices tend to spring up in response to the dispersion of meaning attached to following the band, and in demonstration of the point made by Lifton and others, new forms of community-definition and subsequent self-definition are thus possible. For the Baudrillardian condition – or for that matter Jameson's social schizophrenia – to really take hold, such practices must not appear, or at least never attain a reasonable coherency or effectiveness. The evidence, however, suggests that while there may be a general weakening of the ability for such forms of self-investment to take place, there is nonetheless a real danger in failing to recognize that they do persist; contrary to both Zizek and Baudrillard, otherness, in the sense of a meaningful site of self-location, shows a surprising resilience.

This is partially an issue of some of the assumptions guiding the analysis at hand. One advantage of a neo-Meadian understanding of the subject is that Mead's aforementioned temporal philosophy enables one to escape from theories of a 'perpetual present' that are foundational to Baudrillard's and Jameson's perspectives. Earlier in this chapter, I noted the importance of a historical reconstruction of the past – usually involving one's early fan experiences – in the production of the 'Kisstory'. While this certainly is not the kind of historicism that Jameson may desire (as expressed in his theoretical motto 'always historicize'), it is also not the kind of ahistorical schizophrenia he laments, nor is it really consonant with Baudrillard's viral symbolic self-similarity. While Kiss fans may exhibit certain signs of the virtual selfhood – with othernesss donned 'like a body suit' – of Baudrillard's analysis, the importance of a reconstructed historical consciousness and the subsequent narrativization of self-construction works against this, creating an autobiographical singularity. Again, this does not necessarily diminish the affective intensity of the symbolic arrangement, but, to return to Zizek's point, it allows for a tension that can increase the degree of attachment to this type of fan identity. As Holstein and Gubrium have recently argued, autobiographical self-construction is a key strategy for many individuals coming to terms with the increasingly chaotic environment and the consequent challenges to identity formation (Holstein and Gubrium, 1999, pp. 10–14).

What does any of this mean to an understanding of media audiences, and especially, rock audiences? I began this chapter with a discussion of the work of Frith and Grossberg on the significance of rock music within a larger cultural economy, and I want to return to this material in light of the above analysis. Consider Frith's description of the rock experience as offering a form of self-recognition and a transcendence of the everyday. This is demonstrated superbly in the experience of Kiss fans, and by situating such experiences in terms of an intensely hermeneutic relationship with a formidable and symbolically rich field of otherness, one can move the analysis of this dynamic further. For example, Frith's point that rock makes possible an 'alternative experience of social forces' holds a particular resonance for the fans described above in that the fantasies of social autonomy, singularity, and communal equality are reflective of a particularly potent manifestation of this attempt to create a sense of specialness, to use Frith's term.

Grossberg, though, wants to ask a less internally subjective question in his analysis of rock culture – 'does rock matter'? In other words, what are the potential effects of an affective investment in the rock formation? As mentioned, Grossberg concludes that rock culture ultimately offers only a 'simulacrum' of revolution, connecting his analysis with Fiske's similar (if more optimistically inflected) point about the politics of the popular carnivalesque. I would not quibble with either as there seem to be few direct political implications to rock fan practices in general and more specifically those described above. However, leaving the analysis at the level of the directly political does not seem to be a particularly useful. Indeed, Grossberg ultimately suggests that questions of cultural politics need to be considered in terms of a social plane transected by a variety of forces working to build and dismantle various political alignments. In regard to the specific case of rock and roll, he argues that it 'must be constantly policed, and ways must be found to ensure that it will continue to move only within the lines of a disciplined mobilization of everyday life' (Grossberg, 1997, p. 101). As noted, Grossberg acknowledges that rock can provide a space of separation from the everyday – he finds heavy metal exemplary in this regard (Grossberg, 1997, pp. 100–101) – but suggests that such an escape is always futile, always limited. Again, I agree with this diagnosis at the level of explicit politics, but would add that an expanded social analysis, one examining rock's operation on a larger social plane, a 'horizontal' move, needs to be supplemented with a 'vertical' analysis of the modes of subjective engagement involved in the affective investment in rock and roll.

This repeats a point, then, from Chapter 1 regarding the relative flatness of the subjective dimension in 'articulation theory' and a resultant analytical behaviorism, but I think that this question is worth revisiting in light of the specific focus of this chapter. The world of Kiss fans, as the above research indicates, is marked by strong and persistent discourses of self-affirmation and empowerment. More importantly, though, these discourses are often enunciated within a framework of fantasies involving individuality, communal solidarity and egalitarianism and a masculinist sexuality, fantasies operating in the face of – and perhaps because of – significant symbolic contradictions. If, as Grossberg argues, rock acts as a kind of energy, as a force that is commonly though not automatically harnessed to 'a project other than its own', then it is certainly imperative to examine the ways that such a redirection demands the containment and/or the resituation of subjective engagements at a micro-social level as well as within a broader field of macro-social hegemony. In other words, an understanding of the intensely individual symbolic attachments of rock audience members is clearly not irrelevant to the task of making sense of the contingency of any social effectivity (progressive or regressive) for rock culture. In fact, it is likely that the very contingency of such alignments stems at least partly from the intensity, complexity and multiplicity of the forms of self-relation engendered by one's symbolic investiture in a cultural field, particularly one as symbolically rich as the Kiss Army. Respecting the importance of such attachments in the determination of practices is critical if one wishes to retain some sense of the importance of consciousness – whether construed as 'ideology', 'mattering maps' or 'subjectification' – in the generation of social practices. While it is quite clear from Grossberg's work, and from the justifiably esteemed body of Marxist cultural analysis that proceeded it, that macro-social material arrangements have an enormous impact on the ways cultural practices become registered within the political, the very instability of such practices suggests that other factors need to be considered.

In the specific case of Kiss fans, the emphasis on self-realization, particularly in terms of an autobiographical awareness closely tied to adolescent experiences, suggests a peculiarly narrative quality in which the formation of a self becomes a theme in the discourse itself. Here, Toby Miller's argument regarding the particularly intense nature of popular music's relation to identity, and its potential dissonance from the hegemonic force of a 'well-tempered' mode of subjectivity, is relevant. While Miller notes the inherent tension in such potentially though not explicitly 'unruly' modes of self-relation, he does not offer any extended examples of such a tension and concentrates, in his case studies, on more uniformly hegemonic or counter-hegemonic forms of subject production. The case study at hand, though, suggests precisely this tension; clearly, the fusion of a highly commodified culture of consumption and regressive sexual politics with an ethos of liberty, equality and self-determination cannot be comprehended as uniformly dominant or popular – to reference the Fiskean binary – nor as producing either a well-tempered or an unruly social subjectivity. Instead, this mode of subjectivity, like Grossberg's social plane, is marked by the co-presence of a number of often disparate investments, some resistant and others quite compatible with dominant cultural forms.

I would argue, though, that the only way to comprehend such media-engendered subjective arrangements is through an analysis of the hermeneutic dimensions of the audience experience, an approach demonstrated above. Ignoring the ways that individuals become engaged with practices of interpretation, appropriation and self-relation leaves a gap in the analysis that cannot be remedied by mere recourse to the examination of larger social and material factors or by a return to text as a singular object. To return, finally, to the foundational assumptions of hermeneutic sociology, particularly in its neo-Meadian inflection, one can posit a self that is thoroughly social, built upon a meaningful engagement with socially available symbolic formations – formations inevitability provided by and framed by broader material structures – without requiring a reduction to the same. This has a special resonance to this case study in that it examines a form of mass culture with particularly crass connotations. While the culture of the 'Kiss Army' may seem like the last place to look for a meaningful set of mythico-spiritual discourses of self-discovery and overcoming social obstacles, as well as resources for an aesthetic cultivation of selfhood, both are undeniably present.

4
Screen Subjects and Cyber-Subjects: The Case of *Futurama*

Unlike the previous case studies, which began with a brief vignette describing a characteristic event to introduce the focus of the subsequent analysis, I instead begin this final case study with a description of an ongoing ritual rather than a singular occasion. Each week, particularly during the television season when new episodes of a program were shown, fans of the Fox television series *Futurama* could participate in a vigorous, wide-ranging discussion of the latest episode – and the show in general – taking place on the Internet. The venues for this discussion included chat rooms (e.g., the chat area of the *Can't Get Enough Futurama* site), newsgroups (e.g., alt.tv.futurama), web-based fan clubs (e.g., the Yahoo! *Futurama* clubs) and the message boards and fan forums provided by various *Futurama*-based websites (e.g., *The Futurama Chronicles*). Within these forums, audience members offered evaluations, critical exegesis, historical analysis and a broad spectrum of other genres of discourse; the diversity of this discussion was quite impressive, and the overall volume grew rapidly in the time that *Futurama* was on the air.

There are some obvious and significant distinctions between the kind of public event described in the introductions to previous chapters and the more amorphous virtual interaction presented above. Unlike the Freaky Film Festival and the Kiss record release party, which manifest a firm temporal anchoring, the *Futurama* discussions, while linked to the general rhythms of the network television schedule, are not fixed to a specific time. While the live Internet chats do require simultaneous online presence, the other venues provide for participation at any time, giving participants a great deal of flexibility in terms of both sending and receiving messages. At the same time, there is a relative immediacy to the process, in that such messages can appear almost instantly and can be tracked as they emerge with little or no lag between message creation, dissemination and reception.

More significant than the differences in temporal dynamics, though, are the spatial distinctions that separate the case at hand from the previous events. Rather than the public space of the Canopy Club, the location of both of the aforementioned events, the *Futurama* discussions take place across two locations: the material space of the domestic sphere and the virtual space of the cyber-community. The former, the normal location of both the television and the personal computer, carries associations of privacy and separation from the social world. The latter, conversely, is linked to a kind of freedom from normal communicative and material barriers as well as to the expanded set of symbolic possibilities enabled by the virtual. The *Futurama* cyberworld thus engages spaces which are commonly regarded, respectively, as highly conventional and largely asocial (a judgment which is often applied specifically to television as well), and as radically open and free from most forms of social regulation.

These temporal and spatial distinctions are important elements in the larger issue of the impact of new media, and more specifically the ways that such media – and particularly those associated with the phenomenal expansion of the Internet – are changing the composition of the contemporary symbolic environment. Obviously, such changes have a special importance for the central questions of this book, given the paramount importance of this environment for the model of the social self presented in Chapter 1. The purpose of this chapter is to examine the specific dynamics of a final audience formation operating within the virtual culture of the Internet but tied to the older mass medium of television. The analysis begins with a general examination of recent sociological and philosophical speculation upon the impact of new technology on, respectively, the social composition of subjectivity, community formation, youth culture and pre-existing mass media. This is followed by an analysis of specific aspects of the virtual *Futurama* community: the formal dynamics and 'net ready' character of the program itself; the impact of the Internet on the reception of the program; a discussion of the program itself and the secondary discourses produced by audience members in response to it. The chapter concludes with some speculation on the significance and symptomatic value of this audience formation for the understanding of the wider social implications of these changes.

Cyber-subjects and cyberculture

The rise of the Internet as a communication medium and as a social force has been the subject of an overwhelming degree of interest – and simultaneously anxiety – among scholars of contemporary media. The incredibly rapid spread of Internet use and the literally exponential increase in the range of material available online has made the analysis of this medium an exciting and profoundly challenging enterprise. Nonetheless, a significant body of academic research regarding the virtual world has emerged. While this material is remarkably diverse, one notable aspect of much of the recent material is the tendency for scholars – and particularly those with a cultural or philosophical interest in the Internet – to make strikingly dramatic claims regarding the impact of new media. This is certainly reminiscent of some of the similar rhetoric surrounding television, particularly McLuhan's work, but also that of Jacques Ellul, Walter Ong and many others. As with this earlier work, the recent scholarship often falls into a rather monolithically optimistic or pessimistic stance toward new media. In a recent discussion of some of the debates surrounding cyberculture, Andrew Calcutt points to a nearly binary separation of 'knockers' and 'boosters', and notes that the 'knockers' are just as likely to be leftist progressives as anti-technology reactionaries (Calcutt, 1999, pp. 78–80). This division of views is evident in analysis of the specific question of the impact of the virtual world upon the social subject, though there are some analysts who have attempted a more nuanced understanding.

Work on the impact of virtuality on subjectivity has tended to focus on four aspects of this presumed impact: the increasingly fluidity of the subject; the concurrent hybridity and 'multiphrenia' of the subject; the threat to subjective stability; and the simultaneous opportunity for new forms of self-construction and self-realization. Sherry Turkle, one of the earliest and most influential scholars of computer mediated communication, ties the increasingly fluid character of the technologically-inflected self directly to the social psychological perspectives of Gergen and Lifton, discussed in Chapter 1, as well as to other positions in post-structural theory. Turkle writes,

> Thus, more than twenty years after meeting the ideas of Lacan, Foucault, Deleuze, and Guattari, I am meeting them again in my new life on the screen. But this time, the Gallic abstractions are more concrete. In my computer-mediated worlds, the self is multiple,

LIVERPOOL JOHN MOORES UNIVERSITY
LEARNING SERVICES

fluid, and constituted in interaction with machine connections; it is made and transformed by language; sexual congress is an exchange of signifiers; and understanding follows from tinkering rather than analysis... The Internet has become a significant social laboratory for experimenting with constructions and reconstructions of self that characterize postmodern life. In its virtual reality, we self-fashion and self-create. What kind of personae do we make? What relation do these have to what we have traditionally though of as the 'whole' person? Are they experienced as an expanded self or as separate from the self? Do our real-life selves learn lessons from our virtual personae? Are these virtual personae fragments of a coherent real-life personality? (Turkle, 1995, p. 15; p. 180)

Here, Turkle provides a nice gloss on the argument that the Internet and new media in general provide the means for the cultivation of a more fluid sense of self, as well as some of the challenges that arise from this increasingly fluidity.

Tim Jordan, writing more recently, echoes Turkle and describes the ability to cultivate an increasingly flexible identity as a facet of a wider system of 'cyberpower', which would also include social dynamics and the collective virtual imagination (Jordan, 1999, pp. 15–17). Jordan points out that the relations between on- and off-line identities are extremely complex, arguing that 'identity fluidity is a fact of virtual life' and that 'identity is both present in space and different to non-virtual space' (Jordan, 1999, pp. 78–79). For Jordan, the power of identity fluidity is an intrinsically individual form of power and that if one accepts his foundational assumption that '... the virtual community found individuals and not the other way round', this power is thus limited, reshaped and sometimes negated by the social dynamics in which such identities operate (Jordan, 1999, p. 99). Jordan's argument is extremely important, because it reflects a step back from the automatic assumption that a relative flexibility in identity can be extended automatically into a form of subjective freedom, an assumption that ignores not only forms of economic restriction (e.g., access to the Internet) but also the power-laden interactive dynamics within this symbolic environment. Note that Jordan's orientation here – that the 'community found individuals' – is quite consonant with the social hermeneutic paradigm central to my own theoretical position; this will become particularly important later, when a specific community is examined.

One way of understanding the means by which a symbolic network forms and reshapes subjects, particularly in regard to new media and new technologies, is through the metaphor of the 'cyborg', one developed most notably by Donna Haraway. The cyborg epitomizes the second quality described above, the hybrid character of the virtual subject. In Haraway's vision, as J. Macgregor Wise points out, the cyborg is a liberating blend of the human and the non-human (a literal hybrid) and is thus not susceptible to the standard categorical borders – gender, species, etc. – that limit conventional subjects (Wise, 1997, p. 30). Wise goes on to argue that one of the profound difficulties with a view of the cyborg as a figure of liberation is that, echoing the limitations Jordan raises in regard to subjective fluidity, this figure 'still retains strong links to modern institutions, structures, and drives … the cyborg identity is not synthesis of human and technology, but rather is fragmented – the technical and the human elements in constant struggle' (Wise, 1997, p. 42). Again, this is a critical point and one that emerges from a perspective – in Wise's case heavily inflected by Deleuze – that begins not with the individual subject but with the larger material and discursive environment.

While Jordan and Wise raise some very important caveats to the sense that new technology will necessarily provide a greater subjective freedom, there are other perspectives that see an inherent threat to subjectivity itself in the proliferation of new technologies and new media; again, while the Internet is only a part of these technological developments, it is certainly an important one. This threat is posed by radical postmodernists Arthur Kroker and Michael Weinstein as the potential triumph of the ideology of 'recline', which is defined as the moment in which 'contemporary society gives up to the intimidating power of Technology and Culture, and submits, with fitful rebellions, to the process of virtualization' (Kroker and Weinstein, 1994, p. 161). In recline – a pun on 'decline', as in Oswald Spengler's famous 'the decline of the West' – human life becomes reduced to a set of technological prosthesis, and a paralytic state ensues (Kroker and Weinstein, 1994, pp. 41–44). Here, one can see the heavy influence of Baudrillard and the 'triumph of the object' discussed in Chapter 1, although in this case it is tied directly to a 'will to virtuality' (to use Kroker and Weinstein's terminology) and the specific effects of the rise of cyberculture. This position extends some of Wise's and Jordan's wariness about the impact of symbolic/technological systems on subject formation into a full-blown metaphysical reversal in which the individual is completely consumed by the technological – taking the 'org(anism)' out of the cyborg, so to speak.

While Kroker and Weinstein offer an intentionally provocative and extreme view of the impact of the 'information superhighway', their position is reiterated in a somewhat less dramatic fashion by a number of scholars. For example, Raymond Barglow, from a more conventional social psychological perspective, uses a rather different metaphor, comparing the 'endangered' human subject to the dolphin:

> The image of the dolphin, suffering under captivity or destroyed by modern fishing practices, carries the message that something vitally significant about ourselves gets lost in a world that dissects and manipulates nature without understanding it. The sense of loss – the feeling of emptiness when we peer into the mirror to discern who we are – is by no means dispelled by the wealth of factual information made available to us through access to the new technologies. On the contrary, there are many links between technological abundance on one hand, and subjective deprivation on the other (Barglow, 1994, p. 4).

Barglow later argues, in an analysis combining Meadian social psychology, Freudian psychoanalysis and Frankfurt School Marxist approaches, that information technology, and especially computer-based technology, can serve to colonize the self in ways that reduce the subject to an information processing apparatus (Barglow, 1994, pp. 85–86). This echoes Baudrillard's critique of 'artificial intelligence', although Barglow specifically aims his analytical gaze at individuals who are engaged in technological pursuits, both vocationally and for amusement, suggesting that such individuals are at the forefront of a struggle with the colonizing force of new technology (Barglow, 1994, pp. 39–42; pp. 53–54; pp. 83–89).

Finally, Manuel Castells provides a more general sense of the threat to selfhood and fully-formed subjectivity posed by these technological shifts, linking this threat to the fundamentalist obsession with maintaining a stable identity and the need to preserve autonomy in the face of the hybridizing and vaporizing force of 'the net', which is Castells' term for an entire range of global information networks. In this case, rather than the slide into an enervated subject in recline or the emergence of an endangered subject, there is a reverse movement toward an intensely focused, inflexible attachment to identity forms predicated on the refusal of socio-symbolic contamination. 'When the Net switches off the Self', writes Castells, 'the Self, individual or collective, constructs its meaning without global, instrumental reference: the process of disconnection becomes reciprocal, after the refusal by the excluded [from the Net] of the one-sided logic of structural domination and social exclusion' (Castells, 1996, p. 25). Castells' point is especially

important because, unlike Kroker and Weinstein or Barglow, it addresses those who may not be eager participants in the new, virtual world,
and because he mirrors some of Lifton's arguments about the links
between fundamentalist positions – religious and otherwise – and the
imperiled subject (Lifton, 1993, pp. 160–189).

In all three positions described above, then, there is a strong elucidation of the most pessimistic understanding of the status of the social
subject in the face of the technological changes associated with the rise
of the Internet and computer mediated communication. While the
effects may be bi-directional, pushing the subject toward evaporation
on one hand, or obsessive, archaic attachment on the other, the threat
to a stable, self-reflective subject is a consistent concern for many
scholars. As mentioned, this mirrors an earlier set of arguments from
Baudrillard, McLuhan, et. al. regarding another set of technological
innovations associated with mass media, although the terms are
certainly not identical. Additionally, such arguments always exist in
a dialectic of optimism and pessimism regarding new media; while
Turkle, Haraway and others discuss some of the potentially liberating
elements of the information revolution in somewhat abstract terms,
others have provided a more concrete account of this potential.

For example, Jon Katz's *Geeks: How Two Young Men Rode the Internet
Out of Idaho* provides a compelling narrative of personal transformation
enabled by an engagement with the Internet. Katz tells the story of two
young men from rural Caldwell, Idaho, alienated 'geeks' who found a
degree of self-realization and some amelioration from their local social
estrangement through an immersion in the Internet. Katz's book is
notable because it deals explicitly with the translation of net-based
social participation into extra-Internet personal action. Katz's narrative
ends with the protagonists relocating to Chicago and engaging in edu-
cational and vocational pursuits that would have seemed beyond reach
in their earlier, tightly constrained lives. The use of cyberspace as a
mechanism for exploring a personal transformation that is then realized in concrete, real life spaces is an aspect never really addressed in
the more metaphysically-inclined work of other net advocates and suggests – if only through a rather anecdotal ethnography – that the 'net
self' is not necessarily permanently fixed within the conventional
boundaries of cyberspace.

Absolutely critical to Katz's inspirational narrative is the sense that
cyberspace offers new forms of communal engagement for those who
feel alienated from their more proximal concrete community. As with
issues of subjectivity and liberation, this is one of the most contentious

aspects of virtuality. As Calcutt points out, while 'communities' may be quite commonplace on the Internet, they are often predicated upon a set of attributes – non-presence, exclusion, and self-pity – that are antithetical to most conceptions of a communal relationship. Calcutt argues, 'in cyberspace, community and alienation are mutually dependent rather than mutually exclusive, in that the tie that binds the cyber-communitarians together is their alienation from the rest of the world' (Calcutt, 1999, p. 25). Even Esther Dyson, one of the earliest and most enthusiastic advocates of the transformative possibilities of cyberspace, has expressed serious reservations regarding the communal dimensions of the virtual world, arguing that 'community' can become a term of automatic endorsement, overlooking malignant but thriving virtual communities centered on racial and ethnic hatred, for example (Dyson, 1997, pp. 64–65). Barry Wellman and Milena Gulia temper some of these fears, particularly the variety expressed by Calcutt, by noting that the fear of net-based pseudo-communities replacing genuine human contact is itself rather dubious, deploying a utopian model of community that has long passed, if it ever existed (Wellman and Gulia, 1999, p. 187). The debates continue, of course, as the number and scale of such communities increases steadily and dramatically, and are unlikely to be settled through any existent research paradigm.

The question of web-based communities is critical, though, to the larger issues framing this book, as the question of intersubjective relations and the derivation of self from a collection of others is a central attribute of the hermeneutic paradigm. Recall again Tugendhat's insistence on the search for community as a fundamental aspect of the process of actualizing self-reflection as self-assertion; certainly, the 'geeks' of Katz's narrative, trapped in a largely Mormon and geographically remote Idaho community, mirror this quest, atypical as their personal and intellectual journey may be. On the other hand, the dissolution of self and the enshrinement of a kind of alienated pseudo-empowerment described by Calcutt and echoed in the work of Kroker and Weinstein can act as a powerful barrier to the cultivation of any meaningful sense of individual and ultimately generalized others. The relationship with any mediated community will be complicated, of course, by the focus on a community bound by a set of reception practices involving a different – and paradigmatically less interactive – medium. Nonetheless, the question of community as part of cyberspace and as the foundation for a cyber-subject, remains a difficult one.

If the question of net-based communities is contentious, this controversy pales in comparison to the rhetoric regarding the impact of the

Internet upon youth culture, an important issue in light of the heavy contingent of young participants within the *Futurama* virtual community. There is the predictable handwringing over the potential negative effects of the Internet – a more specific version of the general 'youth media' hysteria described in the introduction – a position nicely characterized and critiqued by Katz as '... misguided, exaggerated, invoked by adults mostly to regain control of a society changing faster than their ability to comprehend it' (Katz, 1997, p. 174). Beyond these rather routine concerns, though, the disproportionately youthful composition of Internet users, and especially of Internet enthusiasts, does raise key questions regarding the place that such new media occupy in a broader cultural formation. Don Tapscott, who coined the term 'N-generation' to characterize those who have grown up with computer mediated communication and new media, notes that the 'virtual revolution' is not controlled exclusively or even overwhelmingly by adults; at both technological and cultural levels, children and adolescents have a real impact on the development of the Internet (Tapscott, 1998, p. 50). Indeed, a considerable legal controversy recently emerged when a 16 year old Norwegian adolescent created software which would allow users to share digital video files in much the same manner as the popular and infamous 'Napster' system (itself created by 18 year old Shawn Fanning) for sharing music files. As these and many other examples demonstrate, there is an unprecedented level of participation by youth in the development (as well as the consumption) of a variety of aspects of Internet culture.[1]

Calcutt notes that this has effects which extend beyond the demographic boundaries of age itself, pointing to a kind of 'youthification' (his term) of culture exemplified by the young *zeitgeist* of the virtual world. Calcutt writes,

> Whereas middle age is traditionally associated with substance, stability, and the long term, cyberculture celebrates instantaneity, fluidity, and the use of illicit substances. But these preoccupations are no longer the preserve of youth. Online and off, the people who share these priorities could be 14 or 45. The Generation Gap has been closing for some time now; and in the new terrain of cyberspace it has never really existed. (Calcutt, 1999, p. 156)

While Calcutt is somewhat vague in addressing the consequences of this youth-inflected culture, there are some important ramifications which can be drawn here. The first is that the boundaries between subcultural, sometimes 'oppositional' formations and dominant cultural formations, difficult to discern in the best of circumstances, are now extraordinarily fuzzy. Secondly, the speed of transformation within virtual culture, at technological and socio-cultural levels, one mimicking the traditionally fluid, rapidly evolving character of youth culture, produces a cultural environment that is profoundly unstable. Finally, there may be deeper socio-psychological implications as well. As Turkle argues, adolescents and children of the 'N-generation' tend to cultivate a fundamentally interactive relationship to computer technology, including a willingness to grant a degree of both intelligence (albeit artificial) and psychological depth to the computer itself, treating the machine as a kind of 'demi-person' (Turkle, 1995, pp. 83–85). This relationship, one that is clearly evident in the development of virtual culture, is particularly important to the issues of community and intersubjectivity noted above, in that it implies a shifting distinction between the human and technological. The willingness to accept computers as communicative partners is unquestionably an important element in structuring the symbolic dynamics of web-based cultural formations.

The issue of youth culture is additionally important to the case study at hand in that fan cultures and other communities bound by an enthusiasm for various forms of media reception are particularly prevalent among adolescents and young adults. These communities, including the *Futurama* culture, necessarily reflect an intersection of media, which of course raises an additional set of questions related to the convergence of multiple media flows – broadcast television and the Internet in the case at hand. Thus, I want to briefly explore four dimensions of this encounter: the historical-ideological parallels in the rhetoric surrounding cyber- and televisual culture; the 'double domesticity' implied by their convergence; the metaphysical implications of this union; and the specific dynamics of the virtual fan community.

Lynn Spigel, writing about the development of network television in the U.S., notes the consonance between rhetoric surrounding the rise of television and traditional American ideals. Spigel connects this to earlier fantasies of utopian communication technologies, and points to the belief that television could transcend social space and create a higher level of interpersonal ties (Spigel, 1992, pp. 109–115). While there was, as Spigel notes, a strong dystopian counterpoint to this techno-utopianism, the popular enthusiasm for television – spurred on by the public relations apparati of the major networks – certainly owed a great deal to the ease of connecting this technological innovation to a long-held ideology of progress and democracy. Interestingly, Kroker makes a very similar argument regarding the Internet, suggesting that the U.S. enjoys a particular ideological suitability for participation within the virtual world:

> In America, the World Wide Web is not just a matter of hyperlinks or hypertext, but is a technological latecomer to a society that, in the most profound sense, has always been a Web. Maybe Nietzsche's 'spider web' capturing passing victims in its fine-spun silk, but perhaps something else. The American mind was born hypertext: virtual consciousness that from the time of the Pilgrims to the astronauts has enjoyed a unique telematic ability to effortlessly link between the media-net and personal history... Like it or not, America is the digital future. However, the problem is that we no longer have the ability to love it or leave it. America is not just a physical presence, but a virtual space. (Kroker, 1996, pp. 13–14).

Even compensating for Kroker's Baudrillardian exaggeration, his point that the rapid acceptance of the Internet and virtual modes of discourse in the U.S. can be linked to a longer tradition of the 'will to technology' is useful for the issue of media convergence as it mirrors research regarding the earlier spread of television. Transcending space, creating a wider public sphere, unifying an otherwise disparate nation – the claims of television prophets and Internet gurus are often eerily similar (Spigel, 1992, pp. 111–113; Calcutt, 1999, pp. 126–127; Kroker, 1996, pp. 7–14).

These ideological similarities are particularly important in light of the global dominance of US television and the ability for the Internet to expand this reach; as I will discuss later, *Futurama*, broadcast in a number of nations, was also available to Internet users (whether or not they had access to the broadcast version) through downloadable video files. If, as Spigel and Kroker claim, the structure and dissemination of media are shaped by ideologies central to American culture, then one might understand U.S. domination in terms of economic control of media industries but also in terms of an attitude toward technology and especially, as Kroker argues, toward the individual's relationship with mediated discourse. This is doubly important, of course, when dealing with the interface of two such media.

Also doubled in this relationship is a 'domestic' quality that has long been considered by scholarly analysts as a crucial aspect of television experience (Silverstone, 1994, pp. 24–51; Morley, 1992, pp. 131–170;

Spigel, 1992, pp. 99–135). At one level, the net-linked computer is simply another screen in the home; in the case of 'Web TV' which allows for Internet access through a conventional television, even this distinction vanishes. In fact, it is probably safe to assume that Internet activity is more likely to involve a single individual operating alone, eliminating even the marginal sociality of the family or couple viewing together. Thus, the interactive qualities central to the more optimistic views of virtual culture – and which are undoubtedly present to at least some degree – are often balanced with an asociality that matches or exceeds that associated with television itself. This material aspect of Internet fan participation thus reflects the intensification of a quality associated with individual media, one ironically emerging from the operation of a community.

There may be more abstract ramifications to the intersection of television and the Internet as well. William J. Mitchell describes a more generalized effect of information networks using the metaphor – recall Haraway and Wise – of the cyborg. 'The Net has become a worldwide, time-zone-spanning optic nerve with electronic eyeballs as its end-points' writes Mitchell, who like Spigel and Kroker, connects these developments with longstanding and in this case international fantasies of global compression through mediated communication (Mitchell, 1996, pp. 32–34). Mitchell argues that information networks allow for a kind of universalization of the televisual, thus completing an ideological and material convergence. Jordan adds to this line of argument, pointing to the rapidly expanding capabilities for high-quality video on the Internet and suggesting that this will not only expand the possibilities for reception but also for a more individualized system of television production and distribution:

> It should be clear that if the Internet can provide both video and audio of comparable quality to radio and TV and provide it already embedded in multi-media – and thus already connected to text, other sites, sales possibilities and so on – then the revolution McLuhan envisaged in the 1960s will have in some form happened... The ultimate media deconstruction seems possible with the Internet making everyone not only a publisher but also a TV network as well. Here the hope, for some expectation, is that the Internet will finally prise open the hitherto closed doors of film, video, and TV to everyone. (Jordan, 1999, p. 160)

Jordan's point is particularly interesting in light of some of the claims of earlier scholars, for example Nicholas Negroponte (writing five years

[margin note, left: Universalisation v. judgement!]

[margin note, left: Everyone can do it.]

before Jordan), who argued that television broadcast systems and computer networks were fundamental opposites (Negroponte, 1995, pp. 180–181). Similarly, Tapscott claims that the Internet would pose a serious threat to television viewing, particularly among younger consumers, who preferred the interactivity and variety of the latter (Tapscott, 1998, pp. 26–31). The kind of binary opposition between television and the Internet that informed Negroponte's and Tapscott's Internet boosterism has been proven grossly oversimplified and perhaps even fundamentally wrong by the increasing interface of the two media.[2] It appears that Tapscott's scenario – 'The Web That Ate TV' – is unlikely indeed, at least in the near future (Tapscott, 1998, p. 26).

The audience study that follows concerns more than a general convergence of television and the web, however; it involves the utilization of the latter as a mechanism for forming and supporting a discursive community unified by an interest in the former. There is relatively little work in this area – and none which takes the question of mediated subjectivity as fundamental to audience study – but there are some recent examples of relevant research. Perhaps the most interesting of these is Nancy Baym's study of soap opera fans who use computer mediated communication (primarily Internet newsgroups) to discuss aspects of their favorite programs. Baym identifies several rhetorical modes in these discussions – informing, speculating, criticizing and reworking – and argues that such conversations expand the interpretive possibilities of the audience, provide a secondary form of entertainment and offer a venue for the safe discussion of personal issues (Baym, 1998, pp. 115–128). Andrea MacDonald makes similar claims in her study of science fiction fans who use the Internet to communicate about the genre, adding that the social dynamics of such groups replicate earlier and broader social hierarchies – the marginalization of female voices, discursive domination by 'interpretation leaders' and a splintering into sub-subcultures (MacDonald, 1998, pp. 131–151). While the analyses offered by Baym and MacDonald address some of the unique features of computer mediated fandom, they were researched and written at a time when this mode of fan culture was dominated by newsgroups and Internet 'mailing lists' and before the vast explosion of a more diverse set of outlets for expression and dialogue – the web pages, multi-media sites, FTP (file transfer protocol) repositories and so on – that are currently available to online fan communities. Discussion, if the term is still appropriate, is vastly more complex both in terms of the volume of discourse and in terms of the media used to communicate this discourse; this is particularly important in the case at hand, as the merger of television and Internet-based media has expanded from the largely verbal culture (words about television) described by Baym and MacDonald to a plurality of verbal and non-verbal modes of communication.

Before moving to the specifics of the *Futurama* community, though, I want to recap the implications of a 'cyber-subjectivity' for the larger issue of audiencehood and a hermeneutic social subject. The issues addressed in detail above can be grouped into three general conclusions. The first involves the increasing fluidity and destabilization of the social subject, a process, as mentioned, that reflects an intensification of many of the general claims regarding the status of the subject within a postmodern media culture addressed in Chapter 1, including the potentially positive and negative consequences of this destabilization. Along with this fluidity, there is the tendency for some of the qualities associated with youth culture to be mirrored in the less age-fixed cyberculture. Additionally, there is the potential for a kind of cyborg-subject inherent in the ability to construct relatively autonomous, disembodied forms of selfhood within the virtual world. The second major implication of cybercultural subjectivity involves the spatial reconfiguration of the kinds of symbolic and material regions, to again invoke Goffmanian terminology, that shape the subject. Here there is both the possibility for trans-spatial 'communities' – again, the term itself is controversial in this context – and the compression of social space noted by Katz and others as well as the double domesticity implied by the intersection of television and computer mediated communications. Third and finally, there is the increasingly prevalent convergence of media flows and modes of symbolic participation, in terms of reception and secondary discursive production, and the rapidly intertwining nature of both. An extended analysis of one such convergence occupies the bulk of this chapter, with a return to some of the above issues in the conclusion.

Futurama: net-ready television

For a number of important reasons, *Futurama* provides a particularly interesting example for the examination of many of these issues. First, the program debuted at a time – January 1999 – when media fan groups and discourse about television programs were firmly established elements within the World Wide Web. In fact, even prior to the debut of *Futurama*, there were approximately thirty websites dedicated to the program, sites that expressed considerable anticipation of the program and which provided speculation and information on the contents of forthcoming episodes (e.g., early publicity materials, 'spoilers', etc.). Much of this can be attributed to the status of *Futurama*'s creator, Matt Groening, particularly among fans of the animation genre. Groening, who is best known as the creator of *The Simpsons*, enjoys a reputation as an established television auteur and has a particularly fanatical following within Internet culture. There are literally thousands of Internet sites dedicated to *The Simpsons*, so there was already a precedent for the explosion of the virtual *Futurama* culture; indeed, there are a number of combined *Futurama/Simpsons* websites and a high degree of cross-linkage between sites dedicated to either individual program. This proximity is mirrored in the scheduling of *Futurama* in the U.S.; while it was shifted around the Fox lineup, it normally occupied the same evening programming block as *The Simpsons*. Most recently and until its cancellation, it ran at 7 p.m. EST on Sundays, one hour before the latter program, as a part of Fox's Sunday evening 'animation block'. At the peak, there were about five hundred Websites dedicated exclusively or largely to *Futurama*, though this number was unstable with new sites appearing and old ones vanishing literally every day. The relative ease of launching sites and the converse ease of allowing a site to disappear – many of which are essentially hobbies for fans – makes it extremely difficult to obtain a complete and fixed picture of the size and diversity of the culture.

A second reason for the ease and scale of *Futurama*'s incorporation within Internet fan cultures involves the high degree of demographic overlap between the program's audience and Internet enthusiasts. *Futurama*, unlike *The Simpsons*, did not have a particularly broad following, at least by the standards of network television; at its peak popularity, it finished between 60th and 80th in the Nielsen ratings, drawing about 4% of U.S. households. However, the program did hold a particularly keen appeal for viewers in the 15–30 age group; this is reflected in an especially intense following among college and university students. This demographic segment has a particularly high level of Internet access and usage – students often have free and relatively unfettered access to the Web, for example – and a generally strong degree of technological savvy. The appeal for the tech-minded is confirmed by the appearance of *Futurama* as the cover story for the February 1999 issue of *Wired* (available before the premier episode was aired), among the most prominent publications for those interested in computer technology and the Internet. There is an additional overlap in the fan base for animated and science-fiction programming

(*Futurama* is both) and Internet use, evident in the vast amount of material related to both genres available on the World Wide Web.

In addition to this demographic convergence, the comic science fiction style of *Futurama* allows for a thematic suitability for Internet discourse. As the *Retro Future* website explains, the show's title is a reference to a major attraction at the 1939 World's Fair in New York, 'The Futurama', that purported to explain life in 1960. The show, set in the year 3,000, picks up this theme with a continual stream of references to bizarrely comic technologies (e.g., public suicide booths, pneumatic people movers, the 'smell-o-scope', etc.) that parody popular understandings of potential future technologies. This mirrors, of course, a similar future-gazing obsession both within discourse on the Internet and in wider social discussions of the impact of the Internet and other technological developments. Often, the program resembles an ironic version of the technological boosterism described by Calcutt and maligned by Kroker. The program's animated fantasy milieu also provides the basis for a number of fan-created computer games which have appeared on the web, such as 'Police Patrol 3,000' and 'Futurama Invaders'; the latter is a parody of the popular 1970's 'Space Invaders' video game. The imaginary technology referenced in *Futurama* is also explored in a number of Web sites that offer 'blueprints' for the Planet Express space ship, mock advertisements for products referenced in the show (robot oil, soft drinks) and other speculative explorations of objects and themes appearing on the program.

Additionally, there are broader aspects of *Futurama* that make it a particularly fertile text for net-based exegesis. The program engages a relentless intertextuality that provides an avenue for fan discussion. One frequent aspect of this discussion involves the compilation of lists of references made on *Futurama* to celebrities, parodies of movies and television shows, nods to some of Groening's other work, and other often obscure elements within popular culture. Additionally, entire episodes were structured around parodies of popular films such as *Titanic*, *Independence Day* and *How Stella Got Her Groove Back*, extending this strategy. For example, the enormous *Futurama Chronicles* Website offers an extensive catalog of such elements, including individual lists of references to popular children's games, advertisements, the obsolete BASIC computer language, the state of New Jersey and numerous other items. *Much Ado About Futurama*, a similarly extensive site, includes collections of references to other television programs, Groening's long-running *Life in Hell* comic strip and a list of celebrities who appear in *Futurama*'s 'Head Museum'.

In addition to such references, the program also includes a number of visual and verbal jokes that lend themselves to a similar process of collection and cataloging. The title sequence for each program is personalized – in the manner of the famous 'couch gag' and Bart's writing on the blackboard on *The Simpsons* – through the use of different satirical messages which appear at the bottom of the screen (e.g., 'Not based on the novel by James Fenimore Cooper' and 'Condemned by the Space Pope') and through images appearing on miniature video screens during the sequence. These elements, often in-jokes designed for fans, appear very quickly and require both attentiveness and often repeated viewings for full comprehension. For example, the video screens sometimes feature brief snippets of historically significant pieces of animation; this connects *Futurama* to an earlier tradition of motion picture art and also flatters the fan with a strong knowledge of this genre. Through the use of such formal strategies, then, *Futurama* opens itself up for the kind of dissection and discussion that occupies a central place in much of the fan discourse concerning television programs on the Internet. In this sense, the program is both an excellent choice for an investigation into a television-Internet audience convergence given the extensive and discursively rich nature of this engagement, and also a slightly unfair example given its rather singular suitability for such an analysis.

Before moving to a more extensive discussion of some of the implications of this convergence, I want to offer a brief textual analysis of *Futurama*, with a particular attention to aspects of the program that are important in shaping Internet-based fan discourse. Following David Morley and Charlotte Brundson who argue for a continued attention to texts themselves as opposed to an automatic reduction to 'readings' and audience responses, I would point out that it is particularly important in the case at hand to examine some of the dynamics of the primary text, before moving to its reconfiguration and rearticulation in secondary discourses. If these interpretive practices are taken here to have a symptomatic value, offering indications as to certain wider aspects of the cross-media dynamic, then an analysis of the primary materials is crucial.

Tony Wilson argues that the production of what he calls the 'veridical effect' is an especially strong factor in giving television a particular hermeneutic grip on viewers and providing for an intense identification with on-screen characters and events (Wilson, 1993, pp. 104–122). From Wilson's formalist perspective, this effect stems from a rhetorical strategy that creates an impression of realism and produces a faith in the truth of the image, even in a fictional program. What is interesting about *Futurama*, however, is that it scrupulously avoids most of the conventions of veridicality, offering a highly fantastic and thoroughly ironic discourse, while still providing for an intense connection with audience members. The central storyline of *Futurama* involves Philip J. Fry, a pizza delivery boy and archetypal 'slacker' from the year 1999 who is transported 1,000 years forward in time by a freak accident on the eve of the year 2000. In the future, he ends up joining the crew of the Planet Express (a play on Federal Express) delivery service, an intergalactic shipping firm headed by the 149-year-old Professor Hubert Farnsworth, who is Fry's 29th generation descendant. Fry works alongside a variety of colorful figures: Bender, an amoral, boozing robot; Leela, a one-eyed alien; Amy Wong, a young Asian intern with the affect of a sorority girl; Dr. Zoidberg, a lobster-like mutant; and Hermes Conrad, a Jamaican-accented bureaucrat. Each episode generally involves a delivery mission to a different alien planet, thus considerably expanding the fictional universe by adding a entirely new set of supporting characters and locations.

Perhaps the most prominent textual element of *Futurama*, though, is the interaction of Fry and Bender, characters that provide contrasting but thoroughly cartoonish – in both the literal and figurative sense – versions of human weakness. Fry is presented as sexually undesirable, addicted to television and junk food, naïve, relatively unintelligent and supremely lazy. Bender is relentlessly carnal, chain smokes cigars, relies on alcohol to power his system, enjoys robotic strippers and prostitutes and has a taste for thievery and violence. The use of Fry and Bender as dual protagonists is crucial in establishing the ironic tenor of *Futurama*, as it provides anti-heroes lacking in any conventional virtues. The character flaws of Fry and Bender serve as anchoring devices for a number of episodes: Fry becomes a billionaire and squanders his money on 20th century relics and the last remaining can of now-extinct anchovies (season 1, #6); he accidentally drinks the emperor of a planet of liquid aliens (1, #7); he becomes addicted to a soft drink, 'Slurm', and in a parody of *Willy Wonka and The Chocolate Factory*, wins a tour of the Slurm factory (2, #13). In other episodes, Bender becomes addicted to power surges – 'jacking in' (1, #9); he flushes Nibbler, Leela's beloved pet, down the toilet (2, #14); Bender also joins the 'robot mafia' (2, #26), participates in 'ultimate robot fighting' (2, #21), and frames his 'good twin' Flexo for his own crimes (2, #20). In all of the above episodes, the overall comic structure and many of the jokes depend upon the incorrigible vices of Fry and Bender; any softening of these character traits, such as Bender's brief conversion to the 'Church of Robotology' or Fry's attempt to save the earth from aliens, is presented as an even greater irony. In the former, Bender becomes a mindless cultist, and in the latter Fry saves the planet by creating a greater future menace. There is a kind of reverse normativity at work here, in which any transgression toward socially approved behavior is treated as contemptible.

In addition to the comic dystopianism of the Fry and Bender characters, there are a few other notable themes which recur within *Futurama*. The most prominent of these are a relentless satire of the mass media, a critique of cynically 'friendly' capitalism and a mocking examination of love and sexuality. The first is present in nearly every episode, with television as the most commonly ridiculed medium; indeed, Professor Farnsworth's name is an homage to television pioneer Philo Farnsworth. The robot soap opera 'All My Circuits' recurs in a number of episodes, with one episode revolving around Bender's eviction from an apartment he shares with Fry when his antenna interferes with the reception of the same program; in a caricature of Freudianism, Bender must cut off his own antenna to stay in the apartment (1, #3). Another episode concerns the reenactment of a lost episode of the vapid and ridiculous 'Single Female Lawyer', a reference to Fox's comic legal drama *Ally McBeal*, that was destroyed when Fry spilled beer on the equipment at a television station 1,000 years earlier (2, #12). The aforementioned 'title gags' include the message 'as presented in BC [Brain Control] where available' and 'in hypno-vision'. In other episodes, we are told that television causes 'eye cancer', that Fry's favorite television genre is 'world's blankiest blank' (another reference to a staple of Fox programming) and that he is 'covered with bedsores' because of his addiction to the 'better than reality' medium of high definition television. Perhaps the most memorable parody of television, though, comes in an episode in which Fry awakes from a dream desperately wanting to shop and is told that advertisers are now able to broadcast commercials into his dreams (1, #6). Here the program directly engages the technological colonization of the imagination envisioned by a number of pessimistic postmodernists – for example, see Barglow's likeminded analysis (Barglow, 1994, pp. 137–150).

While television is the most common media target for *Futurama's* satire, the Internet itself was subject to a particularly detailed and vigorous assault in the twelfth episode of the second season. The episode begins with the Planet Express crew donning virtual reality suits and taking a trip through the Internet; in a play on the notorious technical problems with the America Online Internet Service Provider, the professor has finally connected after a hundred years of waiting. As they enter the Net, the crew is immediately attacked by dozens of advertisements, parodying the annoying 'pop-up' and 'banner' ads which are common to the Web. Intriguingly, the attacking advertisements reflect some of the common anxieties concerning the content of the Internet, referencing political extremism ('Mad? Ammoweb.com'), pornography ('Steamy Presidential mp3s'), voyeurism ('Stalk Anybody. Search.web') and rampant consumerism ('Tired of your car? Trade it for a pig. ebarter.web'). Decoding the advertisements requires considerable attention (and a VCR, DVD player or other digital file), thus reflecting its 'net ready' character. After fighting off the ads, the crew wanders through a pornography-laden city and enters a 'filthy, filthy chatroom'. Bender transforms himself into a 'naughty nurse' – a play on the kind of identity flexiblity posed by Net gurus – and speaks to male visitors in exchange for money. In another chatroom, several 'super studs' turn into cowering nerds when confronted with a real woman, thus parodying both the identity transformation noted above and the presumed geekiness of the real humans behind these fantastic personas. The entire sequence, lasting about five minutes, thus compresses a rather extensive parody of a number of aspects of virtual culture into an extremely concise segment. It also works to flatter the Net-savvy viewer, as many of the jokes – referencing AOL, multimedia technology, the discursive dynamics of chatrooms, advertising and so on – require at least some knowledge of the social customs of the Internet for full comprehension.

Much of *Futurama*'s satire of television and the Internet also reflects the second theme, a parodic critique of the friendly face of modern industrial capitalism. This is evident in the appearance of 'Slurms McKenzie' (a reference to the eighties Budweiser Beer spokesdog, Spuds McKenzie), a lovable worm that promotes the soft drink Slurm that is later revealed to be made from worm excrement. The most notable articulation of this theme, though, is through the occasional appearance of 'Mom', who is 'the world's most lovable industrialist'. Mom, who assumes the persona of a doting Grandmother to promote her popular robot oil, is later revealed as an evil scheming mastermind. In her first appearance, she seeks to produce robot oil from genetically altered 'third world children', but needs to steal Fry's coveted anchovies to obtain a secret ingredient. She then uses her three pathetic, bullied sons to carry out her plans, stripping off her grandmotherly garb to reveal exercise clothes while cursing and chain smoking. Mom, arguably the most striking of *Futurama*'s villains, reflects a particularly acute take on the ways that an avaricious form of capitalism can be concealed beneath an absurdly warm and fuzzy veneer. As with the satire of television, *Futurama* again comes close to a kind of non-academic version of ideology critique, albeit one launched in an absurd manner and with a measure of 'prophylactic irony' (to borrow a term from Mark Crispin Miller) that dilutes the force of this critique.

There is no less cynicism and irony in the treatment of romantic love in *Futurama*. Leela has a brief fling with another recurring character, Zapp Branigan, an egomaniacal military officer happily willing to sacrifice his own crew for personal glory. Their romance ends miserably, but Leela continues to encounter Zapp in subsequent episodes. In a parody of the film *Titanic*, Bender falls for a 'robot countess' who is sucked into a black hole, but he is saddened more by the fact that the bracelet she left him is a worthless fake. Similarly, Fry becomes entangled with an obsessive stalker in one episode and, in another, with a mermaid princess who is disgusted by his human genitals. His romantic fling with Amy ends in a grisly car wreck which temporarily decapitates him. Lastly, Dr. Zoidberg returns to his home planet during 'crustacean mating season' only to be spurned by the object of his desire. As with the broader characterizations of Fry and Bender, any modicum of sentimentality is immediately undercut by an inevitably ironic twist that reaffirms *Futurama's* relentlessly dysfunctional milieu.

While the brief analysis above can only provide a sketch of the remarkably eclectic thematic and narrative character of *Futurama's* fantastic milieu, it identifies some of the most important aspects of the program's content. Overall, the program is notable for its rather extreme extension of many stereotypically 'postmodern' characteristics of programs such as Fox's early nineties cult comedy *Get A Life* (which had a similarly youthful and obsessive following) and of course *The Simpsons*: relentless irony, pastiche and other forms of referentiality, a reflexive mocking of television and a tendency toward anti-heroic protagonists. This quality is critical because it deviates from the verdical modes which are assumed to create audience identification, provides a grounding for a particularly intense interpretive effort by audience members (the 'net ready' aspect noted above) and encourages a kind of discursive productivity on the part of fans. This last element will become important for the following section, which deals with the ways that such secondary discourses are articulated within the Internet fan culture and the ways that the interpretive process itself is likely to be shaped by a changing relation to the television text.

Virtuality and the audience: viewing, secondary discourse and interpretation

In examining the ways that *Futurama* is taken up within Internet-based discourse, I want to separate out three aspects of this convergence of mediated symbolic flows: the physical reconfiguration and recirculation of the television text, the articulation of a variety of secondary fan discourses surrounding *Futurama* and the broader question of shifts in hermeneutic-interpretive practices implied by both. One of the important shifts in viewing practices allowed by the emergence of Internet audience cultures involves the question of the access to and circulation of the television text itself. In ways that reflect an expansion of some of the changes made possible by the rise of the VCR and later DVR and TiVo systems, the text becomes 'unstuck in time' (to borrow a phrase from Kurt Vonnegut) and also becomes a transferable object. The viewer is no longer bound by the scheduling practices and geographic reach of the television network. While videotape exchanges among fans, and, in some cases, commercially released versions of programs provide for an increased physical circulation of television texts, the Internet allows instant access to entire collections of programs that can be downloaded onto one's computer. At the peak of the virtual *Futurama* culture, there were over a dozen websites dedicated solely to the exchange of video files, often containing entire episodes of the program. While the legality of such sites is certainly questionable, enforcement is so lax (at least currently) that anyone with even a minimal degree of net savvy can easily obtain virtually any episode of *Futurama*. This is particularly useful for non-U.S. fans – one need not even have access to the broadcast version in their own nation to view the program. Again, while this was theoretically possible with video cassettes (although there were the inevitable NTSC/PAL/SECAM problems), it is now relatively simple and inexpensive – assuming access to a computer connected to the Internet, of course.

Additionally, the text can be broken down, reconstructed, and/or excerpted in ways that were largely impossible before the emergence of the Web. For example, there are a number of websites that feature extensive collections of both audio and video files and offer thematically organized selections of excerpts based on characters, topics and other elements from the program. These collections thus provide a kind of audio-visual index to notable quotations, particularly hilarious sight gags, songs or unique uses of sound and other memorable moments from the entire run of the program. With these collections, the audience member can selectively replay disconnected textual fragments in a way that would be impossible or at least unwieldy with a conventional television and VCR combination. The smaller scale of such fragments, in terms of file size and downloading time, also allows for an even greater ease of circulation and recontextualization – perhaps a hundred *Futurama*-based websites include at least some audio or video excerpts. Some of the most interesting of such fragments are the remixed versions of the title song for the show available on the Internet, which offer altered variations on the theme music. Here, a relatively insignificant aspect of the program is disengaged from the larger framework of an episode and resituated through a practice – remixing – with an established aesthetic and cultural history within popular music. This is a variation on established 'fan art' practices that will be discussed in detail below, but it is also one dependent on the technologically-enabled extraction, reconstruction and recirculation of a piece of the larger text.

There are other, subtler ways that the viewing experience can be altered by the proliferation of Internet discourses, as in the widespread practice of providing 'spoilers', one common to websites dedicated to television programs. Such 'spoilers' offer information, presumably originating from inside sources, on the plot lines of upcoming episodes. While descriptions of upcoming programs for a given week, or perhaps several weeks have long been a part of published television listings, viewers are now able to obtain often detailed descriptions of episodes that may appear in upcoming television seasons. (In my experience with a number of Internet fan groups, these spoilers tend to be remarkably accurate.) As the name implies, such descriptions serve to spoil the anticipatory mystery, however mundane, associated with upcoming episodes of a favorite program. Conversely, the appeal of such spoilers is that they may serve to increase the sense of anticipation for hardcore fans, who have a deeper formal engagement with the program and are less likely to be concerned with the cross-episodic metanarrative. This is particularly the case with *Futurama*, which unlike most sitcoms and certainly unlike soap operas and other dramatic programs, tends to utilize narrative largely as a vehicle for parody and satire; there is relatively little narrative evolution (beyond the aforementioned recurring characters) or substantial character development. Nonetheless, spoilers undoubtedly work to remove at least some sense of naïvete from the initial viewing of an episode, and further work to dissolve the text's embeddedness with a relatively fixed set of discourses, as well as from the normal rhythms of the network television schedule.

All of the changes described above can be characterized as a shift in the structure of the flow (to use a term favored by both Raymond

Williams and appearing more recently in the work of Appadurai) of the television experience. The kind of linearity and ritual quality of the television experience – relatively uniform broadcast time, limited circulation, relatively stable surrounding symbolic framework – that was already undermined by the proliferation of VCR technology can now be largely discarded. The symbolic flow of the television text can now be redirected, resegmented and reconstructed, and can cross spatial and temporal lines that were previously impassable. Nor are these changes necessary limited to material aspects of the viewing experience discussed above; as I will argue in the next section, a variety of reception practices and especially those associated with fan cultures, practices that preceded the Internet itself, have also been reshaped and refreshed by the emergence of the Web.

A number of scholars, most notably Jenkins, have analyzed the ways that fan cultures create a variety of secondary discourses, most notably fan fiction, fan art and other forms of aesthetic re-production, as a means of personalizing mediated discourses (Jenkins, 1992, pp. 152–277). As mentioned, these practices existed long before the Internet, but they have certainly benefited from the explosion of this medium, for a number of reasons: ease of creating global fan communities, the ability to disseminate and access large amounts of essentially folkloric discourse with relatively little effort and the ability to participate in this culture without leaving the home (e.g., no necessary attendance at fan conventions, club meetings and other events). In this sense, a practice that was largely confined by the limits of physical proximity one associates with a folk community is now expanded into a mass medium, albeit one with its own set of limitations.

One of the most common forms of television fan discourse is the 'fan script', a subset of the larger genre of fan fiction, in which fans offer their own scripts for episodes of the show. Hundreds of such scripts, ranging from one page scene fragments to full 25–30 page episode teleplays, are available from various *Futurama* fan sites. These fan scripts vary considerably, both thematically and in terms of the technical sophistication of the writing, but certain patterns do emerge. Some of the scripts, such as several written by Canadian fan Tammy Corizis, are clearly intended as plausible candidates for actual production (though this is highly unlikely, of course). These scripts are carefully gauged to fit within time parameters (22 minutes), do not use language or situations (e.g., sexual or violent) which would likely be unacceptable for network television, and do not utilize excessively narrow in-jokes. In one script, 'Roughing It', Corizis has Fry and Bender serve as camp counselors to a group of obnoxious children. In keeping with the ironic anti-sentimentality of the show, Fry's girlfriend 'Andrea' (a new character) has a fling with Bender and all three endanger the lives of the children with their reckless conduct.

In another of Corizis' teleplays, titled 'A Little Change (Will Do You Good)', Fry fakes illness to get a day off from work so he can spend time with Andrea. They end up fighting with each other, and after reconciling, the episode ends with Fry returning to his usual, slothful ways. In yet another script, 'Halloween Special I: Attack of the Langolers', Corizis adapts a popular feature of *The Simpsons*, the annual Halloween episode, for *Futurama*. Her version features a highly reflexive horror-film parody which features the cast (including Andrea) fighting off the titular creatures. Once again, Corizis maintains the tone of actual episodes of the program while continuing with the addition of a new character, as well as replicating the conventions of another program associated with Fox and with Groening. Here, the potential for participation within the production apparatus of television – the possibility articulated by Jordan – is referenced in a particularly direct way, and one that does little to alter the aesthetic terms of the program.

While such a multi-layered approach is not exceedingly rare, it is also not the dominant strategy. More common are scripts that accept the basic character and narrative structures of the show but offer some innovation or deviation from standard expectations for the program. Examples of this strategy would include: political satires such as Brandon Smith's 'Ich ein ben Bender', in which Bender becomes a presidential candidate; pastiches of popular television programs such as Aaron's 'Bender Wants to be a Millionaire' (based on ABC's concurrently popular *Who Wants to be a Millionaire* game show); resituations of *Futurama* characters in other television formats such as Marissa's 'Character Interview' in which characters are interviewed, talk show style, as if they were actual people. Of course, the program itself is so relentlessly ironic and so frequently engages pastiche strategies that such fan scripts, while quite unique, rarely appear truly radical in relation to the original text; aesthetic innovation is a real challenge for fans faced with television programming that utilizes many of the strategies common to earlier fan fiction. This is thus reflected in the remarkable aesthetic diversity of *Futurama*-related materials. For example, not long after the 'Character Interview' piece appeared, *The Simpsons* – a companion program to *Futurama* – featured an episode parodying music network VH-1's popular 'Behind the Music' series (which showcases melodramatic tales of show business success and failure), presenting the animated 'cast' in a pseudo-documentary. This is a rather nice demonstration of the increasingly narrow gap between the 'radical' reworkings of fan fiction and the incorporation of such strategies within actual network television programming.

The most controversial element in such scripts is the recurrent use of the Andrea character, who serves as Fry's girlfriend after he brings her back from the 20th century with the aid of a time machine. Andrea appears in scripts by a variety of authors in addition to Corizis, thus becoming a kind of defacto official character. She is a character blending some of the characteristics of Leela – physical toughness and a no-nonsense manner – with Amy's romantic nature and physical attractiveness. Interestingly, it is the addition of Andrea, rather than any of the more drastic aesthetic changes, that has produced the strongest response among fellow fans, both positive and negative. The positive response comes primarily in the form of an incorporation of the Andrea figure within both scripts and other forms of fan art. The negative response is both aesthetic – scripts in which she is killed by Bender, for example – and critical, as in the angry comments of fans that appear in the 'editorials' section of the *Futurama Outlet* website. What is fascinating about this controversy is that it is the use of fairly conventional narrative ploy, the long lost girlfriend, that provokes such debate; perhaps it appears as a violation of the program's otherwise unconventional aesthetic sensibility and thus appears to treat *Futurama* as just another television program. Also interesting is the fact that such secondary aesthetic forms – as opposed to the primary text composed of broadcast episodes – inspire the same types of critical response, albeit on a somewhat limited scale, as the show itself.

In addition to the material noted above, there is a variety of additional *Futurama* fan art appearing on the web that can be divided, usefully, into three categories. The first consists of fairly conventional visual art involving characters and situations from the program, comic strips based on *Futurama* and parody 'Filke' songs that use popular melodies and add lyrics involving the show (for more on this genre, see Jenkins, 1992, pp. 250–276). Many of the strategies used in the scripts discussed above are evident in these forms as well: there are visual pastiches (e.g., *Futurama* characters appearing in *Star Wars* posters or fusions of *Simpsons* and *Futurama* characters); cross-genre parodies (e.g., an 'astrological' chart in which one can locate their personal *Futurama* character-sign); and relatively straightforward extensions of the show's narrative thrust (e.g., the 'Bender's Day' comic strip). This material is quite similar to a long tradition of fan-based aesthetic practices described by Jenkins and other researchers; while often quite inventive, the *Futurama* material is not strikingly different from material related to other programs that is also available on the web. For example, the 'Filke' songs include some set to the tune of contemporary pop hits and an entire group of *Futurama*-themed Christmas carols such as 'I Saw Leela Kissing My Pal Fry', based on 'I Saw Mommy Kissing Santa Claus'.

The most of interesting of these *Futurama* carols, though, is a parody of 'Oh Come All Ye Faithful' that addresses the program's web-based fan formation directly. The lyrics include the following:

> Oh come all ye faithful, obsessed and devoted
> Oh come ye, Oh come ye to Planet Express
> Come and behold it, apogee of tv shows
> Oh come let us adore it...
> Oh sing, choirs of web-heads, sing in exultation
> Oh sing all ye netizens of keyboard and screen
> Glory to sci-fi, all glory in the highest
> Oh come let us adore it...

The references to 'netizens', a recently coined term for avid participants in Internet culture, and those 'obsessed and devoted' to science fiction lend the above parody a level of reflexivity, as it is itself disseminated via the web. The use of a particularly archaic and grand carol is also important here, as it creates a distinctly ironic effect, simultaneously mocking and celebrating the fanatical Internet following for *Futurama*. This ironic sensibility will be explored in greater depth a bit later, but is worth noting here as a significant thematic element in fan art.

A second category of *Futurama*-based creative work consists of material that might be described as 'symbiotic' fan art. In these materials, there is an assumption of the basic parameters of the fictional world reflected in *Futurama*, and the artwork uses this imaginary world as the basis for the whole of its referentiality. There are a number of examples of mock advertisements for fictional products – 'Bachelor Chow', as well as 'Slurm' and 'All My Circuits' – that have appeared on *Futurama*. There are also technical manuals and blueprints for the fictional Planet Express spaceship, decoding information for alien languages, and 'Ask Dr. Zoidberg', an advice column in which the crustacean physician dispenses medical advice.

Perhaps the most interesting element of this material is the 'robot porn' genre, which plays upon Bender's implied love of pornography. In one case, the 'Miss Amphere's Parlour' website, the 'centerfolds' consist of schematic diagrams for electronic devices, accompanied by text parodying the personal profiles included with *Playboy* magazine pictorials. On another site, the porn includes scanned photographs of circuit boards complete with pseudo-lascivious captions (e.g., 'Nice Chips!'). This genre is particularly interesting given the well-known availability of vast amounts of pornographic material on the web, and the controversy surrounding such material. The joke here is certainly dependent upon the hysteria over Internet porn; this is referenced in the parodic disclaimers – 'you must be 18 OS patches (a reference to computer operating systems) to enter' – included with the material. This symbiotic fan art is similar, in some ways, to the fan scripts described above in that it places the fan in the position of doing the same sort of labor that might be expected of the show's creators, who are engaged in a similar effort to rework and expand the fictional world of the program.

The 'robot porn' genre would also be part of the final category of fan art, one consisting of artistic material directly dependent upon or responsive to virtual fandom. While this would also be true to a degree for the 'Oh Come All Ye Faithful' parody, this third group of material is formally as well as thematically web-based. One variation on this approach would be the remixed versions of the title theme and assemblages of video and audio clips noted above; without the ease of reassembling textual fragments offered by recent advances in computer technology and the ability to disseminate the results via the Internet, such practices would be limited to a relatively tiny group of fans. Another is the 'ASCII' art that uses only the standard set of keyboard symbols to fashion portraits of *Futurama* characters, thus deploying an ironically primitive form of computerized art, one largely obsolete in light of today's high-tech computer graphics. Additionally, there are screen savers, computer 'wallpaper' backgrounds, 'alien' cursors and fonts, the video games and a variety of other items which allow for interactive participation and provide the means for the fan to customize her/his computer with various *Futurama*-based desktop graphics. This is a particularly intriguing mode of creative production by fans both because it is so well integrated within the very mechanism that enables such fan communities and because it fuses with a major element of *Futurama* itself, the comic obsession with new technologies. It should be noted that this is hardly unique to the *Futurama* subculture; as MacDonald points out, it has been part of numerous CMC-based science fiction fan groups for some time (MacDonald, 1998, p. 150). There is a kind of reflexive pun at work in such practices in which the

viewer/fan enjoys a simultaneously productive and ironic relati
with the technology of virtual fandom, a quality reflected in pia____
such as playing an ironic pastiche of an old video game (e.g., 'Futurama
Invaders') or using an image of *Futurama's* inept scientist Dr. Farnsworth
as wallpaper for your own piece of domestic technology. These forms of
fan art are only possible – both technically and aesthetically – through the
incorporation of fandom within computer mediated communication and
thus reflect new strategies for the aesthetic reworking of the primary text.

In addition to these forms of creative work, the *Futurama* Web community also serves as a forum for critical and exegetical discussions of
the program. This is another feature that would be much more difficult
in conventional, pre-Web fan cultures, which relied upon paper
fanzines and interpersonal contact – club meetings, conventions and
informal gatherings – for such discussions. There are dozens of chat
rooms, newsgroups, Internet clubs (e.g., the Yahoo *Futurama* club) and
message boards on fan sites allowing for nearly instant reaction to
episodes as they are broadcast. As might be expected, the discussion on
such groups is quite varied, ranging from simple positive or negative
reaction – the discourse famously parodied on *The Simpsons* with the
character known as 'comic book guy' whose trademark phrase is 'worst
episode ever!' – to extended discussions of the implied politics of the
program, recent plot developments and even inconsistencies within
the imaginary world of the program. In addition to these venues for
quick response and, in the case of chat rooms, dialogue, there are also
a number of web pages that include editorial sections that allow for
more carefully crafted critical work. These tend to present essayistic
prose pieces that take on more substantive issues, as in a series of
brief critical pieces addressing the question of social criticism within
Futurama that recently appeared on the *Futurama Outlet* site. The perspectives were quite varied, and the discussion was eventually expanded to include comparisons with other animated programs such as *South
Park* and *The Simpsons*, and ultimately to a general discussion of the
place of political and moral messages within entertainment programming. As noted above, there are a variety of modes of aesthetic production (fan art) available on the Web, so it is not surprising that there
is a similarly multifaceted set of critical practices, many largely or
completely dependent upon the Internet for their dissemination.

While all of the strategies described in the earlier research by Baym –
informing, speculating, criticizing and reworking – are also present in
the *Futurama* Web culture, rather than concentrating on the conversa-
tional genres implied in these discussions, I want to discuss two

functions that they serve within the larger audience community. The first of these, one directly connected to the informational and critical genres, is as a means of fostering a stronger engagement with the program itself through interpretive and archival endeavors. The intertextual character and formal visual complexity of *Futurama* make it an ideal object of such attention, and indeed a good deal of the discussion within various forums, message boards and newsgroups mimics the 'reference' areas within *Futurama* websites. For example, a recent thread on the alt.tv.futurama newsgroup was dedicated to compiling 'an exhaustive list of sci-fi, *Simpsons*, television, literary, movie, musical, and other allusions to [sic] the characters in *Futurama*' (e.g., that 'Leela' is Swedish for 'purple', the color of her famous ponytail; that Fry's middle initial 'J' is a reference to cartoon character 'Bullwinkle J. Moose'). This mode of evolving interpretation, with each new version of a message reflecting the contribution of another list member to the collective effort, is a very common feature of such newsgroups (and of the Internet *Futurama* clubs), and encourages a deeper analysis of the text, by contributors to the thread as well as by non-contributing readers who can now revisit the primary text with an expanded critical perspective.

The collective nature of these interpretive practices is an important facet of the second function performed by such discussions, involving the maintenance of this virtual community and the discussion of its evolving nature. Certainly, the kind of joint critical labor described above is innately communal, but there are other ways that a sense of connection between participants is built. Particularly important here are the internal discussions of the *Futurama* web community, discussions touching directly on issues of communal purpose, connectedness and the role of individual Internet sites within the audience formation as a whole. For example, the *Futurama Chronicles* 'editorials' section includes a number of comments which specifically deal with the state of the virtual community. One such contribution by Jason Barnabe, webmaster of the vast *Roadmap Futurama Database Planet*, used a film reference to structure an evaluation of the then current (December 1999) situation:

> **The Good:** First, you've got all the multimedia sites: AYNIF, the Archive, and the Outlet being the head honchos. Then you have information sites (the Chronicles). Then come themed sites like the Fry file and the Leela Zone, links sites like yours truly and PF, and merchandise sites like Collecting Futurama.

The Bad: There's too much of these. Abandoned sites that people don't bother to take down. The Futurama station was one of the best sites, until it stopped operating one day. Also there are first-time sites, from novice webmasters, too numerous to name.

The Ugly: Two words: original content. There are too many people out there wanting to be 'the best Futurama site on the Internet'. People who start picture sites won't get any hits because the Archive, Outlet, and AYNIF already take care of this. To have a successful site, you have to fill a void. I thought it was too hard to find the site I wanted, so I started a links site. Themed sites seem like the best idea to me. Pick a subject that no other site has. Think to yourself 'Why would people go to my site rather than anyone else's'? I heard an interesting idea for a site a week ago: a site that deals in news and articles only. No other site does that. In conclusion, there are always going to be bad sites out there. My tip is rather than start your own site, just help out another site. This will increase quality rather than quantity of sites. [Boldface and punctuation in original]

This posting offers a concise version of a number of the concerns that arise frequently in such critical reflection by members of the *Futurama* Internet community. There is an appreciation for the diversity of material available online, as well as a somewhat snobbish disdain for the 'novice' participants who are not making the kind of contribution that established virtual fans deem worthy. The twin emphases on originality – coming up with new ideas for sites – and cooperation – working together to avoid redundancy – do suggest a sense of community. However, this is always tempered with the need to retain a critical viewpoint toward developments within the community, and to maintain a level of quality as the community expands.

The webmaster of *The Futurama Outlet*, provided a more populist variation of a similar perspective in his own editorial on the subject, writing,

> ... we are seeing an increasing number of sites being generated for Futurama, and although more sites are good for publicity, quality sites are better... If you make a site and don't update it please delete it or consider not putting it up at all. These sites do take time to update and take responsibility for and if you do not have either of these please reconsider. It is the ultimate goal to get quality and

timely information to fans who are seeking it and if the net just gets clogged with Futurama sites that hold no value it's possible the fans will not be able to get to the sites that do. Also think when creating your site. Don't just steal and pillage other sites to make your site. Come up with original thought, graphics, and concepts to enhance the Futurama experience. Although I can in no way stop you from exercising your freedom of speech and expression I just please ask you to be responsible and to understand the commitment.

Here, the appeal for originality and quality is posed in terms of a commitment to the fans likely to access these sites and for the need 'to enhance the Futurama experience'; service to the community is posed as the primary function of the *Futurama* site, rather than pure expression, though the author does not wish to interfere with anyone's right to free expression, of course. The disclaimer regarding the freedom of expression is particularly noteworthy here, as the *Futurama* community, along with a number of other Internet fan groups, was pulled into a legal controversy involving the right of fans to create sites and the copyright interests of television producers, one which had a significant impact on the community.

Netizens vs. big business: Fox, fan sites, and the law

The legal status of much of the material available through fan sites on the Web has always been somewhat ambiguous, particularly when it includes digital video of entire episodes, audio clips, 'screen grabs' and other forms of direct borrowing from the primary text. While the response from television producers has been varied, Twentieth Century Fox, the producer of *Futurama*, has been particularly draconian in their attempts at restricting this material. Thus, there has been an ongoing battle between Internet-based fan groups for a number of Fox shows – *The Simpsons*, *Millenium*, *Buffy the Vampire Slayer* (which aired on the Warner Brothers network but is produced by Fox) – and the network itself; there has been a similarly long-running conflict between the enormous *Star Trek* fan community and Viacom, *Star Trek*'s production company. This conflict dates back to 1995, when Fox sent a now infamous 'cease and desist' letter to Jeanette Foshee, creator of a very early *Simpsons* site. The letter, quickly made available on the Internet, is quite menacing, with demands to turn over all disks containing copyrighted material, as well as threats of 'substantial monetary damages' and 'statutory penalties of as much as $100,000'. By making the letter accessible for the entire virtual community, Foshee and others who would receive similar letters created a considerable outrage regarding Fox's bullying tactics. The actual legal status of Fox's claims of copyright violation remains somewhat ambiguous. While many sites do use material that is clearly the property of Fox, a case can be made that such pages would be covered under 'fair use' provisions that allow for reproduction of copyrighted material if it would be unlikely to affect the value of the original material, is not used for commercial purposes and meets a variety of more specific criteria. However, the cost of a legal battle with Fox is clearly beyond the means of most fans, and thus there has been a tendency to comply with Fox's demands, although similar material often appears on another site quite rapidly.

The battle between Fox and the fans is part of a much wider set of debates regarding the Internet and the control of copyrighted materials. The concurrent struggle over the Napster file-sharing system is the best-known of these debates, but there are similar battles regarding databases such as the now-defunct 'International Lyrics Server', which provided the written lyrics to thousands of songs; domain names such as 'Roadkill R Us', which was alleged to infringe on a trademark held by retailer 'Toys R Us'; and the many debates regarding the proliferation of pornographic and other explicit materials on the Internet. The larger question here regards the status of the Internet in relation to other forms of information dissemination and the control of both technology and content within the virtual world, a conflict that most commonly pits large media institutions, especially multinational corporations, against individuals and informal organizations using the Internet for a variety of community functions, including the exchange of materials. Although the legal, financial and organizational strength of the former has given the corporate interests a clear advantage in this struggle, net users have devised some intriguing responses.

In the specific case of fans of Fox programming – including the *Futurama* community – the corporate assault has led to formation of a number of virtual organizations, including 'Free Speech is Out There' (founded by *X-Files* fans) and 'The Buffy Bringers' (created by fans of *Buffy the Vampire Slayer*); similarly, the *Star Trek* virtual community has produced both *The Wrath of ViaKahn* (a pun on the title of the second *Star Trek* film) and the *Anti-Viacom HQ*. The strategies used by such organizations include advertiser boycotts, letter writing or more commonly e-mailing campaigns and visual banners on websites demonstrating support for the protest. The most interesting of these, though, was 'Operation: Blackout', an attempt by Fox fans to create a blackout of fan sites by asking creators to voluntarily take their site off line and replace it with a protest message. The event, which took place on 13 May 2000, included a number of *Futurama* sites, as well as several hundred sites for a variety of other programs. Organizers designed the protest to be international, recruiting fans with proficiency in languages other than English to help create multi-lingual versions of the protest message. They also provided additional guidance for fans who do not have their own websites but wished to participate, suggesting that they add a link to the protest site within the 'signature file' in their e-mail correspondence. The protest attracted a considerable amount of public attention, and was featured in stories in mainstream magazines such as *Entertainment Weekly*, as well as a very high level of coverage within the Internet itself. This attention was absolutely critical to the campaign, as the concrete effect on the litigious bodies was obviously very limited. However, the campaign is important because it reflects a rather direct attempt to disarticulate, as it were, the conjoining of broadcast media and virtual flows as a means of protesting the colonization of the net by commercial interests and a direct assault on the autonomy of the fan community. While such an effort, like the other strategies, is always limited in its reach, fans have devised supplementary covert strategies for preserving some of the community services which have been legally restricted.

For example, within the *Futurama* Web world, which has been hit by the same 'cease and desist' letters which were used for other sites, fans have worked together to maintain the availability of 'full episode' digital files – a source of particular opposition by Fox. On the alt.tv .futurama newsgroup, one fan explained that 'BTW [internet abbreviation for 'by the way'] many new DVD's allow MPEG [a common digital video file format], so it shouldn't be hard to burn all the episodes downloaded off the internet onto a DVD'. Thus, fans could create a permanent, offline collection of episodes without the need for a consistent online video source. When discussion on the same group turned to online sources for this material, group members were careful to warn participants of the danger of talking about this in a public forum; within this thread, for example, the discussion included:

> PLEASE try not to give the server names in public. if someone asks for them send them a private e-mail. if fox finds out about all these servers hosting futurama episodes there is a real danger of these servers being shut down by fox, abd we don't want that do we?... As far as I know FOX shut down Cletus' Farm [a *Simpsons* download

site] because people were posting the address at alt.tv.simpsons... If you would like to trade episodes then please e-mail me and we can work something out. DO NOT POST your replys [sic] on where to get episodes here. I am told that is because once we make episode sites public, Fox will shut them down.

The massive scale and flexibility of the Internet is ideal for such covert activity, as sites can be created and placed online and, if necessary, removed with great speed; newsgroups and other interactive forums also provide a relatively easy means of disseminating information about such sites, even if, as above, this consists primarily of requests for private communication. These techniques thus offer a more productive complement to the protest actions described above; they work to create a way around the obstacles thrown up by industrial interests, even as the obstacles are themselves the object of criticism.

It would be tempting to view such practices from a Decerteuian or Fiskean perspective and understand them as working in a subversive fashion to resist the imperatives of capital. While this is no doubt partially true – they are 'subversive' in the sense that they are conducted in a secretive manner and against the formal demands of corporate interests – it is also the case that such maneuvers are often justified precisely because they do no actual harm to the same interests. Many of the fans involved in the Internet protests were stunned by Fox's behavior because they felt that their websites actually worked to promote the programs that were being saluted, a position that was reinforced by the tacit, if guarded, approval of fan sites expressed by *Buffy the Vampire Slayer* creator Joss Whedon and *Simpsons* and *Futurama* creator Matt Groening. This is not to suggest that fan site creators saw themselves as acting purely in the interests of the television producers; however, it is clear that, even at its most polemical, the rhetoric surrounding the Fox actions was a defense of the freedom to behave in a way that would not diminish Fox's profits against the network's senseless bullying. While there are certainly net radicals who see the development of this technology as a clear affront to moneyed interests, they are vastly outnumbered by a large number of quasi-libertarian Internet enthusiasts who perceive the virtual world as a new area for capitalist exploration and promotion. The 'free advertising' position regarding fan sites – one supported directly by the producers of the teen hit *Felicity*, for example – is largely consonant with the latter. Even the protest campaigns reflecting the most ardently independent segments of the community are couched in terms of convincing the producers of the value of these sites, rather than a direct disruption of corporate practices. The freedom to operate and the autonomy of virtual space are posed as complementary rather than hostile to a larger set of media institutions.

Despite the absence of a real radicalism, the Fox actions and fan reactions did serve to strengthen, again through a kind of unified negativity, the communal spirit of the *Futurama* audience formation. The need for cooperation, particularly regarding practices which needed to take place away from the inquisitive eyes of Fox (such as file sharing), worked to forge connections between participants within this culture. In this sense, the incursion of 'the real' in the form of material threats from extra-virtual entities, was a catalyst for, rather than an impediment to, the cultivation of a degree of group cohesion. The shattering of the presumably autonomous world of fan sites and fan culture resulted in a sort of productive contradiction, one reconcilable through group action that nonetheless maintained an essentially consumerist relationship to the primary medium of interest, television. The contradictions in this fight to free one's consuming practices are important here because they exist within a larger set of potentially dissonant symbolic positions that are associated with the *Futurama* web culture.

Coping with mediated multiphrenia: ironic fandom and 'the geek'

While the protest over Fox's anti-fan practices illustrates the unstable and potentially contradictory relationship between the fan-as-consumer and the fan-as-producer in a particularly stark fashion, this relationship is operative at a broader level as well. The condition of the Web-based fan could be described as 'multiphrenic' (in Gergen's sense) in that she must operate within an array of symbolic networks that are not easily reconciled. The consumption/production disjunction is an example of this, but certainly not the only one. The fan also straddles the paradigmatically interactive medium of the Internet and the classically passive, monodirectional medium of television, as well as functioning both as a supporter of the cultural industry through her passion for a product and as an often caustic critic of the same product and of the apparatus that produces it. This position is a tricky one, of course, but strategies have emerged to cope with this multiphrenia. The most telling of these strategies is the cultivation of a form of ironic self-fashioning among fans that works to resolve this tension by utilizing it as the foundation for, rather than an impediment to, one's identity as a fan.

In several ways, an ironic sensibility is well suited to such symbolic challenges in that irony, as a rhetorical strategy, depends upon a kind of semiotic disjunction for its potency. As Paul De Man argues, irony demands the simultaneous appearance of two codes that are both relatively complete in their articulation, and that reflect a significant disjunction (De Man, 1979, p. 300). As D.C. Muecke points out, irony, and especially a kind of self-disparaging irony, also involves the use of a stylistic or symbolic mask which enables the construction of a dual persona – the 'innocent' mask and the 'knowing' figure who dons it (Muecke, 1969, p. 87). Through such a mask, the ironist is able to immerse herself in a symbolic formation while retaining a kind of critical distance from it. In this sense, then, irony is quite useful in dealing with the potential contradictions in a form of self-investment in that it allows one to 'have it both ways', so to speak, and enjoy any inherent contradictions rather than being overwhelmed or disoriented by them. In the specific case of *Futurama* fan culture, this ironic attitude is supported at three levels: by the television medium itself (particularly when set against the 'interactive' virtual world), by the textual content of the program and by a wider, pervasive popular cultural sensibility.

The popular sense that television is a medium of passivity and intellectual junk food, that it is the 'idiot box', is important here in that it provides both a strong counterpoint to the perceived interactivity of the Internet – the basis of Tapscott's and Negroponte's aforementioned arguments for example – and because it implies a lack of any aesthetic substance. This is then merged with the common belief that television does not merit prolonged interpretive effort, that it is intrinsically a medium of distracted rather than attentive viewing – a belief that is standard in many academic understandings of television as well. As noted in Chapter 2 in the discussion of Hejnar's *TV Ministry* and the covering of the television set in the New Art lobby, this understanding of television is one with particularly strong associations with academic and bohemian cultures, and thus with the kind of countercultural aura and often intellectualized milieu of the Web. Therefore, there is an immediate irony implied in the dedication of considerable creative labor to the viewing, interpretation and discussion of the televisual object, one that is clearly not lost on the *Futurama* fan culture.

This ironic understanding is buttressed, of course, by much of the reflexive commentary on the television experience within *Futurama* itself. As mentioned, the program provides a relentless mockery of the social role of television – as 'brain control', as 'better than reality', as the cause of 'eye cancer' and 'bedsores' and so on. Additionally, by presenting the central and only 20th century character, Fry, as a video zombie with a particular taste for the kind of programming that Fox – *Futurama*'s network – specializes in, the program appears to turn on its own patron and even its own audience; this would be doubly so, of course, for hardcore fans. However, it is quite clear that this 'attack' is not so much a form of hostility as it is flattery, letting fans know that they are clever enough to appreciate the paradox of television delivering this message[3] and that the self-awareness implied in 'getting the joke' separates this audience from its satirical target.

This is part of a broader cultural trend, of course. *The Simpsons* has long featured similarly reflexive attacks on television and, more generally, the 'irony epidemic' – as *Spy* magazine succinctly described it – has taken hold across a variety of popular media and genres. Varieties of an ironic sensibility are evident in popular music (They Might Be Giants, Barenaked Ladies, Chumbawumba), film (the Coen Brothers' *Fargo* and *The Big Lebowski*, *Natural Born Killers*), semi-popular and high literature (Carl Hiassen, Mark Leyner) and, as mentioned, television (*Mystery Science Theater 3000*, as well as Fox programming). Of course, the commingling of authentic sentiment and disingenuous masquerade provides specific challenges for fans, who must construct a similarly dualistic response, one that can be registered both at the level of self-involvement within the culture and self-definition as a fan.

This is apparent as well in the ways that devotees of Internet culture often configure themselves, and thus is doubly relevant to the case at hand. The figure of 'the geek' is critical here as it is a part of both virtual and science-fiction culture and thus touches heavily upon the world of *Futurama* fans. 'Geek', a term with origins in carnival culture and strongly derogatory connotations of obsessive behavior and social awkwardness, has been transformed into a largely positive model of a kind of cultural subjectivity. While it would be tempting to understand this transformation as a less politically charged variation on the practice of reversing and/or reclaiming words evident in the use of slurs such as 'queer', 'dyke' and 'nigger' as a means of creating group solidarity, there are important distinctions here. The transformation of 'the geek' involves at least a partial acceptance of many of the existing connotations of the term such as the estrangement from conventional social norms and the obsessive dedication to the seemingly insignificant; these aspects of 'geekdom' are not so much reversed but rather defended as legitimate avenues of self-investment. However, this immersion is tempered both a self-consciousness regarding one's status – a true 'geek', it would seem, would be incapable of self-recognition as one – and through a kind of ironic splitting of the self such that an individual can entertain the monomaniacal passions of the geek while retaining a meta-identity which contains this aspect of the self. Of course, the Internet is ideal for the cultivation of geekdom in that it allows for a particularly easy deployment of multiple personas, as Turkle, Jordan and many others argue. The sense of the Internet as a relatively enclosed virtual world provides the opportunity for an enthusiastic display of one's inner 'geek' with relatively little risk and with the support of a trans-national community of fellow geeks. Perhaps the word retains some of its carnival connotations in this context, as the Internet functions here a kind of midway in which the geek can be put on full display within this liminal space – part human, part technological – while judgment is suspended because one expects to find such unconventional figures in this world. This sense of safety is increased by the domesticity of the cyber-world noted above; the exploration of geekdom and the carnivalization (literally) of the self can take place within the domestic space, thus eliminating the need for a materially public display of one's geek tendencies.

The kind of ironic self-definition intrinsic to the contemporary Internet 'geek' is manifested in a number of ways within the specific domain of the virtual *Futurama* fan formation. It is evident, for example, in the comic obsessiveness with which fans scrutinize the program; the aforementioned blueprints for the Planet Express ship, created from a combination of excruciatingly detailed reviews of the actual program and some speculative filling in of any gaps in the visual presentation of the ship, are a good example of this intentionally silly exegesis. The 'debates' regarding various slips in continuity across episodes of the program – such as the recent discussions of Leela's fluctuating depth perception on the alt.tv.futurama newsgroup are another example, as such discussions often feature disclaimers regarding the minuteness and seeming pointlessness (particularly to outsiders) of such fine-grained analyses.

Another mechanism for the display of a properly ironic sensibility involves the building of connections to other forms of culture which carry heavy connotations of geekiness and pointless obsession. Take for example, the use of outdated video games such as *Space Invaders* and *Defender* as the basis for the publicly available *Futurama* computer games. Here, there is a reference to a prior form of geek culture, recalling an earlier hysteria over the addictive nature of such games and their popularity with asocial 'videopaths'. There are also fan-created role playing games – including one in which the player can assume the character of Dr Zoidberg – that allude to the quintessentially geeky role-playing subculture reflected, especially, in the world of *Dungeons and Dragons* aficionados. Lastly, there are frequent references on websites and within virtual discussions to a larger science-fiction culture, references frequently laced with self-deprecating humor; one of the 'Top 10 Reasons to Watch Futurama', according to the 'Plaid Adder' website is that, 'this show shares my love/hate relationship with *Star Trek*'. In the paragraph that follows, 'Plaid Adder' further explains that *Futurama* both salutes and critiques a variety of elements from the earlier program and that this attitude reflects the author's own ambivalence toward *Star Trek*.

The program itself frequently plays with these connections, a strategy amply displayed in the 1999–2000 season finale. The episode featured cameo appearances – using their actual voices – by United States Vice President Al Gore (whose daughter, Kristin Gore, has written for the show), noted physicist Stephen Hawking (who has also appeared on *The Simpsons*), *Dungeons and Dragons* creator E. Gary Gygax (something of a geek legend) and actor Nichelle Nichols (who played Uhuru on the certifiably geeky[4] *Star Trek* television series). The plot revolved around Professor Farnsworth's invention of a machine which allows users to see the outcome of a 'what if' scenario. Fry views what would have happened if he had not been transported into the future, and learns that he would have accidentally discovered a hole in the space-time continuum. Because of this knowledge, he is kidnapped by an elite squad of nerds, led by Gore, who investigate such breaches of natural law. The episode ends with Fry's ineptitude leading to the expulsion of all of the above from the universe; Nichols' character glumly laments, 'eternity with nerds – it's like the Pasadena Star Trek convention all over again', making a winking reference to fan culture itself. The episode thus provides a rather concise – the segment featuring these cameos is only about seven minutes long – but undeniably intense display of the show's frequent engagement with a full array of classically geeky elements of culture, and the treatment of these elements reflects a wider ironic sensibility, one that is an important part of the culture of *Futurama* fans.

The 'geek', then, serves as an ironic persona which can mediate the sometimes contradictory position of the fans, implying both an enthusiastic embrace of a popular cultural object and, simultaneously, a kind of self-mocking distance from it. One can participate avidly within fan culture without surrendering a critical understanding of the same, and without the social risks associated with an extra-virtual geekiness. As noted, the assumption of this position is enabled in this case by the technological and symbolic possibilities of the web, which make the assumption of various masks and the creation of alternative personas relatively easy; the separation of 'avatars' from the individuals that construct them is ideal for the cultivation of such an ironic sensibility as it allows for a relatively complete immersion within these avatar-identities. In this sense, the ironic mode can also serve as a means of coping with the multiphrenic condition noted above by giving the individual an opportunity to contain potentially dissonant subject positions.

This kind of ironic doubling has an important psychological resonance as well. Within the Freudian tradition, Otto Rank and more recently Lifton have recognized the importance of processes of doubling as means of dealing with disparate demands on a single individual (Strozier, 1994, pp. 86–87). The ability for multiple psychic investments that are not reliant on reconciliation or unification can take on a vast array of forms, with exemplars as extreme as the Nazi doctors Lifton famously studied, or cases of multiple personality disorder. For the culture at hand, one obviously lacking the intense connotations of pathology evident in these examples, the process Lifton describes as 'the division of the self into two functioning wholes, so that a part-self acts as an entire self' is clearly an important aspect of the virtual fan experience (Strozier, 1994, p. 86). Charles Strozier, who studies religious fundamentalism from a psychoanalytic perspective, argues that such doublings serve as a means of providing relief from the need to recognize a 'broken' self, one that could create uncertainty and doubt within fundamentalist communities. In the fan community – the rooting of the former term in 'fanatic' may be instructive here – and specifically among the *Futurama* 'geeks', doubling also served as a means for maintaining belief, albeit of a less conventional variety. However, rather than merely separating out another part of the self, this fan identity allowed for a kind of comforting dialogue to occur, with the 'non-geek' half of the pair acting as a reassurance that the extremes of dedication evident in the faithful half were always held in check, so to speak, by a meta-critical partner. As with the Kiss fan culture, comparisons with contemporary religious belief systems may seem unusual but in fact are quite relevant. The challenge of hanging on to affective commitment – whether through self-affirming and autobiographical piety or self-ironizing – is a key task for both and evident in the hermeneutic practices of each.

Lastly, I want to situate the analysis of the virtual *Futurama* community in light of the issues raised at the beginning of the chapter regarding subjectivity and cyberspace, as well as the broader questions of mass media and identity that structure this book. To do this, I will examine some of the implications of this analysis in three areas: interpretive practices and the individuals' relationship to the media text, the composition and operation of the audience itself and lastly the implications of both of the above for processes of self-formation and self-reflection. The path of this analysis thus follows the Meadian premise that selves are built and shaped from socio-symbolic encounters and also echoes Jordan's theory that cyberspace creates cyber-individuals.

I want to begin, then, by identifying some crucial aspects of the shifts in interpretive practice implied by the above analysis. The first is a kind of simultaneous intensification and destabilization of the individual's relationship to the television text. The text is now subject to a particularly intense scrutiny; it can be dismantled, critiqued, cataloged and recirculated with increasing ease. At the same time, the ritual character of television viewing and the temporal anchoring of this experience is simultaneously undermined, a process already encouraged by earlier technologies including cable and satellite programming, as well as the VCR. The text is much more easily divorced from a standard horizon of related symbolic bodies – the evening 'strip' of programming, the television season, and other factors – and recontextualized within a more flexible discursive framework, one that now includes an entire body of Web-based material. Of course, such processes of de- and re-contextualization have always been part of the mass media experience, but here the issue of speed is critical; the temporal lag between the initial broadcast of a program and its incorporation within a vastly heterogeneous aesthetic and critical milieu is extremely short. This effect is intensified in the transnational context by the fact that many fans from outside the United States do not have broadcast access to a given episode of the program until long after it has been aired in the U.S.; thus, even if they do not view the episode through Internet technology, they are exposed to the descriptive, critical and aesthetic responses before viewing the primary text.

Concurrent with this increasingly rapid process of the rearticulation of the text, there are expanded opportunities for a wide range of reception-based forms of symbolic production. As noted in the analysis of both fan art and discussion, there is an enormous range of venues, media and styles of secondary discourse that are widely available on the Web. Consider, for example, the various interactive features, from video games to chat rooms, designed specifically for the *Futurama* audience. Many of these are inconceivable without Internet technology, and all offer opportunities for audience members to re-engage the primary texts in very different ways. It is reasonable to expect that such practices might in turn affect subsequent encounters with television programs, including but not limited to *Futurama* itself, becoming an important component in the pre-understandings which inevitably shape interpretive responses. In this way, reception and (secondary) production practices become increasingly intertwined, a process encouraged by the rapid integration of various symbolic circuits, including primary texts, fan responses, reproductions and excerpts of these texts and aesthetic production by audience members.

Such changes in the positioning of a primary text in relation to the audience formation enable a number of the interpretive practices common to the *Futurama* culture, particularly those associated with an ironic mode of interpretation. The combination of an intense scrutiny and a simultaneous distance from the text, both enabled by the interface of CMC and a broadcast medium, suggests a real hermeneutic shift; neither the paradigms of television viewership – as 'distracted', as routine – nor those associated with more careful, intense viewing practices – as in film studies and classical literary hermeneutics, for example – really capture the position of the audience member and web-based fan in this context. As will be evident, this somewhat paradoxical condition is homologously present in both the broader context of the audience formation and in the more intimate domain of identity itself.

In the case of the audience, there is the simultaneously trans-spatial, international and highly domestic character of Internet fan communities. This is an extension of some of the qualities associated with national broadcast television, but it is distinctive in its interactivity, in the ways that it enables audience members from a vast geographic and social spectrum to participate in an interpretive community. Of course, much of this participation occurs not so much between individuals as between personas, purely symbolic bodies that can have tenuous connections to the extra-virtual; the vast possibilities for donning various masks and assuming a range of identities gives the community, as mentioned, a somewhat uncertain status. This uncertainty extends into the kinds of secondary discursive production described above, such as art, song parodies and fan scripts; these had been associated with what was essentially a folk culture of fan groups, official and informal gatherings and loosely organized exchanges of various fan-related materials (see, for example, Jenkins' analysis of 'Filkers' (Jenkins, 1992, pp. 268–273)). Obviously, the vast expansion of these practices into cyberspace provides opportunities for participation to a much greater range – in terms of age, location, socioeconomic status, gender – of individuals. However, it also undermines the more intimate sociality of these fan communities and, as described, invites a level of legal scrutiny that was absent in these communities in their earlier, folkloric incarnations; they have been 'detraditionalized', to again recall Habermasian terminology, a process carrying potentially liberating and destructive effects. I had cited Calcutt's observation that the virtual world magnifies the ways that many of the characteristics associated with youth culture have achieved dominance within a broader culture, and I think the effect is similar with some of the elements of a previously alternative, and in some sense oppositional, culture resituated within a much broader symbolic framework.

An important aspect of this process is the way that the structures and practices of the virtual audience formation are connected with a vastly heterogeneous set of discursive fields. The nearly infinite possibilities for linking provided by the Web allow for a myriad of connections between the *Futurama* Web world and other net-based cultures. There are the predictable ties to science-fiction fan culture, especially *Star Trek* fans, but there are also cross-linkages with computer gaming cultures, the 'geek' culture dedicated to an evaluation of the relative 'geekiness' of various cultural objects and to other technologically-inclined Web cultures. This is amusingly demonstrated in discussions which appeared on mailing lists designed for owners of Nokia cellular phones in which Nokia users who were also *Futurama* fans offered instructions for other fans who wanted to program their phone to ring with the *Futurama* title music. While the practice itself is an intriguing extension of the desktop customization described above, the way that it emerges from the interface of two relatively discrete elements from the Web is evidence of the eclectic character of such connections, and the distance they may have from the conventional boundaries of 'the audience'.

Proceeding from the neo-Meadian premise, elaborated in Chapter 1, that the symbolic environment associated with a given audience formation serves as a kind of generalized other, enabling and encouraging various forms of self-relation, the virtual audience formation suggests a radical restructuring of such an environment. As a result, the possibilities for the derivation of a social self from this formation are similarly reconfigured. The fluidity celebrated by Turkle and the dangers elucidated by Barglow, Kroker and Weinstein exist as possibilities here, but they can be reconciled with a kind of ironic attachment to 'geekdom'. This move allows the individual to turn simultaneous threats of self-dispersion – 'being lost in the net' – and the monomaniacal alienation characteristic of the old fashioned geek into a means of embracing one's passions and simultaneously avoiding excessive self-investment.

Kroker and Weinstein's sense of 'recline' is useful here, as the net-based audience formation, with its dually domesticated technological underpinnings and potentially asocial character, certainly bears some signs of this paralytic state. At the same time, though, it is energized by the speed and expanded spatial possibilities enabled both by the reach and velocity of the Internet and by the dissemination of youth cultural energies described by Calcutt. The recline, then, may not be as purely enervating and apathetic as Kroker and Weinstein suggest; on the other hand, the recontextualization of some of the innovative and potentially subversive strategies of sub- and youth cultures undoubtedly strips them of at least some of their original force. In the specific case of the *Futurama* audience, this tension is increased by a primary text (the program itself) that is both suitable for the hermeneutic possibilities of virtuality and relentlessly satirical in its presentation of technology, media culture and the numbing character of contemporary social life.

The kind of ironic and split subject evident in the Web culture surrounding *Futurama*, then, reflects a new twist on the processes of mediated self-reflection posed in theoretical terms in Chapter 1. In one sense, it is supremely self-reflective in that there is an inherent, technologically-enabled distanciation produced by the symbolic structure of the virtual, a process with occasional breaks, as in the legal struggles over fan sites; such interruptions serve to mobilize this community (to an extent) and to produce forms of social attachment impossible in the purely virtual world, but they are also inevitably fleeting. However, the community retains a fundamental separation from the kinds of interpersonal, co-present social formations that Mead and others posed as fundamental to the shaping of the self. The quest to find a place in which one's 'I' can find some fulfillment – even within the terms of media consumption – is enabled by the expanded possibilities and symbolic freedom offered by the Web but also diffused by the intrinsic distance between the real individual and the fragmented forms of self thrown up upon the Internet. This virtual culture thus reflects a third variation on the types of mediated selfhood evident in the previous two analyses. In the following chapter, I will be discussing the comparative implications of all three.

Conclusion: Underground Hybridity, Popular Piety and Virtual Irony as Three Modes of Mediated Selfhood

In the case studies that preceded this conclusion, I examined three very different media fan formations; on the surface, underground film freaks, the Kiss Army and *Futurama* geeks would appear to have relatively little in common. The choice of three diverse sites was intentional, reflecting a balance of media, cultural milieux and demographic and economic scale. In this conclusion, though, I want to pose all three as more than just a diverse collection of audience communities and instead present them as a kind of allegorical collective, representing condensations of larger tendencies in the interplay of media and the self, and more specifically, of the peculiar dynamics of the fan identity. The seemingly absurd character of some of the analysis – the defiant vulgarity of Kiss bassist Gene Simmons refracted through the analytic philosophy of Ernst Tugendhat, or Mark Hejnar's subcultural cinema posed as a form of self-affirming discourse – may seem less so within this context; here, these individual cases exist as exemplary forms of a much larger set of practices. In this final section, I examine the three case studies in more general terms, as reflective of hybridity, piety and irony as strategies for building an identity from the encounter with mass media. Rather than exploring each internally, the task of the preceding analyses, I will examine each mode across three other matrices – roles, regions and practices.

In characterizing the culture of local underground cinema as a hybrid culture and one that encourages a consonant hybridity of identity, I am referring particularly to the ways that this formation weaves together a variety of often disparate cultural threads. The mutability of production, consumption and critical roles, the blending of radical politics with elite and often romantic aesthetic sensibilities and the high degree of overlap with a variety of other subcultures are all evidence of this hybridity. There is a certain unity, of course, in the rejection of mainstream forms of culture among these various elements, but there are also significant areas of conflict, as in the tension between radicals and aesthetes described in Chapter 2. The flexibility of the underground film culture, though, can work to mediate some of these conflicts by giving the 'freak' an opportunity for piecing together an identity out of this plurality. The relentless engagement of 'the self' within the aesthetic objects central to this culture – the films, of course, but also the critical and exegetical work – further encourages a kind of self-scrutiny, one that can produce both a stronger investment within the culture and a critical distance in reference to it. The participatory dimension of the underground, with a frequent blending among circuits of production, consumption and criticism, also deepens the personal engagement with the culture and encourages the subjective polyvalence that is an important part of the broader constitution of this culture from a variety of contributing subcultures.

This hybridity stands in deep contrast to the culture of the 'Kiss Army', one marked by an aforementioned piety in the symbolic constitution of a fan identity. I use the term 'piety' here to refer to the explicit and implicit religiosity of the culture as described in Chapter 3: the fan as 'acolyte', the hierarchical but simultaneously utopian community structures, the self-conscious attachment to a body of mythology and folklore and the iconic status of the band members themselves. The obvious and seemingly daunting contradictions that are an inevitable part of such piety – the silliness of much of the mythology, the relentless commercialization associated with the band, much of the music's somewhat mundane thematic content – serve to increase rather than diminish the symbolic potency of this attachment. The drive to reign in instabilities and to attach one's identity to a stable and utopian image is thus strikingly different from the embrace of heterogeneity in the world of the 'freak'.

The virtual television 'geek', while reflective of aspects of both of the above, adds a third mode of mediated self-construction, one predicated on an ironic distance and a technologically-enabled fluidity. While there are elements of piety in the exegetical obsessiveness associated with the culture and elements of hybridity in the connection with a vast array of virtual and extra-virtual discourses, the dominant character is one of ironic self-consciousness. The possibility for this subjective distance – one enabled by the relative ease of separating real individuals and web personae – creates a context in which the monomaniacal passions typical of more intense fan engagements can be balanced with a self-awareness of one's geekdom. The cultural split between a social isolation engendered by the doubly domestic media of both attention (television) and dialogue (the Internet), and the inevitably expanded virtual community associated with the latter, similarly creates a form of subjective doubling. In this case, engagement with a vast community of fellow fans can be undertaken with few of the risks (and rewards) associated with physical social proximity.

In addition to the distinctions in role noted above, each mode operates within a distinct set of spaces, regions that in the Meadian understanding play a critical role in the generation of forms of social subjectivity. In the case of the underground film scene, a hybridity of role is matched with a similar hybridity of space. There is the use of spaces such as nightclubs and church meeting rooms for the screening of films, as well as the ambivalent relationship to a university that contributes both financial resources and individuals to the culture but also reflects the institutionalization (and perhaps the conventionalization) of the avant-garde. The emphasis on small scale production, zine-based criticism, the aforementioned fluidity of material roles and a D.I.Y. ('do it yourself') ethos also encourages the development and operation of a distinctly local scene, albeit one with ties to a national and international underground. However, economic and logistical necessity demands that such a local scene, particularly in a relatively small city, be assembled from a diverse array of contributing elements. In this sense, as mentioned, the region parallels the kinds of identities it encourages in its contingency and diversity.

One finds similar parallels in the larger cultural world of the Kiss Army. Like the quasi-religious forms of self-imaging and self-affirmation reflected in the Kiss acolyte, highly ritualized spaces such as the concert hall – recall the nearly rapturous discussion of concerts by fans – and the fan convention are particularly important and work to reinforce this odd rock and roll piety. Such spaces are also important in that they reflect the distinctly hierarchical organization of the culture, with an egalitarian audience balanced with a very clear object of devotion. Of the three sites under analysis, the Kiss world has the most direct ties to an international circuit of commodity production and distribution, one that works to bridge geographic territories through unifying practices of consumption. Unlike the valorization of the micro-cultural and the local in the underground film scene, there is a celebration of mass popularity, sometimes even couched in militaristic terms of world dominance (this is the Kiss 'Army', after all). Recall the campaigns to encourage fans to push all of the band's albums into certified gold sales and for a mass marketed Eric Carr action figure; here, the emphasis on a recognition of massive popularity matches a similar emphasis on power and brotherhood in the fantastic and utopian self-configuration of fans.

The spatial dynamics associated with the virtual *Futurama* culture are quite different from both of the above and reflect a kind of doubled space; 'doubled' in the sense that the culture is centered around two technological screens, both largely domestic but otherwise carrying vastly different cultural connotations. This split provides an opportunity for the self-ironization that is an important part of this culture. As in the previous examples, there is a clear homology between a form of mediated identity and the regions in which it operates. Rather than an identity derived from an array of symbolic circuits (the freak) or formed upon a fantasy of coherence and empowerment (a member of the Kiss Army), the *Futurama* geek exhibits the kind of duality that is evident in the regioning of her behavior as a fan.

While the hermeneutic paradigm relies strongly upon this role-region interplay to account for the constitution of a social-symbolic subject, there is a secondary emphasis – particularly in the Meadian inflection of this paradigm – on the importance of action in the generation of a social self. Thus, I want to complete the characterization of these three modes with a brief reiteration of the practices central to each fan formation. In the case of the underground film culture, the major distinguishing characteristics of such practices are the intertwining of aesthetic production, spectatorship and critical and interpretative practices; this is secondarily combined with organizational and practical labor, particularly in the staging of events such as the Freaky Film Festivals. Within the specific domain of filmmaking, there is an emphasis on the personally expressive dimension of aesthetic production and upon its place within a like-minded and essentially folkloric community of fellow artists. This is reflected, within social theory, in Dewey's and Mead's sense of natural esprit de corps and the future-directed tenor of all aesthetic activity.

It would be easy and tempting to contrast this in rather stark terms with the more consumerist bent of practices associated with the Kiss culture, but this would be a regrettable simplification. In fact, one finds much of the same aesthetic ethos behind the types of artistic production associated with the latter culture – particularly in the more elaborate examples such as Sherman's novel, LaRose's poetry, and the theatrical musical created from *The Elder*. However, the grounding for this material is always the primary texts supplied by the band itself; self expression, in such cases, is always a reworking of these texts, rather than the more expansive sense of creative resources evident within the underground film culture. There are also the more conventional practices associated with devoted fans, such as the collection of merchandise and attendance and official and unofficial events; these lack the aesthetic element present in the more producerly (to borrow a term from Fiske) activities described above, but they share a similarly reverent orientation – manifested, in the case of collecting, in a distinctly iconic relationship – towards the band and its products.

The key practices evident in the virtual *Futurama* community have elements of both of the previous formations. There is a similarity with Kiss fans, perhaps unsurprisingly, in the large body of creative materials directly derivative of a primary text, in this case the program itself. However, as indicated, the tendency toward an ironic attitude toward the program and toward fandom creates a distance that is also evident in the practices of the culture. A comparison of two fan-based 'protest' campaigns is useful in illustrating this distinction. While there was the Eric Carr action figure campaign among Kiss fans, the *Futurama* community, along with a number of other fan groups, participated in the protests against Twentieth Century Fox's crackdown on Internet fan sites. The latter involved the assumption of an explicitly critical (if not radical) perspective on the industrial interests associated with the program, while the former reflected a demand for recognition for Carr through an incorporation within the apparatus of mass production. In this light, the *Futurama* fans look a bit more like the underground 'freaks' in their skepticism toward mainstream commercial interests, though these critical passions are usually tempered with a measure of irony.

If the roles, regions and practices associated with these three media cultures illustrate very distinct and telling variations on the subjective dimensions of a fan's engagement with contemporary media, they can also be connected back to the developmental theory of subjectivity in the more general terms of the Meadian social subject. In this sense, all three aspects – role, regions, practices – might be understood as resources for producing a kind of mediated self-understanding, one that could be characterized in terms of the I/me dynamic central to this theoretical perspective. Obviously, any such characterization will lose some of the nuances that have been identified in the individual cases, but it will also provide a clearer sense of the status of all three as allegorical reflections of aspects of a much larger media culture.

In the case of the film freak, discovering subjective coherence demands the incorporation and synthesis, along the lines suggested by Joas, of a variety of 'me' positions – the social conventions associated with filmmaking (and a secondary split between aestheticism and activism), those associated with critical interpretation and spectatorship and those related to organizational tasks – into a more stable identity as a member of the underground community. When combined with the paramount importance of 'the personal' at textual and critical levels, this process of synthesis tends to produce a particularly self-critical, self-reflective subject; this is evident, for example, in the reflexive preoccupation with cinematic representation in many of the films important to this culture.

In the case of the Kiss culture, the task is less one of synthesis and assemblage but rather of maintaining a self-affirming and utopian subject position through a kind of pious dedication to one's place as a Kiss fan. Here there is a need, described in Chapter 3, to achieve a high degree of I/me convergence, and to configure fandom as a site of personal redemption, empowerment, and distinction. The divergences and contradictions that are inevitably a part of this process – as in the status of the fan as paragon of autonomy and as rabid consumer – are less resources for self-examination that impetuses for an intensification of one's symbolic attachment to this culture and of the practices crucial to maintaining this attachment (textual interpretation, secondary aesthetic production, etc.).

This is quite different from the doubled subjectivity central to the virtual *Futurama* community, one in which a gap between symbolic fields is not an obstacle to, but a means for, identity production. Here the task is not so much the assemblage of disparate 'me' positions nor their reconciliation, but instead the creation of a relatively complete persona – the geek – that is both self-critical and obsessive. In this sense, it fuses elements of both of the above through the maintenance of discrete 'me' positions enabled by the relative symbolic autonomy of the Internet. This supports some of the more optimistic speculation concerning the subjective fluidity of the Internet, but it is crucial to note that in this case, at least, the virtual discourse is anchored in the symbolic world of network television, and that this medium provides the jumping-off point for the exploration of one's alternative personae.

The question of the fluid, 'semiotic self' (to borrow Norbert Wiley's term) inevitably raises the issue of the postmodern. In light of the work done in the preceding case studies, I now return to one particularly critical issue – the multiphrenic threat to the self produced by the increasingly dominant role of the mass media in social life, and the subsequent 'disappearance' of the social subject. Recall that in the Jamesonian model, this is posed as a collapse in the signifying chain and the assumption of a schizophrenic state, and for Baudrillard it is regarded as the triumph of the object and a swallowing up of the subject. What one finds in the three case studies, though, is an attempt at a kind of subjective 'appearance' in the face of these threats. While aspects of the postmodern diagnoses are indeed evident – in the speed with which texts circulate, in the overwhelming and nearly instantaneous availability of information, for example – they are balanced with a marked proteanism of the subject itself. It is not as if the maps of meaning have collapsed, but rather that they have become scattered, fragmented and highly contingent. In this light it may be useful to reiterate Habermas' aforementioned argument that when a lifeworld is detraditionalized, there is an expansion of horizons of possibility that complements and perhaps mitigates the concurrent danger of the completely 'spoken' subject of Lacan's theory. Recall as well that if one considers Tugendhat's point that symbolically-constructed role positions can be conceived as offers of meaning rather than automatically determinative structures, then there is an expansion of choices here, although this is always limited by the role positions that are socially provided. Similarly, the struggle to maintain the symbolic parameters of a given self is increasingly challenging in this climate; witness the drive of Kiss fans to maintain the meaning of their fandom in the face of the band's return to widespread popularity and symbolic ubiquity.

If the three fan formations analyzed in the previous chapters imply an uneasy and ambivalent relationship with the postmodern theoretical position described in Chapter 1, they may offer some empirical insights into the question of the subject itself, and especially the binary configurations of socio-symbolic subjectivity. As argued, if the subject can be conceived along neo-Meadian lines as a form of environmental symbolic incorporation, one similar to the Deleuzian-Foucauldian 'folding', then the relapse to one pole in the active/passive binary can be avoided while still maintaining a reasonable depth in the conception of the subject. In relating these binaries to the cases at hand, it would be easy, for example, to pose the underground film community as paradigmatically 'active' given the explicitly political tone of much of the work produced within this community, the emphasis on a mode of artistic production quite distant from conventional capitalism and the linkages with other counter-cultural formations. Against this, one might pose the Kiss Army as paradigmatically passive, given the less critical stance towards commercial culture (and even a celebration of the same), the prevalence of traditional fan-star discourses and the wider quasi-religious character of much of this community. While there is certainly some resonance to this characterization, there are key factors that complicate such an understanding. For example, the Kiss community embraces a utopian model of both the self and the community, one with strong connotations of egalitarianism and autonomy (albeit a masculinist version); this idealism, however deformed by its rooting in a highly commodified culture, suggests the kind of aesthetic-minded future orientation that is an important part of both the Meadian and Jamesonian models of developed consciousness.

Lastly, there is the seemingly active world of *Futurama* web fans, who display a more self-critical attitude than the Kiss fans – though this critical attitude is always refracted and perhaps diffused through the prism of irony – and are certainly more irreverent in their attitude toward the text and the mass medium that supplies it. Nonetheless, it is still limited by the symbolic terms offered by the primary text and by the fragmentation stemming from an ironic stance. While the program itself supplies a critique of the media and of aspects of contemporary capitalism, these tend to be undermined by its relentlessly ironic presentation and by the way that it becomes taken up within fan discourse. What all of the above cultures share is an inability to be placed clearly within one of the binaries described in Chapter 1; for instance, both Althusserian interpellation (one side of this arrangement) and Fiskean popular pleasures (the other side) are inadequate descriptions of identity construction within these cultures. Grossberg's elision of subjectivity for a practice/articulation model, while avoiding some of the oversimplified terms of the above, would still fail to capture the subtle dynamics of these various forms of symbolic 'folding', whether this involves the deep textualism and hybrid environment of the underground freak, the faithful piety of the Kiss Army or the doubled self-irony of the *Futurama* geek.

Of course, one of the central features of all three of these forms of self-creation is the latent utopian dimension that is an important part of all three, and thus merits some final reflection. This utopian dimension is most explicit in the case of Kiss fans. As noted, there is a fantasy of autonomy, distinction and egalitarianism central to the world of the Kiss army, one intensified by a set of associated contradictions: the relentless marketing of the band, the mid-nineties return to broad popularity as a nostalgia act and a more general sense of cultural inauthenticity that has long been associated with Kiss. These fantasies, of course, also reflect the overwhelmingly male and predominantly working-class membership of the fan community. The link made by one informant with Harley-Davidson ownership is telling in this regard, in that both Kiss fandom and the motorcycle culture associated with Harley-Davidson carry similar class orientations as well as similar fantasies of a heavily masculine autonomy and empowerment. The sense of an escape from the everyday is very important here and reflects the claims made by Frith, Grossberg, Waksman and others regarding the power of rock music to offer a transcendence of the mundane. The Kiss Army demonstrates this sort of transcendence, but in this case it is not derived solely or perhaps even primarily from the music, but instead from a much wider symbolic package.

The issue of symbolic breadth is important to the underground film culture, one also featuring a central fantasy of autonomy, but in this case it is the autonomy of an 'alternative' culture; this is conjoined with a secondarily utopian conception of the underground as a kind of common space for the vast array of cultural identities described in Chapter 2. While this fantasy may look rather different from the one described as critical to Kiss culture, it too involves a significant and, in some cases, remarkably similar set of contradictions; there is the threat of colonization by the mainstream, as well as the need to mediate between a variety of often disparate political and aesthetic standpoints. Secondly, in the emphasis on an intensely personalized aesthetic expression, there is a sense of possible liberation from the boundaries imposed by the culture industries and by the more general strictures of conventional social morality. This echoes, as noted, a much earlier rhetoric that surrounded underground cinema in its sixties countercultural heyday. The sense of the freak as a 'free subject' – true to one's own vision, quite literally – becomes an important part of the symbolic milieu of the underground, and as with the Kiss army, this is the case across a variety of discourses, extending well beyond the boundaries of a set of primary cinematic texts. As the *Micro-Film* motto indicates, cinema is not merely celluloid in this cultural world, but 'flesh and blood'.

In the culture of the cyber-fan, however, the limits of flesh and blood act as barriers to be overcome rather than instruments for an aesthetic self-fashioning. Here, the central fantasy is one of a liberation of the self through an escape from corporeality rather than an aestheticizing transformation of the self. The creation of a web persona, one free to engage in pursuits that might otherwise be socially stigmatizing, and the resultant doubling of the self is radically different from the attempt to hone a more authentic self reflected in the above cultures. Freedom is key here as well, but it is an ironic freedom, one that is thus more restricted but also perhaps tied to a stronger awareness of the limitations of fan-based identities. The ability to generate a critical perspective on a discrete symbolic self is unique to this formation. The notion of multiple and relatively complete selves that is important to this culture is also intriguing in that it reflects a break from the more classically modern fantasies described above. It is defiantly inauthentic, incoherent by nature and reflects a disinterest in developing the kind of unified self at the heart of both the film freak and the Kiss army member. 'Being true to yourself' is not a key issue here; 'being creative with your selves' is a more accurate description of the ethos of the *Futurama* web community.

If the case studies confirm some of the theoretical speculation regarding conceptions of subjectivity that have informed scholarship within media and cultural studies, I want to conclude by discussing some of the wider implications of this research for the study of media formations. The first is to note the paramount importance of primary texts, both as the objects of scholarly analysis and as key elements in the ways that forms of media become meaningful to audience formations. The underground film fans and the Kiss Army provide important examples here. In both cases, the primary texts (music and films) are absolutely critical to the ways that such cultures produce modes of self-creation and identity formation. In the former, the continual deployment of a hyper-subjective, self-involved rhetorical strategy within crucial films suggests the articulation of such texts as direct extensions of their creators. For the latter, there is the exegetical intensity of fans who look for inspiration and even instruction in the music, particularly as this becomes activated within a larger set of mythological, heroic discourses. In the final case of *Futurama* fans, a heavily ironic and technologically malleable primary text provides the grounds for a similarly ironic and mutable fan identity.

The important distinction between the approach here and conventional textual analysis, even the hermeneutically rich approach of scholars such as Tony Wilson, is that in this case the text is not simply an object of interpretative practices in a narrow sense, but also a resource for symbolic integration into a social self. This dynamic, it should be noted, is missing entirely in the Althusserian paradigm, in which interpretive practices are given a strongly social dimension but accorded little potential for processes of creative self-construction; the overly deterministic nature of the ideological system simply does not allow for such reflexivity. Likewise, such processes of symbolic incorporation imply a depth missing in the turn toward 'affective investment' as a means of understanding the engagement with media, as in Grossberg; here, affect is folded, transformed and rearticulated in ways that resist description as practices taking place upon a relatively flat social plane. At the same time, it would be a simplification in the reverse direction to claim this process as an example of free subjects making use of media texts at will, as in the 'uses and gratifications' approach. That approach grants the subject a certain depth, but walls her off against the kind of reflexive processes of incorporation through which texts make subjects (as much as the reverse) and thus refuses to acknowledge a certain reciprocity in interpretive practices.

However, if one grants the subject status as a locus of meaning *and* as the site of discursive integration, then both sides of this problem can be avoided. By extending the Meadian premise of the self as the synthesis of otherness, particularly in the version favored by Tugendhat and Kögler, one can begin to see subjectivity as critical to the understanding of media fan formations; the self becomes a meaningful entity (literally) not interpellated by a symbolic order in the Althusserian fashion but constituted by the engagement of a subject with a set of socially-provided symbolic resources. The importance of the mass media in this process is reflected continually in the cases described above. The construction of an entire culture of 'personal cinema' reflected in the philosophy behind *Micro-Film*, the emergence of the 'Kisstory' as an autobiographical genre and the meditations on the nature of 'geekdom' all stand as particularly useful examples of the ways that the subject and media become interlocked in a process of self-construction and discursive production. In the case of the culture of personal cinema and its manifestation in practices of aesthetic and critical production, the emphasis is less on autobiographical narrative per se and instead upon the cultivation of sites – formed, as noted, through an alignment of related cultural formations – for the maximum realization of this self-expressive potential. Within the Kiss army, encounters with media become the narrative center of an autobiography giving individuals the opportunity to reflect upon one's childhood, one's relationship to a community (of both disapproving and supportive varieties) and even upon life-changing experiences. In the final example noted above, the encounter with media becomes the vehicle for a more directly reflexive examination of one's status as a fan and the nature of fandom itself. It should be noted that these are merely outstanding cases; the previous three chapters offer many other examples of this dynamic.

It is appropriate at this point to reiterate that this analysis is not intended to be comprehensive in the sense that it would purport to represent the full social function and impact of the mass media and especially media reception practices. In this light, it is meant as a supplement to the analysis offered by political economics and other larger scale modes of analysis. Such approaches are obviously able to provide a more adequate account of the material dynamics and fiscal and logistical functioning of various mass media. However, these can only provide a partial understanding of the social significance of these media; despite biases against a deeper understanding of the social individual in both Marxist and other, less radical modes of mass communication analysis, it remains a key area of inquiry.

If the impasse of subjectivity in media studies can be overcome, as I have tried to demonstrate, with an approach that takes the hermeneutic, subject-forming possibilities of media seriously, I would secondly argue that this approach can extend the reach of media studies as a discipline. This is most evident, perhaps, in the way that one can understand a set of social conditions associated with a postmodern conception of the social order – and the special role of the media within it – without automatically accepting the overdrawn, pessimistic conclusions regarding the individual that often accompany this diagnosis. Media studies are necessarily drawn into these debates, even as they are launched in philosophy, sociology and literary studies, and it seems only reasonable that scholars develop more sophisticated strategies for entering into them.

In this spirit, I would add that in addition to serving as a means of illustrating some of the theoretical arguments made in Chapter 1, the three in-depth studies are also intended, as mentioned, as allegories for a wider array of media-derived practices of self-construction and, ultimately, forms of social identity. Clearly, they examine particularly intense and/or unique varieties of media audience communities; as noted in Chapter 1, fans are saturated by media in notably strong and sometimes peculiar ways. However, while most consumers of media may seem far removed from the Kiss fans described in Chapter 3, for example, they may also use forms of media as a means of self-affirmation and autobiographical self-construction. While such practices are unlikely to be as striking or as intense, this is a difference of degree rather than of fundamental structure. I would also point out that such an analysis is possible largely through the exportation of theoretical approaches that have often been alien to mass media research, though, as noted, some of these are more common in interpersonal communication research. It also relies upon the use of ethnography in a complementary relationship with the theoretical observations, rather than as a vouchsafe for the authenticity of the observer's perspective or as the sole source of a 'grounded theory'.

Ultimately, I hope, the work can help to fill in an understanding of the role of the mass media in social life by illustrating some critical aspects of this role. I began the book with a brief reflection upon the concurrent public fascination with the Columbine High School shootings and the release of the fourth film in the *Star Wars* series, suggesting that while the treatment of both events often affirmed that mass media can have a real impact on individual lives, the presentation of this impact was grossly oversimplified. The monological character of this impact, at least as it was presented in the mainstream media (and often supported by intellectuals, particularly in the case of Columbine), was reflective of broader binaries that have tended to impede research on the media and the public. In the end, I have provided substantial evidence that there is a good deal of space between such binaries, and that this is rich territory for scholarly inquiry. In this spirit, I hope that throughout the preceding pages I have provided a better sense of what it means to explore the encounter between an 'I' and a 'me(dia)' and what such an exploration might reveal about media and identity in the symbolic world of the contemporary fan.

Notes

Introduction: Media, Culture and The Self

1   See Camille Bacon-Smith's *Enterprising Women* as well as the more recent anthology *Enterprise Zones* (Harrison, 1996).

Chapter 1: Media and Self-Construction: Theoretical Issues

1   Here, 'media studies' refers primarily to the more politically-inclined approaches such as 'British Cultural Studies', ideology theory and postmodern critical theory; the American tradition of media studies (e.g., uses and gratifications, cultivation theory, 'powerful effects') has rarely engaged the question of subjectivity directly, as it is simply not within the normal analytic domain of these approaches.

2   Althusser achieved a degree of infamy for a struggle with mental illness that included the murder of his wife, an ordeal detailed in his autobiography, entitled *The Future Lasts Forever*.

3   'Debate' may be a misnomer in the sense that Thompson's essay on Althusser, 'The Poverty of Theory or an Orrery of Errors' came only a few years before Althusser's full descent into mental illness, thus leaving little room for an extensive reply.

4   John Frow and Meaghan Morris offer similar critiques of Fiske, and both explicitly attach his binary model of 'the popular' and 'dominant' (Frow, 1995, p. 62; Morris, 1988, pp. 165–166).

5   Kögler uses the work of Pierre Bourdieu as an example of this 'social dope' model but it would also be applicable to Althusser and arguably to Grossberg as well.

6   Here, Habermas refers specifically to systems theory as implying a passive subject, but as with Kögler's argument, it could certainly apply to those positions within media and cultural studies that have emphasized passive reception.

7   While Habermas would not use the term 'postmodern' to describe this life-world, it would certainly have some critical similarities with many of the characteristics of the postmodern world identified by scholars using that term.

8   Interestingly, Richard Rorty connects the pragmatists' (which would certainly include Mead) 'sense that there is nothing deep down inside us except what we have put there' with Nietzsche and Foucault. I would argue that Lacan could be included here as well (Rorty, 1986, p. 60).

9   Lifton works within the Eriksonian psychological tradition, and Gergen draws upon a variety of contemporary perspectives in his analysis.

Chapter 2: Every Freak Needs a Show: Polyvalent Subjectivity and a Local Underground Film Scene

1 The quest for a pure experience of cinema within the avant-garde reached an apex in Peter Kubelka's design for a screening room that would eliminate the possibility for any distractions from other spectators, light pollution, or architectural/design features – the 'invisible cinema' – described in the Anthology Film Archives manifesto.

2 Kevin Smith, the auteur behind *Clerks* and *Chasing Amy*, is particularly well-known for his association with alternative comics. He is the owner of a comic book store, Jay and Silent Bob's Secret Stash, in Red Bank, New Jersey, and commissioned a spin-off comic based on characters from *Clerks*. *Chasing Amy*, his breakthrough mainstream hit, is a love story involving independent comic book artists.

3 Baudrillard is presumably referring here to the early work of Foucault; as noted, in the later work, Foucault develops a more nuanced and less mono-logically oppressive sense of subjectivity.

Chapter 3: 'I Believe in Me': Self-Affirmation in the 'Kiss Army'

1 The Band continues to tour in the original makeup, although as of 2002 the two returning members, Criss and Frehley, have left the band again; however, their replacements assume the same 'Cat' and 'Spaceman' personas.

2 Interestingly, Kiss singer Paul Stanley would end up performing as the title character of Andrew Lloyd Webber's musical *Phantom of the Opera* in a 1999 Toronto production.

3 Simmons and Stanley are famous for their abstemious conduct, and Simmons appeared in anti-drug public service announcements for MTV in the eighties, so this lyrical theme is not particularly surprising.

4 There is some fan fiction dealing with teen idols – 'boy bands' and performers such as Britney Spears and Christina Aguilera – but relatively little dealing with mainstream rock acts.

5 The campaign was a success and a Carr figure was introduced by McFarlane toys in 2002.

6 Frustration with the degree of merchandising appears occasionally within the discourse of Kiss fans, particularly when new products emerge – there are literally hundreds – ranging from credit cards to wine to caskets.

Chapter 4: Screen Subjects and Cyber-Subjects: The Case of Futurama

1 This youth orientation is evident, for example, in the subculture of comput-er hackers, and, more conventionally, in the proliferation of so-called 'dot com millionaires', very young Internet entrepreneurs.

2 This convergence is displayed, for example, in the hybrid television networks MSNBC, a joint venture between NBC and Microsoft, and Oxygen, Oprah

Winfrey's network which features a continuous interface with an affiliated website.

3   *The Simpsons* made an explicit joke of this situation in an episode in which Sideshow Bob, Bart's mortal enemy, used television to communicate that he would blow up the world if television was not eliminated.; in the episode, Bob mentions that he is fully aware of the irony of using television to deliver this message.

4   For example, *Star Trek* is the subject of extensive discussion on the alt.geek newsgroup, one dedicated to evaluating the relative geekiness of various aspects of popular culture.

Works Cited

Althusser, L. *Lenin and Philosophy* (London: Verso, 1971).

Anderson, P. *Arguments Within English Marxism* (London: Verso, 1980).

Appadurai, A. *Modernity at Large* (Minneapolis: University of Minnesota Press, 1996).

Bacon-Smith, C. *Enterprising Women: Television Fandom and the Creation of a Popular Myth* (Philadelphia: University of Pennsylvania Press, 1991).

Barglow, R. *The Crisis of the Self in The Age of Information: Computers, Dolphins, and Dreams* (London: Routledge, 1994).

Baudrillard, J. *Cool Memories* (London: Verso, 1990).

Baudrillard, J. *Paroxysm* (London: Verso, 1998).

Baudrillard, J. *The Perfect Crime* (London: Verso, 1995).

Baudrillard, J. *The Transparency of Evil* (London: Verso, 1993).

Baym, N. 'Talking About Soaps: Communication Practices in Computer Mediated Fan Culture', in C. Harris and A. Alexander (eds) *Theorizing Fandom: Fans, Subculture, and Identity* (Cresskill, NJ: Hampton Press, 1998).

Belz, C. *The Story of Rock* (New York: Harper and Row, 1973).

Benton, T. *The Rise and Fall of Structural Marxism* (London: Verso, 1984).

Brakhage, S. *The Brakhage Scrapbook*, R. Hollinger (ed.) (New Paltz, NY: Documentext, 1982).

Brundson, C. 'Television: Aesthetics and Audiences', in P. Mellencamp (ed.) *Logics of Television* (Bloomington: Indiana University Press, 1990).

Burawoy, M. *Ethnography Unbound: Power and Resistance in the Urban Metropolis* (Berkeley: University of California Press, 1991).

Burkitt, I. *Social Selves: Theories of the Social Formation of Personality* (London: Sage, 1991).

Calcutt, A. *White Noise: An A–Z of the Contradictions in Cyberspace* (New York: St. Martin's Press, 1999).

Camper, F. 'The End of Avant-Garde Film', *Millenium Film Journal* 16/17/18 (Fall/Winter 1986/87) 99–124.

Castells, M. *The Information Age: Economy, Society, and Culture. Volume 1: The Rise of the Networked Society* (Cambridge, MA: Blackwell, 1996).

Clark (1992)

Clark, A. (ed.). *The Rock Yearbook 1982* (New York: St. Martin's Press, 1982).

Clarke, S. T. Lovell, K. McDonnell, K. Robins and V.J. Seidler. *One Dimensional Marxism: Althusser and the Politics of Culture* (New York: Schocken, 1980).

Coleman, M. 'Kiss', in A. DeCurtis, J. Henke and H. George-Warren (eds) *The Rolling Stone Album Guide* (New York: Random House, 1992).

Cook, G.A. *George Herbert Mead: The Making of a Social Pragmatist* (Urbana, IL: University of Illinois Press, 1993).

Cronk, G. *The Philosophical Anthropology of George Herbert Mead* (New York: Peter Lang, 1987).

Cronk, G. 'Symbolic Interactionism: A "Left Meadian" Approach', *Social Theory and Practice* 2 (1973) 313–333.

De Certeau, M. *The Politics of Everyday Life* (Berkeley: University of California Press, 1984).

Deleuze, G. *Foucault* (Minneapolis: University of Minnesota Press, 1988).

De Man, P. *Allegories of Reading* (New Haven: Yale University Press, 1979).

Denzin, N. *Symbolic Interactionism and Cultural Studies* (Oxford: Blackwell, 1992).

Dobrotovorskaia, E. *The Collective Image in Popular Music: A Visual History of Style* (Thesis, Bowling Green State University, 1993).

Dunn, R.G. *Identity Crisis: A Social Critique of Postmodernism* (Minneapolis: University of Minnesota Press, 1998).

Dyson, E. *Release 2.0: A Design for Living in the Digital Age* (New York: Broadway, 1997).

Eagleton, T. *Ideology: An Introduction* (London: Verso, 1991).

Eddy, C. *Stairway to Hell: The 500 Best Heavy Metal Albums in the Universe* (New York: Harmony, 1989).

Fiske, J. *Media Matters* (London: Verso, 1993).

Fiske, J. *Power Plays/Power Works* (London: Verso, 1994).

Fiske, J. *Understanding Popular Culture* (London: Routledge, 1989).

Foucault, M. *The Care of the Self: The History of Sexuality, Vol. 3.* (New York: Vintage, 1986).

Foucault, M. *Foucault Live* (New York: Semiotexte, 1989).

Foucault, M. *The Uses of Pleasure: The History of Sexuality, Vol. 2.* (New York: Vintage, 1985).

Frank, T. 'New Consensus for Old', *The Baffler* #12, 3–12.

Frith, S. 'Art Ideology and Pop Practice', in L. Grossberg and C. Nelson (eds) *Marxism and The Interpretation of Culture* (Urbana: University of Illinois Press, 1988).

Frith, S. *Performing Rites: On the Value of Popular Music* (Cambridge, MA: Harvard University Press, 1996).

Frow, J. *Cultural Studies and Cultural Value* (Oxford: Clarendon, 1995).

Gergen, K. *The Saturated Self* (New York: Basic, 1991).

Giddens, A. *Central Problems in Social Theory* (Berkeley: University of California Press, 1979).

Godwin, J. *The Devil's Disciples: The Truth About Rock* (Ontario, CA: Chick Publications, 1985).

Goffman, E. *Encounters: Two Studies in the Sociology of Interaction* (Indianapolis: Bobbs-Merrill, 1961).

Grossberg, L. *Dancing in Spite of Myself* (Durham: Duke University Press, 1997).

Grossberg, L. *We Gotta Get Out of This Place* (New York: Routledge, 1992).

Habermas, J. *Postmetaphysical Thinking: Philosophic Essays* (Cambridge: MIT Press, 1992).

Hall, S. 'Introduction: Who Needs Identity?', in S. Hall and P. DuGay (eds) *Questions of Cultural Identity* (London: Sage, 1996).

Hammersley M. and P. Atkinson. *Ethnography* (London: Routledge, 1995).

Harrison, T. (ed.). *Enterprise Zones: Critical Positions on Star Trek* (Boulder: Westview Press, 1996).

Holstein J. and J. Gubrium. *The Self We Live By: Narrative Identity in a Postmodern World* (New York: Oxford University Press, 1999).

Honneth, A. *The Fragmented World of the Social* (Albany: SUNY Press, 1995).

James, D. *Allegories of Film: American Film in the 1960s* (Princeton: Princeton University Press, 1989).

Jameson, F. *Postmodernism, or The Cultural Logic of Late Capitalism* (Durham: Duke University Press, 1991).

Jenkins, H. *Textual Poachers: Television Fans and Participatory Culture* (London: Routledge, 1992).

Joas, H. *G.H.: A Contemporary Re-examination of His Thought* (Cambridge: Polity Press, 1985).

Jordan, T. *Cyberpower: An Introduction to the Politics of Cyberspace* (London: Routledge, 1999).

Katz, J. *Virtuous Reality* (New York: Random House, 1997).

Kögler, H. 'Symbolic Self-Consciousness: Rethinking Reflexivity with Mead and Semiotics', *Studies in Symbolic Interaction* 20 (1996): 193–223.

Kroker, A. *Hacking the Future: Stories for The Flesh-Eating 90s* (New York: St. Martin's Press, 1996).

Kroker, A. and M. Weinstein. *Data Trash: The Theory of the Virtual Class* (New York: St. Martin's Press, 1994).

Lacan, J. *Ecrits: A Selection* (New York: Norton, 1977).

Lendt, C.K. *Kiss and Sell: The Making of a Supergroup* (New York: Billboard Books, 1997).

Levy, E. *Cinema of Outsiders: The Rise of American Independent Film* (New York: New York University Press, 1999).

Lifton, R. *The Protean Self* (New York: Basic, 1993).

MacDonald, A. 'Uncertain Utopia: Science Fiction, Media Fandom, and Computer Mediated Communication' in C. Harris and A. Alexander (eds) *Theorizing Fandom: Fans, Subculture, and Identity* (Cresskill, NJ: Hampton, 1998).

Marsh D. and J. Benard (eds). *The New Book of Rock Lists* (New York: Simon and Schuster, 1994).

Mead, G.H. *Mind, Self, and Society From the Standpoint of a Social Behaviorist* (Chicago: University of Chicago Press, 1934).

Mead, G.H. *Movements of Thought in the Nineteenth Century* (Chicago: University of Chicago Press, 1936).

Mead, G.H. *The Philosophy of the Act* (Chicago: University of Chicago Press, 1938).

Mead, G.H. *The Philosophy of the Present* (Chicago: University of Chicago Press, 1932).

Mellencamp, P. *Indiscretions* (Bloomington: Indiana University Press, 1990).

Meyrowitz, J. *No Sense of Place* (Oxford: Oxford University Press, 1985).

Miller, T. *The Well-Tempered Self* (Baltimore: Johns Hopkis University, 1993).

Milward, J. 'Destroyer.' *Rolling Stone*, 3 June 1976 (70).

Mitchell, W.J. *City of Bits: Space, Place, and the Infobahn* (Cambridge MA: MIT Press, 1996).

Morley, D. *Television, Audiences, and Cultural Studies* (London: Routledge, 1992).

Morris, M. 'Banality in Cultural Studies', *Discourse*, 1988 (10) 3–29.

Muecke, D.C. *The Compass of Irony* (London, Methuen, 1969).

Negroponte, N. *Being Digital* (New York: Vintage, 1995).

Petersen, J. *Dreams of Chaos, Visions of Order: Understanding the American Avant-Garde Cinema* (Detroit: Wayne State University Press, 1994).

Pfeil, F. 'Potholders and Subincisions: On The Businessman, Fiskadoro, and The Postmodern Paradise', in E.A. Kaplan (ed.) *Postmodernism and its Discontents* (London: Verso, 1988).

Polan, D. *The Political Language of Film and the Avant-Garde* (Ann Arbor: UMI Research Press, 1985).

Probyn, E. *Sexing the Self* (New York: Routledge, 1993).

Rabinowitz, L. *Points of Resistance: Women, Power, and Politics in the New York Avant-Garde Cinema, 1943–71* (Urbana: University of Illinois Press, 1991).

Renan, S. *An Introduction to the American Underground Film* (New York: Dutton, 1967).

Rorty, R. 'Pragmatism and Philosophy', in K. Baynes, J. Bohman, T. McCarthy (eds) *After Philosophy: End or Transformation* (Cambridge, MA: MIT Press, 1986).

Rosenbaum J. and J. Hoberman. *Midnight Movies* (New York: Da Capo, 1991).

Silverstone, R. *Television and Everyday Life* (London: Routledge, 1994).

Sitney, P.A. *Visionary Film* (New York: Oxford University Press, 1974).

Sitney, P.A. (ed.). *The Avant-Garde Film: A Reader of History and Criticism* (New York: Anthology Film Archives, 1978).

Slack J. and L. Whitt. 'Ethics and Cultural Studies', in L. Grossberg, C. Nelson, P. Treichler (eds) *Cultural Studies* (New York: Routledge, 1992).

Spigel, L. *Make Room For Television: Television and the Family Ideal in Postwar America* (Chicago: University of Chicago Press, 1992).

Stake, R. 'Case Studies' in N. Denzin and Y. Lincoln (eds) *Handbook of Qualitative Research* (Thousand Oaks, CA: Sage, 1994).

Strozier, C. *Apocalypse: On the Psychology of Fundamentalism in America* (Boston: Beacon Press, 1994).

Swenson, J. *Headliners: Kiss* (New York: Grosset and Dunlap, 1978).

Tapscott, D. *Growing Up Digital: The Rise of the Net Generation* (New York: McGraw Hill, 1998).

Thompson, E.P. *The Poverty of Theory and Other Essays* (London: Merlin, 1979).

Tugendhat, E. *Self-Consciousness and Self-Determination* (Cambridge, MA: MIT Press, 1986).

Turkle, S. *Life on the Screen: Idenity in the Age of the Internet* (New York: Simon and Schuster, 1995).

Tyler, P. *Underground Film: A Critical History* (New York: Grove, 1969).

Waksman, S. *Instruments of Desire: The Electric Guitar and the Shaping of Musical Experience* (Cambridge, MA: Harvard University Press, 1999).

Walser, R. *Running with the Devil: Power, Gender, and Madness in Heavy Metal Music* (Hanover, NH: Wesleyan University Press, 1993).

Wees, W. *Light Moving in Time: Studies in the Visual Aesthetics of Avant-Garde Film* (Berkeley: University of California Press, 1992).

Weinstein, D. *Heavy Metal: A Cultural Sociology* (New York: Lexington Books, 1991).

Wellman B. and M. Gulia. 'Virtual Communication as Communities: Net Surfers Don't Ride Alone', in M. Smith and P. Kollock (eds) *Communities in Cyberspace* (London: Routledge, 1999).

Wiley, N. *The Semiotic Self* (Chicago: University of Chicago Press, 1994).

Wilson, T. *Watching Television: Hermeneutics, Reception, and Popular Culture* (London: Polity Press, 1993).

Wise, J.M. *Exploring Technology and Social Space* (Thousand Oaks, CA: Sage, 1997).

Zizek, S. *The Sublime Object of Ideology* (London: Verso, 1989).
Zizek, S. *The Ticklish Subject: The Absent Centre of Political Ontology* (London: Verso, 1999).
Kiss Psycho Circus Book I (Fullerton, CA: Image Comics, 1998).
Kiss: The Second Coming (Fullerton, CA: Image Entertainment, 1998).
'The 1994 Spy 100', *Spy* January February 1994, 44–62.
'Readers Respond', *Guitar Player* March 1979, 146–147.

Index

Alston, Macky
  Family Name (film), 63
Althusser, Louis
  criticism by Benton, 18
  criticism by Eagleton, 19
  criticism by Thompson, 17–19
  incorrect reading of Lacan, 18–19
  model of the social subject, 17
  'Screen' Althusserians, 17
Anderson, Perry
  criticism of E.P. Thompson, 18
Anger, Kenneth
  Fireworks (film), 62
  Scorpio Rising (film), 62
Appadurai, Arjun, 7, 43–45
  'scape' model of global culture, 43
  'mediascape', 44–45
Atkinson, Paul, 12

Baillie, Bruce, 56
Barglow, Raymond, 162, 175, 200
Baudrillard, Jean, 45–46, 57, 95, 152–153
  'murder of reality', 45
Baym, Nancy, 169
Belz, Carl, 110
Benton, Ted
  criticism of Althusser, 18
  criticism of Thompson, 18
Brakhage, Stan, 57, 65–66
Broughton, James
  Mother's Day (film), 62
Brundson, Charlotte, 51, 173
Burawoy, Michael, 50
Burkitt, Ian, 30

Calcutt, Andrew, 159, 164, 165, 167, 201
Camper, F., 70
Castells, Manuel, 162–163
Clarke, Simon, 18
Cronk, George, 31

Dash, Julie, 62
DeCerteau, Michel, 21
Deleuze, Gilles
  reading of Foucault's 'folded' subject, 35–37
DeMan, Paul, 193
Deren, Maya
  Meshes of the Afternoon (film), 62
Dewey, John, 103
domestic sphere
  television and Internet in, 167–168
Dunn, Robert, 5, 7
Dyson, Esther, 164

Eagleton, Terry
  criticism of Althusser, 19
Eddy, Chuck, 108
ethnography
  hermeneutic approach to, 50
  importance of primary media texts, 51–52, 211–212
  methods utilized in case studies, 50–52

fan culture, 48–50, 180
fan fiction, 133–134
  fan written *Futurama* scripts, 180–182
  fan written Kiss musical, 134–136
  fan written Kiss novel, 132–133
  fan written Kiss poetry, 131–132
Fiske, John, 20–22, 143–144, 156
  'agency' theory, 20–21
Foucault, Michel, 21–22, 145
  criticism by Zizek, 40
  'folded' subject, 37
  self-relation, 22
Frank, Thomas, 2
Freaky Film Festival, 53, 58, 60–61, 71–80
  abstract films, 84–86
  additional events (non-film), 76–77
  author's involvement in, 54–55

Freaky Film Festival – *continued*
    concerns about *The Blair Witch
        Project* (film), 79–80
    difficulties with 'freaky'
        terminology, 74
    films concerning daily life, 86–87
    films concerning self-construction,
        83–84
    financial concerns, 78–79
    I/me dynamic, 207
    locations utilized, 72–73
    printed programs, 79–80   ·
    programming and film selection,
        73–76
    publicity, 80
    queer and feminist films, 63–64
    self-reflexive media commentary
        films, 88–91
    volunteer staff, 77–78
Freaky Film Festival, films screened
    2 On You (dir. Evan Maderakis), 63
    Affliction (dir. Mark Hejnar), 53–54,
        85–86, 87
    Amy (dir. Susan Rivo), 84
    Bible of Skin (dir. Mark Hejnar), 85
    Cannabis Conspiracy, The (dir. Kenya
        Winchell), 91
    Fame Whore (dir. Jon Moritsugu),
        88–89
    Golden Gate (dir. Eric Landmark), 58
    Happy Loving Couples (dir. Doug
        Wolens), 83
    Herd Mentality (dir. Mark Hejnar),
        85
    Isolation (dir. John May), 83
    Jaded/Outlet (dir. Robert Banks), 63,
        89–90
    Jeff (dir. Mark Hejnar), 85–86
    Job (dir. Lisa McElroy), 87, 99
    Luna (dir. Doug Wolens), 91
    MPG: Motion Picture Genocide
        (dir. Robert Banks), 89
    Next Station (dir. Chaker Ayadi), 87
    Number One Fan (dir. Amy
        Talkington), 89
    Peoria Babylon (dir. Michael
        Kaplan), 88
    Pigskin Orgasm (dir. Jennifer and
        Amber Cluck), 63

    *Red's Breakfast III: Die You Zombie
        Bastards* (dir. Caleb Emerson),
        58
    Ribbed for Her Pleasure (dir. Greg
        Brooks), 63
    Sore Losers, The (dir. John Michael
        McCarthy), 58, 75
    Tell-Tale Vibrator, The (dir. Jill
        Chamberlin), 63
    We Hate You Little Boy (dir. Janene
        Higgins), 83
    Wheels of Fury (dir. Dan Dinello),
        58
    *Yuri Pentrado Al Maravilloso Mundo
        De Los Sunos* (dir. Juan Carlos
        Garay Nieto), 84
Frith, Simon, 102–104, 110, 154
Futurama (television program)
    audience demographics, 171
    Bender (character), 174–175
    capitalism and, 176–177
    content and plot, 174
    deconstruction and reassembly of
        primary text, 178–179, 198–199
    distribution of primary text,
        178–180, 198
    fan art
        dependent on web technology,
            184–185
        production of, 198
        symbiotic, utilizing primary text,
            183–184
        traditional, 182
    fan community
        destabilization, 199–200
        I/me dynamic, 207
        multiphrenic nature, 192
        relation to other fan cultures,
            200
        self-reflectivity, 201
        use of irony, 193–196, 199
    fan websites, 170–171, 185–192
        alt.tv.futurama newsgroup, 157,
            186
        archival function, 186
        Can't Get Enough Futurama, 157
        collective nature of, 186
        file sharing, 190–191
        Futurama Chronicles, 157, 172, 186

Futurama Outlet, 182, 185, 187
    legal action against, 188–192
    Much Ado About Futurama, 172
    'Operation Blackout' protest,
        189–190
    Retro Future, 172
    *Roadmap Futurama Database
        Planet*, 186
    self-criticism among, 186–188
    Yahoo *Futurama* club, 157, 185
fan written scripts, 180–182
'filke', 182–183
intertextuality, 172–173
Philip J. Fry (character), 174–175
plot 'spoilers', 179
postmodern construction of, 177
ratings, 171
ritual viewing, 157
romantic love and, 177
satire of Internet, 175–176
satire of mass media, 175–176,
    193–194
temporal and spatial viewing
    distinctions, 157–158, 199–200
textual analysis, 173–177
visual jokes in title sequence, 173

'geek', 1–2, 194–197, 200–201,
    203–204
Gergen, Kenneth
    'saturated self' and relation to
        Mead, 40–41
Giddens, Anthony, 29
Goffman, Erving, 6, 7, 87
Groening, Matt, 171, 191
Grossberg, Lawrence, 22–27, 103–104,
    110, 113, 154–155
    'affective individual', 24–25
    relation to Mead, 33
    articulation model, 23–27
    'inauthentic authenticity', 25–26
Gubrium, Jaber, 153
Gulia, Milena, 164

Habermas, Jurgen, 113
    criticism of Mead, 35
Hejnar, Mark, 53–54, 76–77, 85–86, 90
    Affliction (film), 53–54, 64
    Bible of Skin (film), 85

Herd Mentality (film), 85
Jeff (film), 85–86
TV Ministry (film), 90, 98
Hall, Stuart, 16
Hammersley, Martyn, 12
Haraway, Donna, 161
heavy metal music, 104–105
hermeneutics
    in Kiss fan culture, 152–154
    in study of popular music, 103
Hill, Jerome
    Film Portrait (film), 67
Hoberman, J., 60, 69, 70
Holstein, James, 153
Honneth, Axel, 16

identity
    flexibility in virtual culture,
        159–160, 170
    'geek', 1–2, 194–197, 200–201,
        203–204
    Haraway's 'cyborg', 161, 168
    hybridity, 202–204
    importance of physical space,
        204–205
    media formation in, 55–56
    multiple constructions in virtual
        culture, 160
    practices, 205–206
    threats by mass media, 207–208
    threats by technology, 161–163
    utopian dimensions, 210–211
Internet
    academic research on, 159–163
    claims of impact, 159
    communal engagement of users,
        163–164
    computer mediated fandom,
        169–170
    construction of the multiple self,
        160
    copyright issues, 189
    domesticity, 167–168
    relationship to television, 169
    spatial reconfiguration in, 170
    use and acceptance in United
        States, 167
    virtual community within, 163–164
    youth culture and, 165–166, 170

irony, 193
    doubling nature of, 197
    in *Futurama* fan culture, 193–196,
        199, 201
    in popular media, 194

James, David, 60, 62
Jameson, Fredric, 57, 46–48, 153
    schizophrenic cultural subject, 47
Jenkins, Henry, 133–134, 180, 199
Joas, Hans
    on Mead's I/me structure, 32
Jordan, Tim, 160, 168, 195

Katz, Jon, 163–165
Kiss (rock band)
    Alive LP, 106, 117
    author's previous research of, 10–11
    author's recollection of, 108–109
    band history, 106–107
    Carnival culture, 143–144
    Carr, Eric (member), 137–140
        action figure, 140, 146–147
        fan fiction, 139, 142
    concert performances, 106
    cultural references to, 107–108
    Destroyer LP, 118, 127
    fantasy personas, 116–119
    Kiss Meets the Phantom of the Park
        (film), 101, 106, 132
    mass media appearances, 113
    merchandising, 106–107, 140, 147
    (Music From) The Elder LP, 115, 123,
        127–137
    fan novel, *A World Without
        Heroes*, 132–133
    fan poetry, 131–132
    high school stage performance
        of, 134–136
    musical narrative, 129–131
    parallels with *Star Wars,* 136–137
    relation to fan experience, 129,
        144–145
    sales, 128
    Psychocircus (comic book), 119–120,
        139
    Psychocircus LP, 101, 111
    religious allusions, 110, 149–150
    reunion of original members,
        110–111, 113
    rock criticism of, 107
    satanic/violent legends associated
        with, 123–127
    Vincent, Vinnie (band member),
        141–142
    youth appeal, 109–110, 117–118
Kiss fan culture
    building identity through, 145, 150
    demographics, 109
    fan economics, 147
    fan self-identification, 114
    female fans, 148–149
    hyper-masculinity, 147–148
    I/me dynamic, 207
    importance of individuality,
        111–114, 116, 119–120, 122,
        155
    'Kiss Army' (fan club), 109
    'Kisstianity', 122, 150
    'Kisstories', 108–109, 111–112, 116,
        120–123, 125–127, 138,
        145–146, 148, 153
    mythological connections with
        band, 120–121
    'real' versus 'other' fans, 114–115,
        146, 150
    relationship to *The Elder*, 144–145
Klosterman, Chuck, 105
Kögler, Hans-Herbert, 144
    criticism of Mead, 35
Kroker, Arthur, 161, 167, 201
Kuchar, George and Mike
    Hold Me While I'm Naked (film), 58
    Sins of the Fleshapoids (film), 58

Lacan, Jacques, 8, 38–39
Lendt, C.K., 105, 107, 111, 120, 128,
    148
Levy, Emanuel, 59
Lifton, Robert Jay, 150–151, 163, 197
    'protean self' and relation to Mead,
        41

MacDonald, Andrea, 169, 184
Mead, George Herbert, 6, 7, 28, 61,
    78, 113
    'aesthetic attitude', 49
    aesthetics in self-construction, 145
    criticism by Kogler, 35
    difficulties in interpreting works, 29

distancing from psychological
behaviorism, 29–30
'generalized other', 32
Tugendhat's comment, 32
Gergen's 'saturated self', 40–41
I/me structure, 30–34, 144–145, 151
in case studies, 207
Joas' comment, 32
relation to Foucault, 36–37
relation to Lacan, 39–40
Lifton's 'protean self', 41
Philosophy of the Present (book), 33
relation to Jameson, 47
'role', 31–32
Tugendhat's comment, 34
media studies
difficulties of applying
postmodernism, 43
effects model, 4
effects model compared to
Althusser-Thompson debate,
19–20
psychoanalytic approaches, 8
social subject and, 4–5
uses and gratifications model, 4
Mellencamp, Patricia, 62, 68, 92–93
Mekas, Jonas, 65, 67
Diaries, Notes, Sketches (film), 67
Meyrowitz, Joshua, 7
'mediated generalized other', 42
Micro-Film (magazine), 55, 58, 60,
95–96, 210
Miller, Toby, 27–28, 155–156
Mitchell, William, 168
Morley, David, 4, 173
Muecke, D.C., 193

Napster, 165
Negroponte, Nicholas, 169
'N-generation', 165, 166

Peterson, James, 57
Polan, Dana B., 64
popular music fan experience,
103–104
Probyn, Elspeth, 21, 27–28
psychoanalytic theory
absence in mass communication
studies, 38–39
'psychotronic' film, 58–59

Rabinowitz, Lauren, 56, 60, 62, 68, 76
Rank, Otto, 197
Reel Queer Film Festival, 63
Renan, Sheldon, 64, 68, 69, 78
Rosenbaum, Jonathan, 60, 69, 70

Schneeman, Carolee
Fuses (film), 62
Screen model of criticism, 96–97
Self
fluidity in virtual space, 170
'folding' of socio-cultural planes,
93
Simpsons, The (television program),
171, 173, 181, 185, 188, 194
sites of analysis
author's involvement in/relation
to, 12–14
selection of, 8–12
Sitney, P. Adams, 56, 57, 60, 67–68
Smith, Jack
Flaming Creatures (film), 62
social subject
Althusser's model, 17
and mass culture, 17
attention to non-media elements, 7
destruction of traditional
construction, 16
effect of virtual culture on, 159
Fiske's 'agency' theory, 20–21
'flattening' of subject, 5–6
hermeneutic model, 15, 28
in a fragmented environment, 6
postmodern concerns, 5–7
media research, 4–5
reconceptualization, 16
threat from new technologies,
161–163
Spigel, Lynn, 166, 167
Stake, Robert E., 8
Star Trek (television show), 1, 196,
200
Star Wars (film), 1, 115–116, 136–137
Strozier, Charles, 197

Tapscott, Don, 165, 169
Thompson, E.P.
criticism of Althusser, 17–19
criticism by Anderson, 18
criticism by Benton, 18

Tugendhat, Ernst, 144
  on Mead's 'generalized other', 32
  on Mead's 'roles', 34
Turkle, Sherry, 159–160, 166, 195,
    200
Twentieth Century Fox, 188–191
Tyler, Parker, 64–65, 69

underground cinema
  'diary'/personal film, 67
  dissonance within culture, 56
  distancing from mainstream
    cinema, 56–60
  do it yourself/multitasking roles,
    98–99
  dynamics of, 68
  emergence in United States, 69
  feminist themes, 62
  hermeneutics in, 93
  'hypnagogic' film, 67–68, 84
  identity politics, 62, 64–66, 97–98
  importance of textual analysis, 82,
    91–92
  need for audience and critical
    models to cross with
    production, 95–96
  need for autonomy, 94–95
  participants' multiple roles, 60–62
  pastiche techniques, 57–58

political themes, 98
  radicalism versus aesthetics, 64–66
  'rhizome' concept, 92
  queer themes, 62
  self-involved character of, 66–67
  shift to academic environments,
    57, 70
  techniques seeping into
    mainstream film, 69–70
  versus mainstream 'indie'/Sundance
    film, 59
Urbana, IL, 53, 71, 101

Waksman, Steve, 105
Walser, Robert, 104, 141
Warhol, Andy, 57
  Hedy (film), 58
  Lonesome Cowboys (film), 58
Weinstein, Deena, 103, 104–105, 111,
    126
Weinstein, Michael, 161, 200, 201
Wiley, Norbert, 28
Wilson, Tony, 173
Wired (magazine), 171
Wise, J. Macgregor, 161
Wellman, Barry, 164

Zizek, Slavoj, 19, 151–153
  criticism of Foucault, 40